Robert Esmonde Sencourt

The Life of George Meredith
Biography of a poet

seVerus

Sencourt, Robert Esmonde: The Life of George Meredith
Biography of a poet
Hamburg, SEVERUS Verlag 2012
Nachdruck der Originalausgabe von 1929

ISBN: 978-3-86347-244-3
Druck: SEVERUS Verlag, Hamburg, 2012

Der SEVERUS Verlag ist ein Imprint der Diplomica Verlag GmbH.

Bibliografische Information der Deutschen Nationalbibliothek:
Die Deutsche Nationalbibliothek verzeichnet diese Publikation in der
Deutschen Nationalbibliografie; detaillierte bibliografische Daten sind im
Internet über http://dnb.d-nb.de abrufbar.

© **SEVERUS Verlag**
http://www.severus-verlag.de, Hamburg 2012
Printed in Germany
Alle Rechte vorbehalten.

Der SEVERUS Verlag übernimmt keine juristische Verantwortung oder
irgendeine Haftung für evtl. fehlerhafte Angaben und deren Folgen.

seVERUS

THE LIFE OF GEORGE MEREDITH

By
ROBERT ESMONDE SENCOURT

TO
NIGEL SUTTON

"Decency's a dirty petticoat in the garden of innocence."
Celt and Saxon

CORRIGENDUM

The Publishers wish to state that the remark on page vii, that Mr. Ellis's study of George Meredith "had to be withdrawn from publication for infringements of copyright," though true of the first edition, fails to recognise that a second, amended edition was put upon the market, and is still to be purchased from the Richards Press Ltd.

PREFACE

It is a curious anomaly that has made a man of the stature of George Meredith wait twenty years for his authoritative biography. But the fault was his own; when he died, Lord Morley and Meredith's other executors approached Sir James Barrie. But Sir James refused, because he knew that Meredith was violently opposed to the idea of anyone writing his life. He wanted to be known through his work alone.

The result he did not foresee was that men would insist on having knowledge about him: that false rumours would be a deforming mirror. In 1912, accordingly, his *Letters* were published with biographical notes by his son, and this, with the excellent article by Thomas Secombe, in the *Dictionary of National Biography*, laid the foundation of a life. Another relative, Mr. S. M. Ellis, made valuable personal researches, which are almost always accurate, and which no biographer can ignore, especially with regard to the material of Meredith's novels, but the book was not reliable in all its judgments and had to be withdrawn from publication for infringements of copyright. A later study revealed the fact that an entirely false estimate of Meredith's character was becoming current; in these circumstances, there was a plain need for an

PREFACE

authoritative life, drawn up from the evidence of those who knew him best.

Each year these become fewer. Lord Morley has already been dead some years: Mrs. Ross and Mrs. Clarke died in 1927; Lord Haldane in 1928; Lady Lugard and Lady Danesfort in 1929. Meredith had outlived most of his contemporaries. But there are seven friends to whom I am particularly indebted for personal information: Lady Milner, Lady Danesfort, Lady Lugard, Mrs. Ross, Mrs. Plimmer, Mr. Buckston Browne and Sir James Barrie. I owe to Mrs. Plimmer and to her son the opportunity of reading some fifty unpublished letters from which I have made extensive quotations. I am enabled to quote from Lord Haldane's unpublished papers through the kindness of his sister, Miss Elizabeth Haldane. I owe to my friend, Mrs. A. W. Anstruther, the opportunity of seeing the letters Meredith wrote to Mlle. Hilda de Longueuil, of whom I heard a further account from Frau von Meister. The text of these letters was printed in the *Nineteenth Century*, in February, 1928, in conjunction with Thomas Hardy's reminiscence. Mr. W. M. Meredith has kindly placed at my disposal many more unpublished letters of the greatest value; Mr. Richard Le Gallienne three others: still more have been discovered in the British Museum. From Mrs. Sturgis comes the miniature which is reproduced for the frontispiece. Mr. Wilfrid Meynell added private information to his books on Meredith's friendship with his wife. The only important collection of letters not consulted is that addressed to Mary and Louisa

Lawrence, which none will be allowed to see for many years to come. But that can scarcely be so valuable as the extremely important collection placed at my disposal by Mr. Frank Altschul in New York. This collection contains, as well as an earlier version of *One of Our Conquerors*, an unpublished poem, "Creed," of Meredith's earliest period, and some forty unpublished letters, of which the most important are to Samuel Lucas, to Jessopp, to Janet Ross and to Robert Louis Stevenson; it contains also many more comments on works submitted to Meredith when reader to Chapman and Hall than those noticed by Mr. B. W. Matz in his article in the *Fortnightly*. From all these the generosity of Mr. Altschul has enabled me to quote. I am bound also to acknowledge the kindness and hospitality of Mr. and Mrs. Wood, who now live in Meredith's delightful house at Box Hill. I reproduce from the Longueuil letters an unpublished poem and extracts from others in the British Museum, collected by Mr. Matz, and excerpts from some unpublished manuscripts in the Widener Library at Harvard. Neither Mr. W. M. Meredith nor I, however, can accept the whole of Mr. Matz's little collection as George Meredith's work.

The account of Frau Cosima Wagner is based upon that given me by Mrs. Henry Beaumont of Baden-Baden.

My especial obligations are of course due to Mr. William Meredith himself, whose knowledge of his father is incomparably more complete and more accurate than anyone else's. I have taken the greatest

PREFACE

pains to harmonise my statements with the knowledge of Mr. Meredith, as indeed with that of the other friends I consulted, but I must make it perfectly clear that I, and I alone, am responsible for this book. I have striven to write it with a detachment which would be as unbecoming in a son as it is needful to a critic and to a biographer.

In published work, my debt to James Moffatt's *Primer to the Novels*, and *Les Cinquantes Premières Années* of M. René Galland, needs emphasis, with that to J. A. Hammerton's book, to Mr. Ellis's *A Mid-Victorian Pepys*, to Professor Trevelyan's *Poetry and Philosophy of George Meredith*, and to various articles in *The Times Literary Supplement*. Parts of my concluding chapter have already appeared in the *Fortnightly Review*, of my eleventh in *The Bookman*, and of my thirteenth in *Scribner's Magazine*.

In the years since George Meredith died, the pattern of biography has altered. Mr. Lytton Strachey has commended, and exemplified, a subtler strategy than full narration: it is to attack the living person at unexpected points. What Mr. Strachey has done with a detachment that all found delightful, and some suspected to be sinister, M. André Maurois has done by the charm of his sympathy. His mischievousness is gentleness itself, and, though it is with the most delicate of fingers, he touches our hearts. Even though one has none of the accomplishments of such admirable writers, one could not but learn from them that the

PREFACE

time for cumbersome biography has gone by, and that what is asked even of an official biography is to dwell on salient intimacies as material for the portrait of the living man.

But even so, a dilemma still remains. One must either adapt one's materials to one's taste for piquancy, as, for instance, in the case of Florence Nightingale, and of Essex, Mr. Strachey did; or one must adhere to them so closely that, like M. Maurois, one will find unscrupulous enemies accusing one of plagiarism. Between these two choices, I have never hesitated. As in the case of my earlier book, *Outflying Philosophy*, this Life is an almost uninterrupted reference to my sources, and when no other reference is given, it is to be understood that I am relying on private information.

There was in George Meredith a gift so singular that even now, a hundred years after his birth, the world of letters which saw him die supreme in England is again divided into that same opposition of a minority of enthusiasts and a crowd unwilling to consider him which greeted his advent as a poet. But the fame of great writers shines slowly, presaged alone by morning stars of judgment. Dante waited two hundred years for the Renaissance to set him in his place. The first to express a classic appreciation of Shakespeare was Dryden. We are only now beginning to arrive at the idea that Wordsworth is as great as Milton. What the ages to come will think of the eminent Victorians, therefore, we can best guess by the foresight of men of distinction. The men who admired Meredith were such as to argue that he will be not the least in an era of great men, and the true picture of him which scrutiny's varnish brings out from the memories of those who knew him will catch the best eyes in a gallery of masterpieces. Like the heroes and heroines he created, he was a figure on the grand scale.

ROBERT ESMONDE SENCOURT

HYÈRES, 1929

CONTENTS

I	The Opening of Life	page	1
II	The Morning of Romance		21
III	Craving the Buried Day		44
IV	The Friends of Genius		75
V	Janet Ross and *Evan Harrington*		104
VI	Arthur's Abdication		118
VII	The Function of Woman		135
VIII	First Years at Box Hill		149
IX	France and Germany		171
X	Criticism and Comedy		188
XI	The Longueuil Episode		220
XII	When Autumn Days Strip Bare		238
XIII	Some Later Friends		260
XIV	The Last Few Years		283
XV	Genius in Action		301

I

THE OPENING OF LIFE

§ I

MEREDITH was born of a family who in the High Street of Portsmouth breathed, as the subjects of George IV, an ample air. For three generations the business of naval outfitters had brought them into intimacy with the traditions of the Navy. Nelson may well have known them. Hardy, who received the embrace of the dying admiral, stayed, himself an admiral, under their roof. Thoughts of a high ancestry in the Welsh mountains, perhaps of Powys chieftains —who knows but of actual Tudors?—tuned them to something in their blood which gave them distinction of looks and bearing. So that Meredith's aunts found their natural spheres in a world very different from the shopman's. One married a banker who in 1833, when Meredith was five years old, was Mayor of the town; another married a naval officer who in 1832 was Consul-General in the Azores, and whose daughter, after marrying into the noble Portuguese family of Cabral, died in Rome, the Marchioness de Thomar, an ambassadress at the Papal Court; a third married an officer in the Marines, who died a general, Sir Samuel Burdon Ellis.[1]

[1] *Dictionary of National Biography*, 2d. Supplement. *Letters of George Meredith*, vol. i.

The father of these beautiful daughters was as remarkable as they. His features were distinguished, and his personality fascinated women. He visited at country houses: he kept a stable of good horses: he rode to hounds, and raised and commanded a squadron of yeomanry: he had gallant adventures, and when he did business in the tailor's shop he shook hands with the officers whose splendour his tradesmanship could enhance, fitting them complete in a single day. He died in 1813,—"a fine figure of a man and there ain't many marquises to match him." Such was the verdict of Mr. Kilne the publican on Old Mel in *Evan Harrington*. For Melchizedeck Harrington was no other than Melchizedeck Meredith. From the aunts and their memories, Meredith drew his first knowledge of the aristocracies with whom his family had for two generations found themselves at home. And all the equivocal positions in which he found himself, as a tradesman's son moving amongst a race of sportsmen and of cosmopolitans, were the education offered to the sensitive and handsome boy who was born there in 1828. *Evan Harrington* records the impression the life left on George Meredith, as we see his youth there identified with his own shaping spirit of imagination, just as we see Dickens identified with his own ideal life in *David Copperfield*.[1]

Between a tailor and a naval outfitter, however, there is a distinction which gives the keyword to the enigmas of Meredith's youth. When the boy was five years old his mother died. A memory remained of the

[1] *Letters of George Meredith, Evan Harrington.*

splendour of womanhood; and her Irish ancestry had endowed her with something more than one expects from the daughter of a tavern. Her brother exchanged the tavern for the pulpit. For his father Meredith never cared much, and even to his old age there was no softening of his judgment. Augustus Urmston Meredith had not been a great success in his business, either at Portsmouth, in St. James Street, or, where he later settled, in South Africa. To a bad business head was joined a certain instability of character.[1]

Meredith was dependent upon his aunts, and it was his impressions of them to which he returned again and again for his portraits of magnificent women. These handsome creatures were well equal to the world of comparative elegance into which they married, but when he saw them they were perforce back from their memories of Army people, or of foreign aristocracies, to the fact that they were daughters of the shears.

The little boy felt already there was something intensely real about them; and, already conscious of the personal splendour he shared with them, his imagination was happier in the world of their stories than in the street of shops. At three years old, as he showed his toy horse and a cart that made music as the wheels went round, he had realised that there was something in his white frock and blue ribbons, or in some deeper power of impression, that made him feel far above little Jimmy Price, the bookseller's son, who came in sometimes to play with him, even though

[1] *George Meredith*, by S. M. Ellis.

Jimmy was already five. And George remembered that his birthdays were feasts, to which the neighbours' children were invited as an honour, and given almonds and raisins to eat. Little George Meredith moved among them always as one above them. He never bowled a hoop with them, nor played with their marbles, nor whipped their tops. His aunts had already formed in him a taste for other things, and it was given a firmer base when, at eight or nine years old, he was sent to St. Paul's School at Southsea. For already, in the English system which gives boys throughout life the social label of their schools, this little private one in Southsea raised him on an Etonian pinnacle above tradesmen's sons. He would descend from it only to admire a sporting effort, as when Neale, the coffee-house keeper's horse, came in second at the races at Stokes Bay in 1839.[1]

His spirit raced from the shop and its sailors, from the boys at school, from the chapel where the chastened flesh fidgeted in the pew during the long services, from the lessons, which he could not or would not learn, to the wild country and the woods and the sky above them. There his spirit from his earliest to his latest days was at home. "I am of the woods," he wrote to Mademoiselle de Longueuil as he was nearing sixty: and while a boy he felt a dim delight tingle in him when in the spring he lay under boughs of breathing May, his soul singing with the birds, blooming into the flowers, as under the drooping leaves, the sunny vistas, pregnant with immortal romance, tempted

[1] S. M. Ellis, *George Meredith*.

him on with delicious hopes. For it was the peculiarity of his genius to wed nature in a generative union to all his most sensitive depths of love and spiritual ardour. "O skylark," he would cry in after years,

> . . . I see thee and call thee joy!
> Thy wings bear me up to the heart of the dawn;
> I see thee no more, but thy song is still
> The tongue of the heavens to me!
>
> Thus are the days when I was a boy;
> Sweet while I lived in them, dear now they're gone:
> I feel them no longer, but still, O still
> They tell of the heavens to me.

None of the intimations of immortality which came to Wordsworth in early childhood found expression in so keen a rapture.[1]

§ 2

When George was a boy of thirteen his father married again and went to London, sending his son to another private school near Petersfield; and life from this time was crowded with new romances. Friendships thrilled him, the old comedy of the aunts in the tailor's shop, with all its jabs into his sensitiveness, was exchanged for the adventures of a boarding-school, for games, and for the companionship of

[1] *Letters of George Meredith. Poems:* "Spring Song" and "To a Skylark." *George Meredith*, S. M. Ellis.

country scenes. Just as *Evan Harrington* gives the record which the comedy of Portsmouth left on his childhood's imagination, so *Harry Richmond* records his later boyhood. He knew already that power of feeling with and through others which is the meaning of a heart. He detested conventional religion. He loved heroes, not only the heroes of his early childhood, Hardy, Nelson, Pitt, William the Conqueror, Harold, Alfred, not only the great characters of Shakespeare, Falstaff, Lear, Hamlet, Shylock, but boys of flesh and blood at issue with inadequate ideals or weak authority. The boy who loved his head-master's beautiful daughter, whom Meredith's readers know as Heriot and again as Weyburn, fascinated him as Steerforth fascinated David Copperfield, and united him with his Temple in the fervours of boyish eagerness. In such ardours emerges the spirit of the hero, eager not only for the life of action, but also for the imaginative creation of deeds of the heroic temper, the spirit which is ready to act and to endure.[1]

The Spartan schools of the time offered the boy his chance of both. All his life Meredith was devoted to boxing as he was to swimming: all his life a whipping was his favourite metaphor for inward discipline. His flesh then was not only the organ but also the teacher of his spirit. The thrill of youth and spring in his veins was one with the impulses of love: cricket came often into his memories and pictures of boyhood; while fists and the birch taught him to bear pain cheerfully. A bleeding nose and the chastening of bared flesh

[1] *George Meredith*, by René Galland.

each took its place in the great tradition which has made Englishmen what they have been. Shelley's white fury found expression in fights, and released itself by rolling on the ground after his whippings. But George Meredith, no matter how nervous he might feel nor how his sensitiveness might wince before imagination's terrors, mingled something robust with his intensity.[1]

His spirit too found freedom and roamed far. In his own words, he walked "the glittering lanes of boyhood's fairyland."[2] He was coming to that age when, retiring into himself, "he was growing to be lord of kingdoms where Beauty was his handmaid, and History his minister, and Time his ancient harper, and sweet Romance his bride; where he walked in a realm, vaster and more gorgeous than the great Orient, peopled with all the heroes that have been. For there is no princely wealth, and no lofty heritage, to equal this early one that is made bountifully common to so many, when the ripening blood has put a spark to the imagination, and the earth is seen through rosy mists of a thousand fresh-awakened, aimless and nameless desires; panting for bliss and taking it as it comes; making of any sight or sound, perforce by the enchantment they carry with them, a key to infinite because innocent pleasure." Imagination and eagerness crowded each experience with issues of poignant life. "I forgot," said Harry Richmond, "the existence of all save of what I loved passionately, and that was shapeless, was

[1] *George Meredith*, by J. A. Hammerton.
[2] Unpublished poem in British Museum.

like a wind."[1] That experience was the result of riding in the mist, when a magical exhilaration roused that dim sense of secret joy which all through his life was the essence of his romance. But just as it was always associated with his love of action, so too it mingled with an intuitive knowledge of the inward working of the characters around him; like Harry Richmond, he could guess and trace the workings of a master passion, and exulted in the power this gave him over those who could not themselves guess how deep, how varied, how delightful were the views he saw before him down the long avenue of life.

§ 3

And while he was here and still only fourteen, his ambition took another turn. He did not trust his father; he was not satisfied with what was being done for him. He had learnt meanwhile that he was a ward in chancery and that sums of his own money were available for his education. He heard, doubtless through one of his school friends—was it Hill?—of a school in Germany which was not beyond his means. To this he determined to go. In 1842 it was no small adventure for a boy of fourteen to send himself to school in Germany, but the boy was determined, and he once said that he obtained an interview with the Lord Chancellor to press his proposal. This, however, is more likely one of the romances he would invent as a joke.[2]

---

[1] *The Ordeal. Harry Richmond* and René Galland.
[2] *Letters of George Meredith.*

THE OPENING OF LIFE

The school he chose was a remarkable departure from the English traditions. The Herrenhütte, a Moravian sect with many admirable resemblances to the Society of Friends, had found as early as 1765 an asylum under Prince Alexander of Wied, and had started a school which flourished and still survives. It was the aim of these good men "to bring boys up for the Lord Jesus." But they sought to recommend their religion not so much by the discipline of doctrine as by practising what they commended. Their object was to do as they would be done by; but whether they would have relished the Jesuit surveillance they gave their boys is a question. An usher eyed the young creatures at every moment of work and play, and slept in their crowded dormitory, where the beds were so close together as to be practically touching, and not a window open. The boys went to a school chapel, but a deeper influence came from their contact with their teachers, whose gentleness took all envy, hatred, and uncharitableness out of their lives and filled them with an eagerness for being real Christians, and this mingled something mystical with the Modernism growing up over against the Catholic revival. A mood of evangelical fervour passed over Meredith here and he could not repress his anxious curiosity about the ultimate fate of the souls around him; looking with intense solicitude at the boys who undressed beside him, or ran out to play Chevy Chase, he would ask: "Were they saved?"[1]

But what conquered this, and remained, was something vaguer, something deeper, something commoner.

[1] Professor Henry Morley. S. M. Ellis.

Meredith, though he wrote to Tom Taylor that the style Dickens encouraged was tricky, was to have many affinities with him, and this was one of them. Dickens, as he wrote to a son who was leaving for Australia, did not attach much importance to religious forms: "and so you will understand only better," he wrote, "that I insist solemnly now on the truth and beauty of the Christian religion, such as it was given forth by Christ himself, and on the impossibility of your doing much wrong if you respect it humbly and with all your heart. Only one word more on this subject; the more we are steeped in religious feelings, the less we are inclined to speak of them." Meredith's feelings were a different temperament's expression of a like conclusion. "There cannot be any goodness unless it is a practised goodness," he put into the mouth of Nesta Radnor, as he was growing old. It was but an echo of a letter he wrote at Neuwied. One feeling, through all his quarrels or his happiness with his friend Hill, had been in both their hearts. It was fellowship. "O my God, grant that all may have the same feeling towards you to make your life happy. But true fellowship is not to be had without Christianity, not the name but the practice of it. I wish you the greatest of all things—'God's blessing,' which comprehends all I would or could otherwise say." In his religion, the boy of sixteen was already mature; his tone paternal.[1]

---

[1] *Letters*. The religion of the Moravians finds recurring expressions in the *Monthly Observer*. Unpublished letters.

§ 4

But Germany itself was more to the boy than the charity of the Moravian brothers. Its rivers, its woods, its villages were filled with a sweet old romance which took one back to all that was beautiful in the Middle Ages: and, as in the Middle Ages, nature offered its own simple delights to mingle with the tinglings of youth. Winter, spring, summer, autumn were so much more marked than in England as to make the mere course of the year a matter to fill the minds of lovers of nature: in the winter snow and storm:

> And white untrodden mountains shining cold,
> And muffled footpaths winding thro' the wold,
> O'er which those wintry gusts cease not to howl
>   and blow, . . .

or at times a wild storm which marked in its tension a relief, or a sort of crisis, in his own inner life, as it did in those of Farina and of Feverel,—the dense clouds rising mountainous in the west, while the storm, tearing shreds from it, swiftly hides the moors. A violet light would light up the hill below the Drachenfels, and the Rhine would shine for an instant in the depths. Then the fury of the storm would burst on forest and mountain, trees torn from their roots would whistle in the whirling gusts, while torrents of rain would foam down the hills, or fly like white plumes in the intervals of darkness.[1]

But the Rhineland offered also what was sweet and lovely: the fruit trees, exquisite in spring with the

[1] *Poems*: "Pictures of the Rhine," "Farina."

tints of blooming cheeks, made him intensely alive, after weeks of snow, to the meaning of spring, as they bloomed among the gabled villages or at the edges of the pinewood. The later months were lovelier still: long walks in the country around made him intimate with the clear summer of the Rhineland. Before Whitsuntide the school would give itself up for several days to *Wanderlust*, each boy with a knapsack and an *Alpenstock*, like a young German of to-day. To drink from the brooks they passed, to pick up their meals in farm or village, to sleep in a haystack or some peasant's immense old kitchen, to watch the winding river at intervals as it curved among the meadows, or to lie in peace on some sheltered slope of the hills, half murmuring words of thanks, were adventures that thrilled him into intimacy with Germany.

> Every day was golden-leaved
> With wonders rich and new.[1]

It was Germany in its gentlest and most romantic grandeur, where the castles rose above the Rhine in the rare loveliness of slow decay, and where the hour was rich in legend of an antique time. Elves dancing among the mushrooms, Undine in a robe of silver lightning wonderful to see, Siegfried after a merciful combat killing the monster of the Drachenfels, Satan busy with the Cathedral of Cologne, or the Minnesingers singing their gay or tender tunes to hearts which gave an answer: all these were Meredith's inspirations, as they were Wagner's. And into this rich

[1] Unpublished poem in British Museum.

soil new and beautiful growths had come to a wondrous bloom.¹

Goethe had been dead ten years, but his glowing phrases had re-animated the hearts and brains of all who spoke his language. He had felt the profound intimacy of nature with human life. The earth and the sun met him with a thousand thrills and voices that awoke him to a joy, which he identified with love, in a simple sentiment that drenched his being. Love was the deep experience which brimmed the streams of life, whether it led up in a leap to heaven or wore men to a semblance of death,

> Glücklich allein
> Ist die Seele die liebt.²

But life itself, life lived not by each single man alone but as one of mankind, as part of nature, was so romantic, so august, that Goethe hardly wished for further of divineness. The earth, in fact, was God's visible garment, and the forces of life and being in their complex and endless interplay were weaving for Him His living vesture. Man was indeed a spirit and unutterable mystery of mysteries; looking inward, he finds himself gazing at a whole sea of light and love. Plato in a great passage of the *Timæus* had spoken of time as the mirror of eternity: time, the mirror of eternity, was to Goethe man's realm and man's bequest:

Die Zeit ist mein Vermächtniss, mein Acker ist die Zeit.

[1] "Farina."
[2] Translated by Meredith, in the *Monthly Observer:* "Happy alone are the souls that love."

With an inward happiness that was royal and supreme, Goethe could speak of divine depths in sorrow, and honour adversity in its most repugnant forms.[1] It was the lesson of *Wilhelm Meister* "not only to be patient with the earth, and let it lie beneath us, we appealing to a higher birthplace, but also to recognise humility and poverty, mockery and despite, disgrace and wretchedness, suffering and death as divine." He saw both the unevenness of life and his own character resolved into a larger harmony: *Ungleich dem Gleichen bleibet nicht fern.* Man was to be helpful and good: to set his aim on nobleness, which in the storm and fiction of existence was what man was meant for. According to vast, everlasting, venerable laws must we all complete the course of our existence.[2]

Goethe had given these ideas as leaders to Germany, and Meredith breathed them from the air of Neuwied. French and German literatures were the chief study there. The heritage of Goethe had inspired not only the philosopher, but also Fichte, Jean Paul Richter, Novalis, Eichendorff, Mörike and Freiligrath. If Meredith found his first great teacher in Goethe, and through Goethe in Spinoza, it is true that his philosophy was also stated by Novalis and Jean Paul. Jean Paul, who learnt much from Sterne and his sentimentalism, had, as Justin McCarthy said, a warmer heart, a quicker soul, a richer quaintness of fancy. He saw human life in the light of the heart, which was the light of nature.

[1] Ὁ μὴ δαρεὶς ἄνθρωπος οὐ παιδεύεται was the motto of *Dichtung und Wahrheit.*

[2] *Das Gottliche.*

He was a man who turned his whole energies not to strain away from life to some higher form, but placing himself nearer to life, to support the soul on the body and through the body; a man who detected in the picture of the hero a danger for the purity of immediate experience, who would not renounce that immediacy for all the honours in the world; a man who embraced a task of endless difficulty because he created no representative men, no Greeks, no types, but irrational creatures of the senses, German men and women with their thirsts and longings, with their desolations and absurd buffoonery, "but, above all, not only the princes and nobility of the past but the mean, the poor, the oppressed, the wretched and the suffering, those who rejoice in their constraints and are exceeding wise in their lack of wisdom. And then he brought a light which victoriously dispersed all the twilights of life, and turned man's sojourn on earth, which is too hard to endure, into a holiday service, invested with sublime pathos. So the whole chaos of life, its mysteries, its fatalities, the sportiveness of fate, the imminence of death, the fragility of happiness, the restlessness of fancy—all must be accepted and set forth not symbolically but as the fact it is. There, the clear guiding principles made like architecture to look firm and according to the laws of building; here, an unbroken ivy around the conjuration of great unrevealed mysteries, Man—Fate—God."[1]

Novalis, also, mystical and transcendental, emphasised the spiritual value of man's fellowship with

[1] Dr. Heinrich Simon.

man. But among the great German names, none was so dear to Meredith as Heine's. In the deep simple sentiment of Heine, he found the voice of something which in early youth was all in all to him, and which never left him; after his sixtieth birthday he would quote the poems of Heine ten at a time: in Heine, as in Goethe, he found the life of the heart compared with nature:

> Du bist wie eine Blume,
>   So schön und hold und rein,

and these simple similes and metaphors of flowers, of pearls in the sea, of stars and streams and waves, to express the raptures of the lover, renewed his raptures, and he was content.

§ 5

Such were the ideas, such were the impressions that crowded on the eager, rapturous, active boy from the ages of fourteen to sixteen. They form his inspiration, his religion; they mould his genius. It was not to be a thing of reasoned order like the great Latin geniuses; it was an intuition and expression of the crowded complex issues of human life; it was of the same order as Shakespeare's and Goethe's, and when it vaunted the function of brain, it exemplified brain as a curb, or as itself an intuition, not as a force meeting nature as lord and master, with power to arrange it, as it were, in a creative order, looking at the wealth of human life from a point above it. The defects of Meredith are essentially German defects: the result of a German, as opposed to a Latin discipline, of a Celtic sensitiveness of passion and pride. It was the age of Beethoven, and Wagner was almost his contemporary. In Meredith, as in the great musicians, passion becomes sublime, and the air conveys this sublimity, as the wind's urge and keening is in *Tristan und Isolde*.

And did he not in those early and impressionable years meet his first Blumine, fair and pure? The winter morning of Germany, compared to Ottilia, was no doubt suggested by an inspirer. It was part of the system of the Herrenhütte to allow their boys to meet girls from time to time. Meredith, to whom women were always the first of wonders, could not have failed to drink from the offered cup. He thought of her in terms of a German dawn on snow. "Her face was like the quiet morning of a winter day when cloud and sun intermix and make an ardent silver, with lights of blue and faint fresh rose, and over them the beautiful fold of her full eyebrow on the eyelid like a bending upper heaven. These winter mornings are divine, they move on noiselessly. The earth is still as if waiting. A wren warbles, and flits through the lank, drenched branches; hillside opens green; everywhere a mist, everywhere expectancy. And they bear the veiled sun, like a sangreal, aloft to the wavy marble flooring of the stainless clouds." Did this girl provide a sitter for the portrait we know as Princess Ottilia? Did she speak a judgment on England to the boy of sixteen? One cannot think he wanted, or would have tolerated, so much. It was enough that she was young and lovely, and attuned to the spirit of May, providing a personal rapture to mingle with his sense of summer.[1]

All German then was the world of wonder that met him in those springing years when the poetic imagination ripened in the physical warmth of young adolescence. And to all this the Moravians allowed the spaciousness of their sympathy. It was their wish to allow each boy to develop the life of his own mind, and give play to his own fancy, and even to write poems and stories. These gentle preceptors (for to these whipping was a barbarity) kept their pupils' birthdays as they liked their own to be kept. And they filled their winter days with their elaborations of the sweet simple old ceremonies of the German Christmas. For weeks before, they were busy with the tree, and on Christmas Eve, a blaze of candles and glittering gifts, it showed beneath it the Holy Child in the manger, while the thrilling hymns of *Stille Nacht, heilige Nacht* mingled with the gay pathos of *Tannenbaum! O Tannenbaum! Wie grun sind deine Blätter!* In their warmth of heart, affection and religion were indistinguishable.

The boy who went down the Rhine in 1844 had grown almost out of recognition in two years. As the fort of Ehrenbreitstein left his sight, as Rolandseck came into view, as he passed below the Drachenfels and looked from Königswinter at the wooded heights of the Siebengebirge, as he passed from Bonn over the watery curves which broke the level plains, to watch for the high outlines of Cologne (which were then waiting for their spires), the impressions that

[1] René Galland.

mingled with the old legends, which the Rhine evoked, had raised him from the sense of the comedy of Portsmouth, and the conventions of Anglicanism, and the battles of his English schooldays, to a sense of a union made eternal with the river of life, as his spirit united with that of inhabited nature. The dim rapture had found a solid ground of traditional thought. He was joined to Coleridge and Carlyle in that fellowship of transcendental idealism which was Germany's gift to their ages:

> O the one life within us and abroad!
> That meets all motion and becomes its soul,
> A light in sound, a soundlike power in light,
> Rhythm in all thought and joyance everywhere.

But the high pulse of human life, and an interest rushing from one detail to another in an endless change of fun and fervour, made Meredith akin not to Coleridge but Carlyle. The best essay on the basis of the Meredithian philosophy is *Sartor Resartus*. Carlyle has himself referred to a source for that from which Meredith drank with the thirst of athletic youth. It was the first uproarious comic nature like their own, who had found a prophet in Goethe. It was Jean Paul Richter. Carlyle himself drew a contrast between Jean Paul's grotesque tumultuous pleasantry and the spirit that pervades and ennobles the delineations of common life, or his wild and shadowy imaginings. "His thoughts, his feelings, the creatures of his spirit walk before us embodied under wondrous shapes, in motley and ever fluctuating groups; but his essential character, however he disguise it, is that of a philosopher and moral poet, whose study has been human nature, whose delight and best endeavours are with all that is beautiful and tender and mysteriously sublime in the fate or history of man." The words are as true of Meredith's comedy as of Richter's, and they are true of Carlyle himself.

II

THE MORNING OF ROMANCE

§ 1

FOR twenty months after his return to England, the young Meredith did nothing in particular. His chief preoccupation he found in his quarrels with his father, against the background of the shop. Just before the boy went to Germany, Augustus Meredith, as we saw, had moved from Portsmouth to St. James. He had married, his choice falling upon his housekeeper. Her name was Bucket. In this household there was little to please the handsome boy with his red-gold hair, his large mouth, his taste for amplitude and his transcendental idealism. He was back again among the crowding incongruities of the comic world, and if he often laughed at them, he often felt desperate. He found relief in violent exercise, and in Carlyle. There was about Carlyle just enough of the uncouth to give Meredith a savourous mixture of idealism and oddness making him able to laugh at the strain which irked him in his own life, and Carlyle kept half his brain in Germany, after his return to England: in those years of moulding, Carlyle who dominated his thoughts also formed his style.[1] He wrote to Raffalovitch that Carlyle "was one of those who stood constantly in the presence of those 'eternal verities' of which he speaks:

[1] S. M. Ellis.

> Thou hast bared the roots of life with sight
> Piercing; in language stronger than the lyre.[1]

Years earlier he had given his account of Carlyle, in *Beauchamp's Career*, saying that his style was so loose and rough that it resembled early architecture in utter dilapidation; it was "a wind-in-the-orchard style that tumbled down here and there an appreciable fruit with uncouth bluster,—its sentences without commencements came to abrupt ends, like waves against a sea-wall, learned words jostled by slang, and accents falling haphazard, like slant rays from driving clouds." The effect on mind and joints was an electrical agitation: and that was what was always vibrating through the fibres and passions of Meredith. He seemed to generate electricity from the air he breathed, and it flashed from him in unending sparks and lightnings.

The effect of the German philosophy of Carlyle was to deepen his enjoyment of his own intense and agitated life. Meredith did not meet Carlyle till fifteen years after his return to England. The sage, smoking his pipe, listened in a stony silence during the whole visit. As young Meredith rose to go, Carlyle broke it with the words, "This has been a very pleasant evening. Come again."

Meredith had in those days another great enthusiasm. It was the poetry of Horne. We have forgotten Horne: he is recalled now because Meredith read him and admired him not only as an Ishmael in the world of letters, but as a philosopher-poet. Horne's adventures as a young man in and near Mexico had been nearly

[1] *Letters.*

cut off by sharks, by shipwreck, by mutiny, by fire and by fever. But he was preserved from these to declaim against the "barriers excluding men of genius from the Public," barriers against which he hurled himself, in the confidence that he was a genius, by producing an epic which was sold for a farthing. It was at this price, for this epic, that George Meredith fell under his spell, and read in his vague verse, sometimes eloquent, sometimes graceful, sometimes magnificent, a Miltonic sort of philosophic allegory impregnated with Hegel. For even Horne kept him to his German philosophy. The epic was *Orion*. "The poem," he said to Mrs. Browning, "is destined to represent equally the real and the ideal, the dream, the theory or the shadow, and the substance or action which are born of them." What interested Elizabeth Barrett was praised by George Henry Lewes, who saw in it the moral that man cannot rest happy but, driven by his instinct for progress, must always struggle on. "The direct tendency of my allegory," said Horne himself, "in so far as it relates to the passion of love, is to counsel this combination of the mind with the senses which best helps the noble progress and happiness of certain beings." One must pass, by suffering, through a love which combines both action and passion, before one reaches the fulness of sympathy which makes for true happiness, just as poetry itself was the work of a soul imposing form on matter. Horne was a spirit of morning, and shared with Meredith a love of the stars that lose themselves in the colours of dawn. Orion in the end becomes a star—

> Installed 'midst golden fires which ever melt
> In Eros' breath and beauty; rising still
> With nightly brilliance, merging in the dawn,—
> And circling onward in eternal youth.

And one of his celebrations of the beauty of the dawn (and as he wrote, " 'Tis always morning somewhere in the world") is finer still:

> The long clear shadows of the morning differ
> From those of eve, which are more soft and vague,
> Touched with old day-dreams and a mellowed grief.
> The lights of morning, even as her shades,
> Are architectural, and pre-eminent
> In quiet freshness, 'midst the pause that holds
> Prelusive energy. . . .

Through this verse, which is not incomparable to Wordsworth's, the ideas of Horne sunk deep into the mind of young Meredith, who worked them out in masterpieces after an intenser realisation of their significance. A copy of Meredith's *Poems* of 1851, in the Widener Library at Harvard, is inscribed to R. H. Horne, Esq., "by whose generous appreciation and trusty criticism these 'Poems' were chiefly fostered." And Horne himself was far from contemptible: "in this poet," said Carlyle, "burns the fire of the stars."[1]

There was another poet of the time, with whom George Meredith found affinity: it was George Darley, who first used the metre we know so well as that of "Love in the Valley." Darley, who died in 1846, was

[1] *Letters.* "Orion." Horne in *Dictionary of National Biography* and Chambers's *Encyclopædia of English Literature.*

also a poet of nature, a lover of earth, and he sums up the feeling he shared with Meredith, in "The Wild Bee's Tale."

> They may talk of happy Heaven—
> Of another world of bliss;
> Yet, were choice and freedom given,
> I would ask no world but this.
>
> Have they lawns so wide and sunny?
> Have they such sweet valleys there?
> Are their fields so full of honey?
> What care I for fields of air?
>
> Give me Earth's rich sun and flowers,
> Give me Earth's green fields and groves.
> Let him fly to Eden's bowers,
> He who such cold bowers loves.[1]

§ 2

Tutored by Horne and Carlyle, Meredith in February, 1846, was articled to a solicitor, a Mr. Charnock, who had chambers within the shadow of St. Paul's. Tall, dark and thin, sometimes untidy, often dirty, with something goat-like in his bearded face, Charnock, in the early 'thirties, was a droll personage amongst solicitors. An antiquary of some distinction in his day, Charnock was not really interested in the intricacies of his respectable profession. He much preferred to smoke, to take long walks, to

[1] Darley's *Poems*. René Galland.

pour out robust or cynical jokes, to idle away a day fishing, to hunt out the meaning of place-names, to plan a walking tour in the Hartz or the Tyrol, or to meet Dickens or Horne at the Arundel Club.[1]

He was not ill content, therefore, to find a clerk with a taste for literature, and, in fact, he encouraged his young friends to write a little manuscript monthly of their own. To do something remarkable in this struck him as worth more than a knowledge of Coke on Littleton, or of the law of gavelkind, and he was sufficiently struck by his young articled clerk to introduce him to the son of Thomas Love Peacock. These with a few others were encouraged by Charnock to write together. The plan of the *Monthly Observer*,[2] as it was called, was for each contributor to edit and criticise in turn. Charnock was himself the leading contributor, and began with his "Tour in the Hartz." But neither the patron, nor any other, escaped the pungent and uproarious criticisms of the young Meredith. Charnock had a sort of Turkish pseudonym which gave Meredith his cue. To be an ambitious writer unappreciated, said Meredith of Charnock, was to be in heaven without houris, and if Charnock's claim could be appreciated only by those who knew the languages he knew, he would need a tribe more numerous than the more energetic Moslem could generate in the most flourishing harem.

Mr. Daniel, who aimed at a higher effort than he

[1] René Galland. S. M. Ellis.

[2] This is now in the possession of Harvard University. Cf. *Contributions of George Meredith to the Monthly Observer*. Edited by M. B. Forman, Edinburgh. Printed for private circulation, 1928.

could attain, was invited to a comparison not only with Icarus, but also as Meredith said had a sublimer prototype: Satan, who, dissatisfied with immortality, allowed himself that unrestrained desire which led him to damnation. Meredith inserted several of his own translations from the German poets. Each contribution of his—he himself was editor in June, 1849—shows his temperament, and the amalgam it was making with his genius. Exuberant, and at times grotesquely sportive, it glowed like a fresh rose of dawn. "The universe," he wrote, "is but a succession of links, and we are all united in nobility and gentleness and love."[1] His mind had a vitality that even to the end was for ever escaping from discipline to harlequinade, and his immense zest released itself in fun, and recurring roars of laughter, only to renew itself in a fresh and passionate tensity, which grew serene in rapture. His first poem was this on Saint Theresa:

> With holy earnest eyes enshrined
>   She bendeth on her knees,
> Her voice is heard, above the wind
>   Shrill from the northern seas;
> The sisters stoop on either hand,
>   She smileth mild on each,
> And in the wind a choral band
>   Comes singing to her speech.
>
> Her hands are tested, palm to palm,
>   Then folded as in rest;

[1] Unpublished MS. in Widener Library at Harvard.

Beneath her dawning eyelids calm,
  Upon her snow-white breast.
Her snowy garments rustle clear,
  As snowflakes rise and mix,
And to her neck there presseth near
  A silver crucifix.

Around her gloried form the air
  Is starred with falling snows
That cover all the convent bare
  With symboll'd pure repose.
Above her halo'ed head the sky
  Is studded thick with spheres
All swimming to one blissful eye
  Whose beam is bright with tears.

She knoweth that the time will come,
  And in the deepened night
Discerneth well her heaven home,
  The morning and the light—
And thro' the shadow and the pain
  A seraph sister voice;
But now she kneeleth once again
  That others may rejoice.[1]

§ 3

THE most interesting of the other contributors to the *Monthly Observer* was Peacock's daughter, Mary Nicolls. She was a naval officer's widow, approaching

[1] From an unpublished MS. in the Widener Library.

thirty, with a little girl of four or five. A keen wit, a lack of nervous stability, and a nature extraordinarily susceptible to the attraction of genius or talent in men, had inclined Mary Nicolls to a fatal interplay of sarcasm and sentiment. No premonition of this crossed the mind of the young man of twenty-one who met her in Edward Peacock's rooms. Her hair parted in the middle, and a girlish simplicity in her round face, she had a wit which enabled her to use to the full the charms of her temperament and person. Her eyes were languishing, and her upper lip the bow of Cupid, her arched eyebrows meeting above the nose of a child with nostrils dilating to air. She was at once interested by the exuberant young athlete whom her brother introduced and who gradually carried her by storm. His vitality, as we saw, was electrical in every movement, his features were handsome, his expression tense, and his thick red-brown hair gave a hint of the health and strength and youth which were then wedded to the intensity of his nature. He was already an admirer of her father, and they shared an enthusiasm which for him was the enthusiasm of a lover. His inexperience gave him no hint of the disappointments his idealism might find in a temperamental widow of nine-and-twenty. She herself, in spite of keen attraction, hesitated before settling down to marriage with a man with no endowments but his youth and genius. But they swam out upon the flood of rapture; across its warm and sparkling stream, the growths of earth swarmed with a new enchantment as wonderful to them as the holiness of heaven. A love which suffused every experience thought of all nature as united with him in joyful expectance, in a longing so delicious that it was more than half fulfilment of what he had already dreamed and written in verse.

Happy happy time, when the green star twinkles
    Over the fields all fresh with bloomy dew;
When the cold-cheeked dawn grows ruddy up the twilight,
    And the gold sun wakes, and weds her in the blue.
Then when my darling tempts the early breezes,
    She the only star that dies not with the dark!
Powerless to speak all the ardour of my passion,
    I catch her little hand as we listen to the lark.

Clambering roses peep into her chamber,
    Jasmine and woodbine breathe sweet, sweet,
White-necked swallows twittering of summer,
    Fill her with balm and nested peace from head to feet.
Ah, will the rose-bough see her lying lonely,
    When the petals fall and fierce bloom is on the leaves?
Will the autumn garners see her still ungathered,
    When the fickle swallows forsake the weeping eaves?[1]

The two lovers escaped from town to mingle their appreciation of each other with the pleasures of the country. The thought of her mingled in the green flashing plunges of the river, below white and yellow lilies swaying at anchor among the reeds. He would look at her with all his eyes, and young love has a

[1] "Love in the Valley," in *Poems*, 1851.

thousand. And when in the summer air, the little skylark went up above her, all song, to the smooth southern cloud lying along the blue; when from a dewy copse, dark over her nodding hat, the blackbird fluted, calling to her with its mellow note; when the kingfisher flashed emerald out of green osiers; or when a low-winged heron travelled aloft, seeking solitude; then he too seemed to wing the air with the birds, and the gracious glory of heaven fell upon his soul. No sight or pageantry of nature escaped his keen glances; each was mingled with the fulness of his love, and the voices of the birds and of the winds and of flowing water sang serenades of which he drank every note. Loveliest of all was the descent of evening in the woodland of early summer, when the rich lights gave a lucid green to the young leaves of oaks and planes and beeches, and turned the pine stems to red-gold, and gilded both meadows and streams. At such moments colour was only a symbol of the glow which radiant love spreads among the cooler lights of life. "Peeps of the revelling splendour above and around enliven the conscious full heart within. The flaming west, the crimson heights, shower their glories through voluminous foliage. But these are the bowers where deep bliss dwells, imperial joy that owes no fealty to yonder glories." All heavenly pageants are the ministers and slaves of the throbbing content within, for here "into eyes and ears and hands the lovers pour endless ever-fresh treasures of their souls," and their rapturous being mingled in the exchange of one another's names. "Their natures had unblunted edges and were keen for bliss, confiding in it as their natural food." Then the poet knew the supersensual spring of the ripe senses into passion: when they carry the soul with them, and have the privilege of spirits to walk disembodied, boundlessly to feel.[1]

And what did Mary feel? Was she a dead body, or did she too languish and taste ecstasy? For she was not the child of nature who thrilled and dreamed beside her. The fascinating young widow lived too much in the deliciousness of her own feelings and the tension of her nerves for which she sought relaxation, now in sentimental outpourings, now in sharp flashes of wit.

§ 4

The bridegroom encouraged this lady to write her most ambitious essay, which was to trace the connection between civilisation and good fare. Madeira and grouse seemed to her to nourish better politics than abstemious plainness. And she observed that republicans had inclinations to turnips and cold mutton, as, under some monarchies, the art of cooking and eating had been degraded to fantastic gluttony. National peace and individual taste were the two conditions necessary to the cultivation of the science of gastronomy. But while her mind, in a mingling of pedantry and wit, would at one time explore such themes, at another she would become more metaphysical and argue that death was also birth, taking up the arguments of Butler's *Analogy*, that nature's processes lead us to expect what faith reveals, and that there is every reason to think

[1] *The Ordeal*.

that through the weakness and corruption of the body the new, real life passes into a fuller and more brilliant mode of being. What Mary Nicolls argued in January, in the *Monthly Observer*, was restated by George Meredith in the March number.

> Thro' rapid glances of the inner eye
> The soul is sentient of its own salvation,
> And in the Faith that such a knowledge brings
> Feels the great glory of its future wings.[1]

[1] The *Monthly Observer*. Cf. the following extract from the unpublished poem "Creed" which was originally in the Thornton-Leigh Hunt Collection and which is a colloquy between a temple worshipper and one who was not.

> "And, before this structure I design,
> The multitudes shall kneel, beholding there
> Impersonate the splendour that they worship!
> And unto us His ministers anointed,
> Us, martyrs in divine humility,—
> That splendour shall be poured, so that the people
> Gazing on us shall see poor human flesh,
> Elsewhile so frail and feeble, fill'd with Grace,
> And able to dispense the gifts of God!
> O grandeur of the thought! That this great work
> Should image His Eternity, and stand
> Eternal on the earth for evermore."
>
> . . . .
>
> "O Brother, Brother,
> To do thy duty is to act a prayer,
> More earnest in the conscious Eye of God
> Than all the formulas of earth-built creed:
> Duty is prayer, and truth to humankind
> And glad devotion unto Him who made
> The conflicts of the Soul will sink the knee
> But not in temples built of the cold stone!"
>
> They parted, and those brothers to this day,
> With kindred love and one religious aim,
> Are strangers to each other's heart and home.

A thousand intellectual sympathies united the young couple, and their intercourse was to the end a lightning of wit, at first radiant with rapture, and, later, sinister with disillusion. They were married at St. George's, Hanover Square, on August 9, 1849. Marriage burst upon the bridegroom with those wonders which thrilled his being with a mystical sense.[1]

> No longer, severing our embrace,
>   Was night a sword between us;
> But richest mystery, robed in grace,
>   To wrap us close and screen us.[2]

They went off soon after, for their honeymoon, for a tour on the Continent, in which she first introduced him to France, and then he led her back to where he had been happy on the Rhine, five years before. The delights of the honeymoon are recalled in poetry:

> Home friends we pledged, our bridal maids,
>   Sweet wishes gaily squandered.
> We wander'd far, in faëry glades,
>   Up golden heights we wander'd.
> Like King and Queen in royal bliss
>   We paced a realm enchanted,
> A realm rose-vista'd, rich from this
>   Though not from this transplanted.[2]

His boyhood's dreams and thoughts found a fresh hold in his developing maturity, and there was a new precision in his new pictures of the Rhine. At each moment observation and thought gave more strength

[1] *Letters.*   [2] Unpublished poems in British Museum.

to that life of intense feeling in which earlier youth can live simply on sights and sounds. In the autumn they were back in England.

The centre of the next few years of their life was Lower Halliford on the Thames: and the reaches above and below Windsor made Meredith as intimate with the Thames as at Neuwied he had been with the Rhine. Meredith loved his wife's little daughter, Edith, then five years old, and would carry her about on his shoulders for miles, telling her wonderful stories.

And here he came under a new influence which developed certain permanent characteristics of his thought and attitude, as Carlyle strengthened him in that unity of the ideal life with the exterior world which was his inheritance from Goethe. "We gather heroes as we go, if we are among the growing; our constancy is shown in our not discarding the old ones."[1] The great intellectual adventure of Meredith's early married life was to assimilate his keenness for sport and his German idealism to the classic and egotistic mellowness of a superb epicure. This survival of the eighteenth century was his father-in-law.[2]

§ 5

Peacock was not a great writer, and as a man no more remarkable than the cultured world has thought him. But apart from his being the father of Mary Meredith, he had many claims on the sympathy of his son-in-

[1] *Lord Ormont and His Aminta.* [2] *Letters.* S. M. Ellis.

law. Neither had been at universities, each had climbed by his own effort into the world of elegance; and Peacock had a love of nature as strong as Goethe's kinship to the classics. He thoroughly enjoyed his cynical humour, and what life offered him with it, and if he showed an intense dislike for sports, for political economy, or for Lord Brougham, he had a mellow appreciation of nature, music, Madeira, and gastronomy. With all these he now imbued his son-in-law whose feeling for him became a grateful and affectionate respect. Peacock had seen some great days: his first love had been an intense passion; he had spent years of his life among the Attic folios and marbles of the British Museum; he had taken an important part in introducing iron steamships into the trade with India, and he had shown extraordinary powers and accomplishments in his defence of the East India Company against the charges of Mr. Silk Buckingham.[1] Above all, he had been the intimate friend of Shelley from 1812 to 1818: knew all about his relations with Harriet and Mary, and had in fact made Shelley, as Scythrop, the hero of his novel, *Nightmare Abbey*. Shelley in his fervour had written of the pagan egoist with an extreme of generosity:

> his fine wit
> Makes such a wound, the knife is lost in it:
> A strain too learnèd for a shallow age,
> Too wise for selfish bigots;—let his page,
> Which charms the chosen spirits of the time,
> Fold itself up for the serener clime

[1] *Times Literary Supplement*, 1927. *Poems* of 1851.

Of years to come, and find its recompense
In that just expectation.[1]

To his love of Greek poetry, and the mountain scenery of Wales, was added a geniality that captured the affection of ardent poets and which made young Meredith feel towards him what young Shelley had thought twenty-five or thirty years before. With Peacock the wedded couple found a home in the intervals of their sojourns in lodgings, now by the seaside, now on the Thames.

But even their lodging-houses were distinguished. At "The Limes" at Weybridge their hostess was a widow of Macirone who had been an A.D.C. to the King of Naples, and whose daughter, afterwards Lady Hornby, was the original of Meredith's Emilia. Here too came Horne, and Eyre Crowe, an A.R.A., who wrote two books on Thackeray, and here also Bulwer Lytton was a guest. Here the two Merediths lived, now writing poetry together, now writing on cookery. "Economy in a wife," they began, in Peacock's style, "is the most certain Charm to ensure the affection and industry of a husband." Cooking, they argued, in its influence over health and life, was an art which philosophers of the highest class, and they alone, would understand. It was a part of that wider art of housekeeping which kept humanity happy, and was not to be divorced from the adroit management of servants. Familiarity, they said, breaks the neck of obedience, but praise was necessary: "to cherish the

[1] " Letter to Maria Gisborne."

desire of pleasing in them you must show them that you are pleased." Ah, how clever, and how delightful, to gild with philosophy the sauce-pan and prepare an aphorism to mark the oven door![1]

§ 6

But Meredith, while reading *Gryll Grange* or *Nightmare Abbey* (for *Crotchet Castle* was not yet in the writing), lived a fuller and more intimate life with the sea and the clouds. From the sordidness which mingled with the attractiveness of London, and from the "sad slaves of obscene jokes," he would escape to gleaming waters, to circling hills, to forest flowers, and starlight on the pebbled stream, and to a contemplation at once rapturous and precise of all the pageantry of day and night in the open air, with grass and plants and flowers growing in their rich variety, and the birds above them singing. What had been his joy, in his childhood, was now his joy and his wisdom too. For him the mystic secret was, already, to be made one with nature. He loved especially the southwest wind: its play with clouds and lights; and its music in the woods:

> Hazels close,
> Thick brambles and dark brushwood tufts
> And briared brakes that line the dells
> With shaggy beetling brows, had sung
> Shrill music, while the tattered flaws
> Tore over them, and now the whole

[1] S. M. Ellis. René Galland.

> Tumultuous concords, seized at once
> With savage inspiration. . . .
> And round the oak a solemn roll
> Of organ harmony ascends,
> And in the upper foliage sounds
> A symphony of distant seas.

As the wind blew up wildly from the lingering lines of sunset over the hills, he felt that he was one with all that air meant to the life of nature:

> Great music under heaven is made,
> And in the track of rushing darkness
> Comes the solemn shape of night,
>   And broods above the earth;
> *A thing of nature am I now,*
> *Abroad, without a sense or feeling*
> *Born not of her bosom;*
> *Content with all her truths and fates;*
> *Even as yon strip of grass that bows*
> *Above the new-born violet bloom,*
>   *And sings with wood and field.*

The life of nature, the changes of the light, were the imagery which taught him most about the life of his own spirit: his soul should learn to be true to the primal joy of the dawn and

> Like aspens in the faintest breeze
> Turn all its silver sides and tremble into song.

And mingling with all these came that wholesome enchantment which poured upon him, when the colour of the dawn, flushing heaven and throwing an exquisite intensity into the colourings of earth, seemed nature's mirroring of the love which beat backwards and forwards between his pulses and his spirit. The rising moon, crowning June's long twilight loveliness with her glowing beauty, woke the secret of his love:

> Far up the sky with ever purer beam,
> > Upon the throne of night the moon was seated,
> > And down the valley glens the shades retreated,
>
> And silver light was on the open stream.
> > And thus in me, and thus in me, they sighed,
> > *Aspiring love has hallowed Passion's tide.*

And then the hallowed rapture offered him a still more intimate understanding of the beauty of flowers and their secret: was he not, like bird and flower, the possessor of his bride?

> When at dawn she wakens, and her fair face gazes
> > Out on the weather thro' the window panes,
>
> Beauteous she looks! like a white water-lily
> > Bursting out of bud on the rippled river plains.
>
> When from bed she rises, clothed from neck to ankle
> > In her long nightgown, sweet as boughs of May,
>
> Beauteous she looks! like a tall garden lily
> > Pure from the night and perfect for the day!

In the intervals of these raptures was the excitement of taking exercise. He found another rapture in reading poetry. There was the poetry of Tennyson, as there had been the poetry of Horne: but there was also the poetry of Spenser, of Shakespeare, of Milton, of Coleridge, of Shelley, of Wordsworth, of Keats and even, as Peacock reminded him, of Southey. Each of these had for him its peculiar felicity: with Spenser he dwelt among

> Lakes where the sunsheen is mystic with splendour and softness;
> Vales where sweet life is all Summer with golden romance.

Wordsworth was to him the voice of great nature, and sublime with his lofty conceptions. Shelley he compared to Shelley's own skylark:

> See'st thou a Skylark whose glistening winglets ascending
> Quiver like pulses beneath the melodious dawn?
> Deep in the heart-yearning distance of heaven it flutters—
> Wisdom and beauty and love are the treasures it brings down at eve.

Each of these poets was his teacher and ensample, and their mystical harmonies were for ever chiming to him through the loveliness of the fresh air, till he himself became the echo of their poetry. He was already one among them, and wrote immortal verses. Not yet mature, he knew; the fruits of extreme youth and, with some exceptions, of labour; they would serve their purpose if they made his name known to those who look with encouragement on an earnest student of nature who is determined to persevere till he obtain the wisdom, the inspiration, the self-possession of the poet.[1]

[1] *Poems* of 1851. Letters in British Museum.

Such was his account of himself to Ollier, a man of distinguished literary friendships, the friend of Peacock, as he had been the friend of Shelley.

> Enough for me,
> To paint the flower in all its natural hues
> And plant it.

So he had written with equal modesty to Horne. He could hardly have dreamed of an awakening to fame, still less of money. The young writer, the young poet, has expressed its youth, and is unwilling to remain hidden. "I believe," he wrote to Horne on May 10, 1849, "that I am now steadily improving. I have but flickered heretofore."[1]

Youth, when all is said, has its own charms. We could not dispense with these early poems of Meredith, when he perfumed the freshness of dawn with the aroma of his personality. Health and sweetness were what made them delightful: and these struck the attention of Kingsley, who in a long article of acute but sympathetic criticism gave Meredith the best appraisal and the best advice, in *Fraser's Magazine:* "One idea has risen before his mind, and shaped itself into a song; not perfect in form, perhaps, but as far as it goes, healthful and consistent and living, through every branch and spray of detail." Kingsley compared Meredith to Correggio, inviting him to see how Correggio, in spite of his exquisite lusciousness of colour and chiaroscuro and form, prevented his pictures from being tawdry, or overwrought, by so

[1] Unpublished letter in British Museum.

subjecting his parts in harmonious gradation to the severe scientific unity of the whole as to make a picture a single glorious rainbow and his Magdalen a living emerald. If Meredith could but have followed this counsel! He was, as William Michael Rossetti already noted, too vivid, excitable and diffuse. But with this, as Rossetti also noticed, went another quality, one which makes Meredith a supreme poet for romantic and rapturous youth. It was warmth: "warmth of emotion and to a certain extent of inspiration, like the high mantling blush on a beautiful face, or a breath glowing upon your cheek." There was in this something so open and so engaging that, once recognise it, one had an intimacy with the poet as with a close friend. Such warmth, such openness, such freshness were the best promise one could ask of youth. So Kingsley noted: "Only he who begins honestly ends greatly." But to Meredith, the greeting of contempt, which met him too often, worked like agony on a system which was once again run down for lack of food, as it had been when he lived in Ebury Street. There were times when in his paroxysms of desperation he would run round the Park till he dropped.[1]

---

[1] *The Athenæum*, Aug. 23, 1851; *Fraser's Magazine*, Dec., 1851.

III

CRAVING THE BURIED DAY

§ 1

IF Meredith had been only the wholesome and rapturous poet, he would have reached into a realm of his own. But what made him rarer was that he was no less a sportsman than a poet. To one of his own sons his keenness for sport seemed the key to his mystery. He had the countryman's fondness for dogs and horses. When he lodged in Ebury Street he would, in the month of May, walk to Esher, doing thirty or forty miles a day. He looked on hard exercise as an essential of a boy's life, and vital in a man's. There is an article in an old *Wykehamist*,[1] an article long forgotten, where in his own style he urges the joys of the Spartan life on and for school-boys. Mrs. Totgrass addresses Mr. Theophilus Thews:

"DEAR MR. THEWS—I have been alarmed and distressed by hearing that my dear boy, whose health you *know* is delicate, though I am assured his constitution is sound *in the main*, has fallen into the ways of modern young men, with this mania for increasing the size of their muscles. That he should be afflicted with a desire to rival his companions is not at all astonishing, but it does indeed surprise me that *you*, to whom I entrusted my dearest, with the very fullest belief that he was

[1] June, 1872.

under Providence, in the safest, *discreetest* hands a mother, unhappily a widow, could hand him over to, *both* for his body's welfare and his soul's, should consent to countenance, nay, encourage, a pernicious system leading to numberless vices and evils, to the destruction of his health, (I refer you to the recent letter of Dr. Syncope in one of the papers—a morning journal, I believe—I do not think a penny paper, so it is creditable) heart-disease is one of the commonest; *remora* of the heart, he says. And my boy! my Julius! They never get over the effects, Dr. Syncope says. They appear strong men, and in a moment—! This is a *medical* opinion. For a social and religious one, Dr. Oldport will, I do hope, have weight with you, and he condemns it utterly as tending towards a toleration of *low society*. You have met him; he is one of your cloth, and he is decidedly *against* it, and can scarcely understand a brother clergyman's approval of a system so subversive of our principles. Pardon me, if I speak impressively; I am a mother, and feel the welfare of my son is at stake. . . . I may have misunderstood dear Julius; he writes in such spirits, quite *unlike* him! and if I have, I am sure you will find excuses for a mother. It may not be exactly that horrid *training* and public-houses, and young men, like engines, caring for nothing but speed and stakes and *betting*. I do not object to cricket, of course. We have had cricketers in our family. But I have seen dreadful examples. Dr. Oldport's son—or *his* wife's brother's nephew—I am not certain which—but the young man is a wreck in consequence—through *Training!* . . .

"I entreat you, for my comfort, tell me if I have indeed misunderstood dear Julius.... The newspapers. ... Medical men ... habits of *gentlemen*. But the dear boy's letter is so happy in its tone, and well expressed, that I really am afraid to put it to him, lest it should really be true that he has, in the words of Dr. Oldport, *abandoned his station* like Esau, and I apply to you to confirm it, most devoutly trusting that you will not ... In conclusion ...

"Dear Mr. Thews, believe me, yours sincerely,
"Matilda Totgrass.
"To the Rev. Theophilus Thews."

"Dear Madam—After carefully perusing the letter you have done me the honour to address to me, I believe I am in a position to appreciate its full significance. Your son is in training, and with my approbation. He has not merely 'gone' into training, which implies ordinarily an intention of going out of it as soon as convenient; but he is in a state of training, and means to keep in it. Accept the unwonted cheerfulness of his letter for a proof of the present excellent results. We began last winter. I have not to inform his mother that Julius commonly commenced his winter with a cold that accompanied him to the end of the spring, and reduced him to a machine calculated to emit twenty sneezes to the hour. Medicine availed nothing, nor would a surgical operation have helped me to drill a grain of knowledge into a head tenanted by that inveterate enemy. The question for us was whether it was sent by malignant Fates to stunt the poor boy's physical and intellectual growth, or whether we could combat it by human agency. I decided to attempt the latter. We trotted him at first for fifteen minutes in flannels before breakfast; after which, bath, scrubbing, and the moderate satisfaction of an increasing appetite. Symptom the first:—a singular vivacity, brightness of eye, readiness of tongue. We trotted him faster and longer. Symptom the second:—extraordinary appetite, combined with power to wait for his food. Trotted him half-an-hour to a pump, stripped him, drenched him, gave him an icicle to suck, wiped, groomed, dressed him, trotted him at a brisk pace home. Symptom the third:—not a vestige of catarrh, immunity from atmospheric changes, promptness to spring to his feet to perform services. He craved permission to take lessons in boxing; granted. Proposed to join a gymnastic club: agreed to. Offered to match himself to run against any of his comrades, vault and box them; here I interposed, dear Madam, and accosted his mind. He confessed that he did hanker after the stimulus of rivalry, and we had a long discussion. I will not inflict it on you, but will condense what I told him. 'England wants men, and our Creator virtuous creatures. Your training is not an end but a means; you want no more than to keep an established health up to the mark, that you may feel the pleasure of animal health on your method of preserving it; so that this shall always seem a greater delight to you, as well as more friendly to your wellbeing than any whatsoever of the baser temptations. Aim to be athletic, not an athlete; and shun Olympic laurels, they are not for our time.' And so forth. I think

I may say, Madam, that he listened to me profitably; at all events, he sticks to his work and challenges none. England is desperately in want of men of the kind he is coming to be. The newspapers show that the want is felt; otherwise we should not see them fanning and puffing the young athletes to extremes, exciting the vanity of the lads, until they lay themselves open to a warning from Dr. Syncope. I shall use my utmost influence with Julius to prevent his rowing in matches in outriggers, when he goes to the University. It might do him no harm to row a match in a barge; and a punting match is good, if he must (and it is one of the errors of our English nature to incline that way) enter into matches. But the trim taper outrigger driven for speed, at any cost, is death to the lungs. The lungs affect the circulation, and the circulation the heart. Dr. Syncope is right there.

"If you have any remaining doubt concerning the wisdom of my treatment of your son Julius, I beg you to commission Dr. Syncope to pay me a visit, that he may inspect our young gentleman.

"Believe me, dear Madam, it is you, and not your son, who have taken to an extreme course in athletics. You are guilty of the *skiomachia* of the ancient professed athletes, the *skiomachia* or shadow fight, a fair enough exercise when not carried too far, and when we begin with a determination to thrash the shadow out of sight and consistency, but undoubtedly bad when we allow it to dodge us and renew the contest when it pleases, instead of we.

"Have I convinced you, Madam? I shall be happy

to continue the correspondence and advance further reasons in support of the system, and especially upon the point of 'low society,' a question that places me at variance with the respected Dr. Oldport; for *I* hold that it is for the good of the country that gentlemen should not shun 'low society.' The diversion is already —to quote your words—one to 'alarm and distress' patriotic minds; and, moreover, if the gentlemen are of so delicate a cast that instead of assisting to uplift, they are dragged down by 'low society,' of what particular value are they by comparison? But this is another and a wider subject.

"I am, dear Madam, with profound respect,
"Your obedient servant,
"THEOPHILUS THEWS.
"To the Hon. Matilda Totgrass."

This letter, though written when Meredith was over forty, is full of counsels he put into practice in his twenties. For years he walked to and fro over the downs to Epsom, arriving in time for a great race, watched the long row of horses breasting the hill, ran across to see them again passing Tattenham Corner into the straight, and waited for the winner's name, which soon filled the air.[1]

During his walks Meredith recalled with particular zest his memories of boxers, men who, matched for a purse of fifty sovereigns, found pride of place in *Bell's Life*, and with some of whom he himself had sparred. One of these, driving his young woman from London

[1] *The Times*, Feb. 12, 1928.

into Kent in a high dog-cart, heard a chance remark to her disparagement from three navvies, at which, flinging the reins to her, he casually laid the three navvies flat on the road. Men look at their best when they are sparring, Meredith noted in *Rhoda Fleming*. And Skepsey showed that his keenness for boxing survived up to the time when he was over sixty.[1]

Writing, however, to a friend from Esher, he confessed that boxing, though good, was a little brutal. "Fencing brightens the eye without blackening it." Fencing, in fact, he thought the best exercise in the world, giving thorough exercise with fit measure of excitement, better than anything going to occupy brain, while it braces nerves and tightens muscles. But for himself, he added, "my best solitary exercise is throwing the beetle—a huge mallet weighing 18 or 19 pounds—and catching the handle, performing wondrous tricks therewith." Wrestling and walking, his endurance was unwearying; his muscles wire and whipcord, without an ounce of flesh to spare. In the old days when walking was itself a sport, he was an eager walker; in the great days of walking-matches—from London to Dover or to Canterbury and back—he walked part of the road with the champions. He remembered one who, entering a tavern at Canterbury, called for a bottle of their special Red Seal in a tankard, drank it off and started back to London again. Such men were heroes to him. He made walking a thing to set the blood tingling. "A man should sweat once a day—then he will have a clear brain," he used

[1] *The Times*, Feb. 12, 1928. *Rhoda Fleming. One of Our Conquerors.*

to say, and "Sweating saves from impurities at all events." He never sauntered, never lounged: an old friend noted, he strode with the stride of a giant.[1]

As for cricket, he preferred a game of hard hitting and scores quickly run up. A drawn game was his anathema; he liked the village cricket of his boyhood, when each side went in to win, and he was bored by stone-walling. But he followed first-class cricket in the newspapers when he was an old man. In those days lawn tennis, like croquet, was a soft game, and he did not play it: he was an excellent diver and swimmer, and every morning until late in life he took his cold tub, which was indeed at that time part of the solemn ritual of the sportsman's day.[2]

Hard exercise gave him a good appetite, and his ideas were clear on the subject of diet. A connoisseur, he was never a drunkard nor a glutton. He preferred, in fact, vegetarian food to meat. Beer he found not too easy to digest and a good sound claret made blood without heating; to aid the digestion of late dinner he advocated a choice of music, dancing, dialogue, laughter and billiards. Everywhere there was the same extraordinary and exuberant vitality: in every moment a phenomenal energy, the physical forces rivals and equals of the mental. In his sports came out those mastering qualities of his character as they were of his fitness, courage, and strenuousness. He saw in them life's central need and joy, the very reason for living.

[1] *Letters*. S. M. Ellis, *George Meredith*.
[2] *The Times*, Feb. 12, 1928.

> Life is but a little holding, lent
> To do a mighty labour. We are one
> With heaven and the stars, when it is spent
> To do God's aim. Else die we with the sun.[1]

These he would quote as his own favourite lines. Life, more life and fuller, life where the body and the brain pour their energy into full tides of feeling is what men should seek while it may be found. Not to whine into a past that had turned and fled, but to look up bravely, planted on the honest present, to the problems of the pressing future, never content to live in a fool's paradise,—to court activity, making use of each moment as it came so that it would be transformed into the energy of character instead of hanging behind to haunt one with the sloughed chrysalises of vanished butterfly hopes and impulses; this was the ideal that Meredith developed in his natural zest for sport.[2]

§ 2

But the sportsman-poet, however rare and however admirable as such, is still far removed from being an angel. The very intensity with which he lived made him difficult to live with, impatient not only of life's little worries, but of its irksomeness. He could not suit himself to trivial rounds or common tasks, and his exaltation of natural life was far from being supernatural. It needs a heroism all its own, and not unholy, to live in cheap lodgings, and diet cheerfully on the coarse cuisine of poverty, which could drop down to a mere

[1] Their opening is quoted on his tombstone.
[2] J. A. Hammerton. *Vittoria. Letters.*

plate of porridge for the day. And it would have been much to ask of intense natures like those of George and Mary Meredith. Each was highly strung, each imaginative, each emotional: but more than this, each was quick to anger and cuttingly satirical in dispute. The cuts of the rapier of ridicule are not worth making, and fencers so skilful had not learned the skill of living that demands suppression of skill in satire. These two were witty enough to be such fools as to enjoy quarrelling; flashes of amazing brilliance shot from their altercations, and their rages would be interrupted by his roars of laughter. But at the basis of their relation was disillusionment. They had set out for the upper air on wings of rapture too loosely attached for changes of temperature, for contrary winds, or for the cyclonic uproar of their unusual temperaments. His chivalry towards women, since not infrequently it was hardly on the hither side of adoration, did not make a dangerous marriage any safer. Before she ever married Meredith, Mary had fallen into the habit of pining for what is not and of questioning the reality of joy. She found an expression of her widowed life in thinking of a blackbird whose mate had been shot:

> To him the pulse of Love doth seem
> The vision of a hopeless dream
>   And mockery,
> That sea of air where others sport
> To him a mist where shadows float,
>   No verity.[1]

[1] MS. in Harvard Library. *Letters*. This poem was adapted by Meredith himself for "The Two Blackbirds" in a later number of the *Monthly Observer*.

That habit was to return on her with fatal ease when Meredith's alienation widowed her a second time while he was yet believed to be her rapturous lover. "To know when a thing has perished or is vital," Meredith wrote after his wife's death, "is one of the tests of wisdom. Figure to yourself a lover who hears a voice in his ghostly bosom, demanding answer to the question, 'Was it all delusion?'" And thus he bases his logic—"Impossible; it could not be delusion, for the dream was so immense, the rapture so heavenly."[1]

To be the sticks and stones of a glorified past, to cling to the days that were, in this he found his great temptation. And all his chivalry was sensitive at the knowledge that he was an equal disappointment to the woman whom he had worshipped and whose sensibility had no body of robustness, and, still worse, that she could not tell him so:

> The strange low sobs that shook their common bed
> Were called into her with a sharp surprise,
> And strangled mute, like little gaping snakes,
> Dreadfully venomous to him.

He knew that she already loved another. Jealousy added its pang to disillusionment, when her eyes glowed with a rich light as they swam to the man whom she had newly singled. Living with her in married intimacy, her familiar lineaments could be at times more keenly tempting than new loveliness:

[1] *Letters.*

> The splendours, mysteries, dearer because known,
> Nor less divine: Love's inmost sacredness
> Called to him, "Come!"

but he knew that in heart, if not in body, she was unfaithful. She had feasted on sensation, while he had thought, even in his raptures, of a life of energy and service. In love's deep woods, he dreamt of loyalty to life:

> My crime is that, the puppet of a dream,
> I plotted to be worthy of the world.[1]

His difficulty was that he could neither rid himself of the past, nor yet build on it. He must remember every throb of joy, and realise in remembering that the whole of life is mixed:

> And if I drink oblivion of a day,
> So shorten I the stature of my soul.

Nor could his principles help him to serenity:

> Cold as a mountain in its star-pitched tent,
> Stood high Philosophy, less friend than foe:
> Whom self-caged Passion, from its prison bars,
> Is always watching with a wondering hate.
> Not till the fire is dying in the grate,
> Look we for any kinship with the stars.
> Oh, wisdom never comes when it is gold,
> And the great price we pay for it full worth:
> We have it only when we are half earth.
> Little avails that coinage to the old!

[1] *Modern Love.*

The terrible fact, conceived in a style of traditional splendour and beauty, made memory like despair. At one moment

> Hushed we sat
> As lovers to whom Time is whispering.

But he must turn from this to an emptied present.

> A kiss is but a kiss now! and no wave
> Of a great flood that whirls me to the sea.

Passion in anguish has never in English expressed itself in an austerer eloquence, or wedded thought more pregnantly.[1]

§ 3

Poverty, neglect, and disillusionment severely scourged Meredith's intense and at times morbid sensitiveness. He had found relief in writing a story of the Rhine where Farina, the inventor of eau de cologne, was the hero. It was Meredith's first essay in lending romance to tradesmen, and excessively brilliant in descriptive splendours. In it he relieved himself of some of his feelings about the difficulty surrounding his social position at the same time that he recalled all that the Rhine and its legends had meant to him in his youth. This had been preceded by a still more brilliant essay in the style of the *Arabian Nights*, an oriental fantasia, rich in jewelled imagery and quaint descriptions; its theme was the need of discipline to bring out the finest in character; the recurring blow, he urged,

[1] *Modern Love*.

is but celestial hail, and steel is tempered by the hammer. Endurance must teach effort:

> Out of hundreds who aspire,
> Eighties perish, nineties tire.[1]

While he turned to these distractions to build up a literary career on the solidity of prose, he was attempting to infuse prose with the subtler aroma of poetry. For it is the excellence of Meredith that he can endow prose with a poetic rarity of beauty, as it is his fault that he jars the temper of prose with the oddness which, in poetry, we not merely tolerate, but accept with a glad surprise. Poetry is more obviously art than prose. Those who accept its discipline are allowed more idiosyncrasies. Meredith gave himself in prose the double discipline of an unflagging novelty of expression, and a style which, in the intervals of oddness, sought to recreate beauty in transcribing the elusive shows he discerned in his busy communion with nature. In all these he had already left Peacock far behind. His mind was both mellower and more elevated, and all his experiences were heightened by being pervaded with his sense of rapture. Discerning eyes saw already what this promised. "In exuberance of imagery, in picturesque wildness of incident, in significant humour, in aphoristic wisdom *The Shaving of Shagpat* is a new Arabian night": so George Eliot wrote; she admired particularly the constant alternation of passion and wild imaginativeness with humour and pithy sense. In *Shagpat*, ingeniousness had already

[1] *The Shaving of Shagpat.*

created its peculiar expression. For an example of it George Eliot cited:

"She clenched her hands an instant, with that feeling which knocketh a nail in the coffin of a desire not dead."

For freshness: a maiden's eyes that were "dark, under a low arch of darker lashes, like stars on the skirts of the storm."

For poetic exquisiteness: "stars that were above the purple heights, and the blushes of heaven that streamed up the sky."

For vividness and vigour: how horsemen "flourished their lances with cries, and jerked their heels into the flanks of their steeds, and stretched forward till their beards were mixed with the tossing manes, and the dust rose after them, crimson in the sun."[1]

The young man who at twenty-six could write such sentences was sure of a name that English literature could never forget. But the ripening of his maturity first showed itself in his refusing to suit his orchestration to the nine years' seniority and the firmer social position of his wife. There was within him a struggle between chivalry and manhood, as there was between romantic sentiment and vigour. It was inevitable that his wife should wish that he had a settled income like her father, and be content to give his leisure to writing. She went so far towards this end as to make an appointment in London for him. But he forgot on his way to the station, and spent the day in one of his long cross-country walks.[2]

[1] *The Leader,* Jan. 5, 1856.   [2] René Galland.

§ 4

From that day on, she had to realise that a man of genius will nurse his genius as a mother sacrifices her own welfare to that of her child. Anything which threatens its life or success will awaken his ferocity. And while he devoted himself more and more to his art, she became more the housekeeper and the mother. For a child had been born in 1853, half-way between the *Poems* and *Shagpat*. Mary Meredith was religious, needing both for will and feelings the support of faith. Not a sacramentalist, she found her religion with Maurice and Kingsley. George Meredith had much in common with them, but his enthusiasms were all for the poetry of nature. In support of this, he inclined towards the paganism of Peacock; Charnock, Horne, and his new friend, Fitzgerald, who had already in youth the mellow cynicism of Adrian Harley, all drew him out into the current of rationalism, and amid the raw partialities of the time, he failed to distinguish between superstition and faith. That made him sinister to Mary Meredith where she most needed a friend. Religion is more than usually necessary to women who are nervous invalids, and Mary Meredith had inherited from her mother a tendency towards insanity, which it needed only a strain to develop. Between her and her husband there was a spiritual discord, jarring the worse on temperaments too similar in a nervous tensity which made them mystical in different ways. Nor could any wife fail to resent the generosity with which Meredith admired the women he did admire. A great virtue grew inevitably from his chivalry towards women; the friendships which grew out of it, even when most platonic and most innocent, were decked in the robes of passion, and even when he had grown old, his closest friends could not always detect when his attractions towards a woman were, or were not, amorous. Both *Modern Love* and *Richard Feverel* show that he felt intensely the need of faithfulness, and its strain:

> I am not of those miserable males
> Who sniff at vice and, daring not to snap,
> Do therefore hope for heaven. I take the hap
> Of all my deeds. The wind that fills my sails
> Propels, but I am helmsman. . . .[1]

He knew that he was to blame as well as she, and when they suffered, it was most because of their intimacy, and of the moments when at times it renewed, or poignantly recalled, the vanished ecstasy:

> . . . If I the death of Love had deeply planned,
> I never could have made it half so sure,
> As by the unblest kisses which upbraid
> The full-waked sense; or, failing that, degrade!
> 'Tis morning: but no morning can restore
> What we have forfeited. I see no sin:
> The wrong is mixed. In tragic life, God wot,
> No villain need be! Passions spin the plot:
> We are betrayed by what is false within.[1]

[1] *Modern Love*.

To Mary's questioning eyes the oddness of dress in Charnock or Horne was as sinister as their rationalism.

The intimacy of husband and wife survived for seven years. But a year after the publication of *Shagpat* they decided not to spend Christmas together. She remained at Blackheath, he went back to Seaford. At Seaford, two years later, the tragedy reached its height. Mary was now in love with Henry Wallis, a young painter whose work in the Academy had shown some promise of greatness, who had been urging her to elope with him. She had spoken of her intention to her husband. He remonstrated. He admitted that for their lack of unity he had been partly to blame: he recognised the tragic situation: he told her he knew already of her relations with Wallis. "But if you leave our roof," he said, "you commit an intolerable wrong to yourself and our child: you make yourself an outcast; you are bound to stay." But she paid no heed. In after days

> he learned how silence best can speak
> The awful things when Pity pleads for Sin.

He realised that her openness with him had been the daylight of honest speech. Furthermore, she had suggested, for she had persuaded herself to believe, that in leaving him she left him free to unite himself to another he preferred. And in his friendships, as in his fury, he realised that he had shown a lack of regard for her sensitiveness. He asked himself:

> If for those times I must ask charity,
> Have I not any charity to give?

And this the more because of the sensitive fragility of her own nature:

> It is no vulgar nature I have wived.
> Secretive, sensitive, she takes a wound
> Deep to her soul.[1]

The wound Meredith had given was repeated quickly and more fiercely by Wallis, who had taken her to Capri. Abandoned by him, and returning to England with a child not her husband's, she sought reconciliation with him. He refused. She sought to see her son. Meredith used to the full his right to separate them. Through all this, her brother remained his friend. But then the unhappy woman grew desperate and her reason gave way. Even when she was dying, Meredith did not relent further than that in the last days he allowed the little boy to go to see his mother.

But when at last she died, and Meredith realised that his last opportunities were gone, he was overcome. One of those profound emotional crises of which his nature was capable racked and tore him. This was the woman who, when all was said, inspired his masterpieces, *Modern Love* and *Richard Feverel*, and in whom he had realised the dream of *Love in the Valley*:

Thus piteously Love closed what he begat:
The union of this ever-diverse pair!
These two were rapid falcons in a snare,
Condemned to do the flitting of the bat.
Lovers beneath the singing sky of May
They wandered once; clear as the dew on flowers:

[1] *Modern Love*.

But they fed not on the advancing hours:
Their hearts held cravings for the buried day.
Then each applied to each that fatal knife,
Deep questioning, which probes to endless dole.
Ah, what a dusty answer gets the soul
When hot for certainties in this our life![1]

But before the tragedy had closed its curtain on her death, Meredith had sought relief in writing a book about the education of a boy. *Richard Feverel* was a new *Emile*. But unlike *Emile*, he was to prove the excellence of the education according to nature, by showing the tragedy of education according to a system. Sir Austin Feverel, as Meredith wrote forty years afterwards to Mrs. Meynell, had built up a system on his unforgiveness of his wife. If Meredith was able to criticise Sir Austin, it was because he recognised that he himself was false to his standards in being relentless to his own wife. And this terrible defect of the quality of mercy, which accounted both for his broken friendships and his faults of style, was to torture him, and torture others to the end. *Modern Love* and *The Ordeal* are Meredith's *De Profundis: If thou, Lord, wilt be extreme to mark what is done amiss, Lord, who may abide it?*

When a man or woman has deeply loved, when their fortune and their happiness have grown around one object with tendrils fast as flesh and blood, and when this object, escaping them, has left their being without a centre, they return again and again to their

[1] *Modern Love.*

memories of it, and with endless questionings debate the nature of their possession, and the way they lost it, and remorsefully ask whether they might have retained it. It is not one circumstance alone which determines what might have been: a hundred are interdependent, being essential to their nature, and the very nature of their possession made their loss inevitable. But they can for long relish no object but that which has a connection with the centre of their lost happiness, and cherish painfully those fleeting moments when it seemed about to return. There was one of those which Meredith recalled with especial vividness:

We saw the swallows gathering in the sky,
And in the osier-isle we heard them noise.
We had not to look back on summer joys,
Or forward to a summer of bright dye:
But in the largeness of the evening earth
Our spirits grew as we went side by side.
The hour became her husband and my bride.
Love, that had robbed us so, thus blessed our dearth!
The pilgrims of the year waxed very loud
In multitudinous chatterings, as the flood
Full brown came from the West, and like pale blood
Expanded to the upper crimson cloud.
Love, that had robbed us of immortal things,
This little moment mercifully gave. . . .

It was from the straining tension of such memories, touching him to his quickest depths, that he sought relief in a work of art congruent to all that was most real to him. His own youth, and his son's, his young romance, the rapture of his love, the tragedy of it, the place, in other words, which feeling must give to energy and to nature, the horror of his own unforgiveness and what it might mean in poisoning the life of the son to whom he transferred the adoration he could no longer give the mother: these are the ingredients of Meredith's first complete novel, which is his most popular and his greatest. Nowhere in English literature is love so ardent, so poignant, so romantic as in *Richard Feverel*. Here the beauty is richer, and the tragedy more intimate, than in *Romeo and Juliet*.

It is full of wisdom that grows round and full from the vivid poetry of life's joy, but its theme is nature, which means that—

                         the grace
Of heaven seems holding earth in its embrace,[1]

and that the body, which is the vehicle and wing of love, is essential to nature's worship and religion. This book is, in fact, the poetic counterpart of *The Origin of Species*, which appeared in the same year. In man's kindred to the animal was a truth of his nobleness.

For such a truth, with all that it implies, of the intimacy of love with life, the prudery of early Victorians was but ill prepared. Respectable families "objected to it as dangerous and wicked and damnable."[2] That was an age when nothing was thought so hideous as nakedness, and nothing so wicked as impassioned love. "My constant error," Meredith was to write in

[1] *Modern Love*.   [2] Unpublished letter.

Evan Harrington, "is in supposing that I write for the wicked people that begat us."

§ 5

The Times found the book penetrative in its depth of insight, and rich in its variety of experience, but of impurity it found none. Such, it said, could only come from corrupt imaginations which pervert the fine purpose of the author; but the book was more than the clergy or the critics as a whole could stand. "I find I have offended Mudie and the British Nation," Meredith wrote to Lucas. "He will not, or happily dare not, put me in his advertised catalogue. Because of the immoralities I depict! O canting Age!" Henceforward the clergy were never to be free from his boisterous anathemas. Like people of lesser genius, he found the symbol of ineptitude in the poor clergyman. So, in a verse letter, to Janet Duff-Gordon, he wrote:

> But what is this? Ah, thought of dread!
>   Ah, thought of rage and shame!
> That, lower when I lean my head—
>   I hear—the CURATE'S NAME.

Tennyson's Arthur, he said, was "a crowned curate." In one unpublished letter he even referred to a *carnal curate*. "I am thinking of becoming a socialist," he once said, "and then I shall have been everything, except a curate." And so, as the very acme of absurdity, he proclaimed to Lady Danesfort: "They tell me that the curates—the *curates*, my dear!—are beginning to quote me in their sermons." It was true. A time was to come when curates could be other than Victorians, and when in fact they could welcome the catholic wholeness of his truths.[1]

But there is no curate in *The Ordeal of Richard Feverel*—only a very pious child, born of a clergyman's widow—"he was a postermost child, and afore his birth that woman read nothin' but Blair's *Grave*, over and over again, from the end to the beginnin'; that's a serious book!—very hard readin'!—and at four years of age that child that come of it was really the piousest infant,—he was like a little curate. His eyes was up; he talked so solemn." The child was an acquaintance of the wisest of cooks, a cook that knew you can't have men's hearts without their stomachs. Many were the hours that Meredith relished with Mrs. Ockenden at Seaford, before he transformed her into Mrs. Berry, as he transformed Maurice Fitzgerald into Adrian Harley and Charnock into Hippias the dyspeptic, and Richardson or Peacock into himself; there are finer figures than Hippias or Adrian; Sir Austin, Lady Blandish, Austin Wentworth, Clare, Lucy, Richard.[2] The book is not the denunciation of a system, but a pæan in praise of nature, in the person of heroic youth, better understood by cooks and farmers than by philosophic egoists waving censers before their own wisdom. The man who wrote it, though so masterly and so mature, was still only twenty-eight or twenty-nine. He had known disillusion, after love had opened

[1] Unpublished letters. *The Times*, Oct. 14, 1859; Feb. 12, 1928. *Memories of George Meredith*, by Lady Butcher.
[2] S. M. Ellis, *George Meredith*.

to him immense dreams and heavenly raptures; he had a little boy whom he adored. And he created in imagination a world as rapturous and as tragic as that which he knew, peopled with splendid forms, and seen through a haze of gorgeous renaissance grandeur, till Victoria's people seemed like those of Titian and Veronese, and England's air as full of coloured light as a picture of Lorrain's or Turner's. What was objected against Meredith was in fact objected against Turner. "I never saw such colours," said a lady before one of his pictures. "Ah, madam," Turner at once asked her, "don't you wish you could?" Beauty is not less real because dull eyes are blind to it. Only the musicians know true music.

The test of Meredith is not the verdict of contemporary curates, or of any commonplace men. It is the judgment of those who live on the scale on which he himself lived. What shocked the world of 1859, in his great novel, was that for which he will be blessed for ages by natures which are richer and more sensitive to life. It was the height and wholeness of his passion. We associate such height, such wholeness, with the names of Shakespeare and of Goethe. But neither have written with such warmth, either in measured or looser rhythms, of the heart's link with common earth, or worked it out with such fine energy of elevated thought. Hardman wrote, after reading *Modern Love:* "No other man but himself could have written it. No other man possesses that wondrous knowledge of the human heart, that weird power of analysis of feelings, that deep and pitiless probing of the soul."

And the words were true also of *The Ordeal of Richard Feverel*.

The book begins by picturing the disastrous influence of a wife's desertion on a husband of fine mind and heart. The philosophy of his ripe bitterness was to be worked out in the life of his baby son. This philosophy was to put nature and virtue in the foreground, but at the same time to remove the boy from the contagion of the common world, and in fact to make the son a brighter and fresher mirror of the virtues of his father.

Was not that Meredith's own temptation with his delightful little boy? Was not the son kept from his mother? Was he not condemned to make his father his special companion? And did he not in the end resent it and insist on his own freedom? The story of Arthur Meredith, as we shall see, explains the problems of *The Ordeal*. Richard Feverel's history begins with a fight, and a thrashing, pictured vividly by a painter at once prodigal and subtle in his comic effects. The boy from earliest youth is in conflict with the farm, where his young love finds youth's instinctive idealisms outraced in a fair young creature of flesh and blood. The first seventh of the book is given to Richard's revenge on the farmer who had thrashed him for poaching and for insolence, and shows how an immensely complicated situation arose, when the boy bribed a yokel to set the farmer's rick on fire, when the yokel was arrested for arson, was saved by bribery and forgery, and how Richard told all to the farmer in the end. His father, playing Providence in this preliminary ordeal, was satisfied.

But a few years later, and Richard's nature, rich and wild with passion, cheated by false philosophy of natural outlets, yet splendid and untainted, finds his high idealisms outdone in the lovely bloom of the farmer's niece, Lucy Desborough, the daughter of a naval officer. Once more the father intervenes; but the boy carries off his bride. The baronet relents, but prescribes a temporary separation from the lovely innocence his son has wedded. "The strength of his love for a pure woman is a success till the father strikes down his own fabric," Meredith wrote to Lucas.[1] Thwarted nature takes a terrible revenge when Richard, after a champagne supper, succumbs to a siren's wiles. In a torture of remorse he flees to the Rhineland. He feels unable ever to face his wife again. When, however, he hears, after some months, that a son is born to him, the spirit of Life illuminates him, vivid as lightning, and he hurries back. As he goes, two letters meet him: one is from Lucy; the other, from the enchantress, tells him of a Lord Mountfalcon having paid court to his unsuspecting wife. As he passes on his way through London, he calls on Mountfalcon, and they arrange a duel. He goes on home to avow his infidelity to his father and to Lucy: and through this Ordeal the sweet wonders of life at their tenderest are made real to him. Yet he leaves them, and returns.

In the duel he was severely, but not dangerously, wounded. The family went to him, but the doctor

[1] Unpublished letter.

would not allow his wife to see him. Before his acuter stage was over, she had died of brain-fever. Sir Austin Feverel "went to Richard and said in so many words that his Lucy was no more. I thought it must kill him. He listened and smiled. I never saw a smile so sweet and so sad. He said he had seen her die, as if he had passed through his suffering a long time ago. He shut his eyes. I could see by the motion of his eye-balls that he was straining his sight to some inner heaven. . . . His father was right for once, then. But if he has saved his son's body, he has given the death-blow to his heart. Richard will never be what he promised. . . . Have you noticed the expression in the eyes of blind men? That is just how Richard looks, as he lies there silent in his bed—striving to image her on his brain."

These are the last words of *The Ordeal of Richard Feverel:* and it cannot be denied that the poignancy of them is the fruit of great bitterness. Meredith found, as every tragic writer finds, that death, and death alone, is the sublime conclusion of high romance. It has been said over and over again that there was no need for this ending. But impatience and pain cannot change the truth that things need must be so. The inward calm, which shines lambent within when the wild tumult of sin and passion assault a great nature, is something which comes neither from nature, nor from science, and has its home out of this world. Meredith was no Dante to unveil those mysteries. He wrote of human life, not of eternal life: and it is not, after all, surprising if his touching story gives a cue to discerning curates. The whole significance of tragedy is that, showing man in all his grandeur, of which not the least is joy in beauty, it shows him overwhelmed by the inadequacy of this world. Man is indeed heir of a life beyond the bourns of reason. We can never realise his grandeur without seeing that this world is but one scene in the theatre of its perfection. One's reading of life breaks off in the middle of a paragraph.

Meredith knew that which with unique vividness and beauty his art paints. His book is full of an intense amusement at the quaint confusion of life: but the rapturous dream had left him puzzled by his own exhaustion: science, playing with nature, is more likely to offer destruction than joy to the finest stuff of youth. His longing was beauty,—as his love had been,—a high romantic beauty. There was no high romantic beauty in his own parting from his wife. A pictured wife, whose reason gives way under the strain of her faithfulness, leaves a very different impression of romance from one whose brain gives way because she cannot return to the husband who will not forgive the openness of her adulteries. Between the Catholic Lucy and the daughter of pagan Peacock a great gulf was fixed; Meredith found in his imagination some sort of solace for the wound of his own tragedy. All his art was to be the reaction of his energy against his sensitiveness. The tailor's son pictures his hero as the heir of Raynham Abbey. But as nothing in life was to touch him so acutely as his failure to maintain rapturous romance with Mary, so none of his works were to be so intimate and so powerful as *The Ordeal*. It is the link between *Love in the Valley* and *Modern Love*. And *because art is itself action, this book is as much the story of his life as his life itself is.* It has the intimacy of a confession, and in it heart speaks to heart. For there his inward nature asserts itself against its own outwardness disfigured by jarring circumstance. Meredith's nature was as wild and high, as proud and pure as Richard's; so, like Richard's, it needs must be wrenched and jarred: in this story, where comedy and romance and tragedy are one, he asserts the force of nature's laws at the same time as he reveals the failure of the high natural excellence of chivalry and honour to deal with human nature when a young husband, made to adore, faces the fact that his wife is an adulteress, which she need not have been if he had not taught her to await so much from life and from himself.

What Meredith had done in art, he did not do in his other life. The book was two years old when Mary Meredith was freed from insanity by death. She died repeating the words of a poet, words which she wished to have written above her grave. The words were not those of her husband, but another:

Come not, when I am dead,
   To drop thy foolish tears upon my grave,
To trample round my fallen head,
   And vex the unhappy dust thou would'st not save.
There let the wind sweep, and the plover cry;
   But thou, go by.

These words were not written above her grave. No words were written. No tombstone marks it. There the power her husband hymned spread undisturbed its incessant vicissitudes of warmth and chill, of bloom and decay. His record of her death was one convulsion of grief, and one shocking cynicism. But her monument will live for ever in three of his masterpieces. The stricken, deranged, lonely, erring, brilliant woman will not be forgotten among those who live by the heart in their youth: they will know her in associations too general, intimate, and dear to need her name attached to them. And though her husband dropped no tears upon her grave, his memories of her are her aureole.[1]

[1] *Letters*, S. M. Ellis.

IV

THE FRIENDS OF GENIUS

§ 1

WHILE Mary was thinking of the grave in which her body was so soon to rest, her husband, in the intervals of writing tragedy, plunged into open-air life among choice friends, with roars of unconscious laughter where humour gave wit repose, while Falstaff lived again, robust in love of cheer. Lazy incompetence of judgment hurries forward the word insincerity: but Meredith's cheerfulness was as genuine as noble words show his feelings to have been when they touched the heights and depths. His good spirits are as integral to him as his tragic thought, and if, his art's monument lost, he lived but in the remembrance of his friends, the record would be of "a fellow of infinite jest"; his laugh was generally short, but it was a roar: and if it was not short (and his boyish enjoyment of pure absurdity could tickle him tremendously), the tears would soon be rolling down his cheeks, and he would put his hand to his mouth to hold back another outburst. But cynicism was not absent from his fun.

In the intervals of laughter, he would pour out talk with a voice which had the deep full resonance of a bell, and was phenomenally penetrating, his accent that of the set who knew the sense of splendour they could give by the way they pronounced their words.

His dress was that of an artist on the heaths: a soft and shapeless hat, a scarlet tie loosely knotted in the collar of a greyish flannel shirt, grey stockings below knickerbockers, and strong laced boots, a walker's. That garb was by no means ill chosen for the splendid head above it, with curling auburn hair unparted, a strong peaked auburn beard, a straight nose, finely tipped, with sensitive nostrils, and over these a fine brow and grey darting eyes. Holman Hunt said of him that he was a perfect example of the well-bred Englishman. Rossetti found Meredith's face so striking, so noble, so full of feeling that, painting his "Saint Mary Magdalene," he used his profile for the Christ.[1]

Meredith's especial friends were Maxse, Frank Burnand, Hyndman, Maurice Fitzgerald, who stayed with him at Seaford; and an incarnation of Pickwick as a publisher, jovial, ruddy, white-haired, and stout, in Mullet Evans, who was a proprietor of *Punch*; and then Rossetti, Swinburne, Hardman, the Duff-Gordons, and Bonaparte Wyse. These are a stout company. Fitzgerald, son of John Boulge Fitzgerald, of Boulge Hall, was a first-rate scholar, a sybarite and even a cricketer, if it did not mean violent exercise. Born six years after Meredith, he suffered in his childhood from a step-mother, and it was decreed that a father's choice should provide him with a wife or he go penniless. He appeared as an ideal bachelor, and was devoted to cooking and Euripides. Meredith met him on these grounds. He was the original of the wise youth in *The Ordeal*.

[1] S. M. Ellis.

In due time, however, he found a handsome woman and married her. To escape the father's knowledge, they lived as Mr. and Mrs. Marston. Once when Maurice Fitzgerald was in the train with his wife, his father got into the same carriage, and only with great cunning did the young man succeed in passing his wife off as a stranger, scribbling about his difficulty on a newspaper he politely offered her. Some years later he arrived at Boulge and fell very ill. His father promised him anything he would wish. He avowed that his longing was for his wife. The old man kept his promise, and was not a little surprised to find that his daughter-in-law was the woman who had fascinated him in a railway-carriage years before. Fitzgerald never recovered, but by dying he secured for his wife and family the inheritance they would have forfeited had he avowed their relation to him on any occasion but his death-bed. This was in 1877. Fitzgerald was then forty-two.[1]

Hardman was the most concrete of the company, a Tory, a practised critic, a gourmet, with a flat forehead, a ruddy face, and short legs, and a suggestion of Henry VIII about his figure, who would insist on Meredith defining his terms, and who faced him with the arguments of the entrenched class, when Meredith gave reins to his enthusiasms for the future of mankind. "Let me set you right, sir," he said sometimes—and that, said Meredith, was his modesty. "On the question of politics, I venture to state," he remarked in anything but the tone of a venture, "that no educated man of sense who has visited

[1] S. M. Ellis, *A Mid-Victorian Pepys.*

our colonies will come back a Liberal." As for a man of sense and education being a radical, he scouted the notion with a "pooh" sufficient to awaken a vessel in the doldrums.[1] He and Meredith were both great walkers, and great talkers, with a taste for refined flavours in food and wine. From Hardman, Dickens in fact had accepted in 1848, for *Household Words*, a paper on "The Rôle of Cookery." They had in these long rambles a sort of ecstasy as they breathed in the scent of Surrey pinewoods, or watched in autumn the changing tints in elms and beeches. Returning to the cottage, they would eat a plain meal of bread with jam or honey, and start out again, while Meredith would read in the evening the work that he was doing. There was little poetry in Hardman, however: he was a hearty being, and met Meredith on his own levels of a good appetite and a trusty pipe. He was at this time encouraged to write a work on William Cobbett which, with his love of school-boy jests, he called his W.C.

Hardman had many a broad joke to crack with Meredith. In his studies of Cobbett, for example, he came on an advertisement in the *Farmer's Museum*, published in Philadelphia, about the same time as the *Lyrical Ballads:*

"Wanted, for a sober family, a man of light weight, who fears the Lord, and can drive a pair of horses. He must occasionally wait at table, join in household prayer, look after the horses, and read a chapter in the Bible. He must, God willing, rise at seven in the

[1] *Beauchamp's Career.*

morning, and obey his master and mistress in all lawful commands. If he can dress hair, sing psalms and play at cribbage, the more agreeable.

"N.B. He must not be familiar with the maidservants lest the flesh should rebel against the spirit and he should be induced to walk in the thorny paths of the wicked. Wages, 15 guineas a year."[1]

Such were the jests that they repeatedly exchanged.

§ 2

On a May evening of 1862 Hardman and Meredith started from Copsham to walk to Burford Bridge. Roars of laughter and absurd rhymes diversified their exercise, and they would improvise or recall improvisations to good old nursery tunes. They were "Tuck" and "Robin" to each other, and made as much fun out of these nicknames as though still boys. As dark was falling, they settled in the inn at Mickleham and listened to nightingales singing by the banks of the stream near by. The poet, in his melodious voice, addressed the melodious birds, in the verses of Keats, which he loved:

> I . . . guess each sweet.
> Wherewith the seasonable month endows
> The grass, the thicket, and the fruit-tree wild;
> White hawthorn, and the pastoral eglantine;
> Fast-fading violets cover'd up in leaves;
> And mid-May's eldest child,

[1] S. M. Ellis, *A Mid-Victorian Pepys*.

> The coming musk-rose, full of dewy wine,
> The murmurous haunt of flies on summer eves.[1]

The night-jar and the frogs threw out their own tunes on the night air. At ten or so, the walkers returned, and sought bed at eleven. With tipplers arguing below, and Meredith shouting jokes through the wall, Hardman lay awake, and in the intervals of silence still heard the nightingales in the trees. At half-past five in the morning Meredith wakened him, but was content to let him rest till seven. At nine they strode off over the Ranmer Common, on through Shere and St. Martha's chapel, and so over the Merrow downs. They slept in an inn at Milford.

Next day they went on in hot sun to Hindhead, and lunched at Haslemere, drinking copious ale. At three they drove to Godalming to catch the train, dropping Meredith from it at Esher, while Hardman went on to London. Such walks were Meredith's inspiration: they are central in his history; he was at the same time giving hard exercise to brain and flesh and spirit; for, as Lord Morley said, he "lived at every hour, day or night, with all the sounds and sights of Nature open to his sensitive perception." All this flooded out in his keen talk; and with Hardman he was engaged in very frequent argument. "I should so like you to know him," Hardman wrote of Meredith to a friend. "You would like him immensely, and disagree with him constantly."[2]

---

[1] "Ode to a Nightingale." S. M. Ellis, *A Mid-Victorian Pepys*.
[2] Lord Morley, *Reminiscences*. S. M. Ellis.

THE FRIENDS OF GENIUS

It was on this walk, in May of 1862, that Meredith found at Guildford, as he passed through, a *Spectator* with a review of *Modern Love* which cut him deeply. Even the *Westminster*, which, though it complained of their frequent roughness and occasional obscurity, praised the poems for their freshness and vigour, for the sharp observation they showed and skilful analysis of human nature, still lamented that the poems often dealt with a woman's temptations and guilt. Meredith's treatment of those subjects stirred the *Spectator* to a violence of invective which sounds far more personal than literary. It began by describing Meredith as a clever, bold man, and finished by designating the volume as vulgar and tawdry. It accused Meredith of pandering to the beastliness in men, and of finding indecency picturesque. "Mr. George Meredith is a clever man, without literary genius, taste or judgment, and apparently aims at that sort of union of point, passion and pictorial audacity which Byron attained in *Don Juan*. . . . On the whole, the effect of the book on us is that of a clever, meretricious, turbid picture, by a man of some vigour, jaunty manners, quick observation and some pictorial skill, who likes writing about human passions, but does not bring either imaginative power or true sentiment to the task."[1]

Meredith as he read this at Guildford on the 24th May was stung and flushed. Hardman argued that anything so unreasonable could only have come from an enemy who knew him personally. But to that Meredith did not agree, arguing rather that it was written

[1] May 24, 1862.

by a woman! In *Richard Feverel*, as it stood then, woman indeed had been compared to a wild-cat. Only one of the wild-cat kind, in other words, could have written that savage review. But when Browning met Meredith a few days later, he told him that this volume, which had struck the *Spectator* as so vulgar, so muddy, and so audacious, had astounded him with its originality, and had delighted him with its naturalness and beauty.[1]

There was much in this poetry that was like Browning's own; the love of fun and surprise which made him tolerant of the grotesque and the obscure, the same keen thought, the sense of the wholeness of life, and vivid pictures of inward and outward beauty, which are so brilliant in *Men and Women*. Each poet had sweetness, sincerity, and vigour.

"As to the Poems," Meredith wrote to Jessopp on September 20, 1862, "I don't think the age prosaic for not buying them. A man who hopes to be popular must think *from* the mass, and as the *heart* of the mass. If he follows out vagaries of his own brain, he cannot hope for general esteem; and he does smaller work. 'Modern Love' as a dissection of the sentimental passion of these days could only be apprehended by the few who would read it many times. I have not looked for it to succeed. Why did I write it? Who can account for pressure?

"Between realism and idealism, there is no natural conflict. This completes that. Realism is the basis of good composition: it implies study, observation, artistic power, and (in those who can do more) humility.

[1] S. M. Ellis, *Letters of George Meredith*.

Little writers should be realistic. They could then at least do solid work. They afflict the world because they will attempt what it is given to none but noble workmen to achieve. A great genius must necessarily employ ideal means, for a vast conception cannot be placed bodily before the eye, and remains to be suggested. Idealism is an atmosphere whose effects of grandeur are wrought out through a series of illusions that are illusion to the sense within us only when divorced from the groundwork of the Real. Need there be exclusion, the one of the other? The artist is incomplete who does this. Men to whom I bow my head (Shakespeare, Goethe; and in their way Molière, Cervantes) are Realists au fond. But they have the broad aims of Idealism at command. They give us Earth; but it is Earth with an atmosphere. One may find as much amusement in a kaleidoscope as in a merely idealistic writer; and just as sound prose is of more worth than pretentious poetry, I hold the man who gives us a plain wall of fact higher in esteem than one who is constantly shuffling the cards and dealing with airy delicate sentimentalities, headless and tailless imaginings, despising our good, plain, strength-giving Mother. Does not all science (the mammoth Balloon, to wit) tell us that when we forsake Earth we reach up to a frosty inimical Inane! For my part, I love and cling to Earth, as the one piece of God's handiwork that we possess. I admit that we can refashion; but of earth must be the material."[1]

[1] Unpublished letter in the possession of Mr. Frank Altschul of New York.

§ 3

Keen arrows were to be shot for Meredith's defence. There was at that time a young atheist, who was an old Etonian and the son of an admiral, who, passing through an astounded Oxford like a male mænad, had burst upon the world as a writer of verse which flowed clear as a song. This passionate and primeval young man, now twenty-five years old, whose hair was red as a blown flame, and whose eyes, in Meredith's words, were of a "gray-green hue that may be seen glistening over a wet sunset,"[1] poured out his talk like molten lava. He had brought out a little volume at his own expense, and had had poems accepted by the *Spectator*. This was Swinburne. He admired Meredith intensely: he loved *Modern Love*. He set to work at once, and by June 7th his vindication had appeared in the *Spectator*. He argued first that praise or blame should be thoughtful, serious, and careful, when applied to a work of such subtle strength, such depth of delicate power, such passionate and various beauty as *Modern Love*. He compared the venomous critic to a child which babbles "after the dangling delights of a child's coral, and jingles with flaccid fingers one knows not whether a jester's or a baby's bells." He took as specimens of fine power, and depth of imagination at once intricate and vigorous, the two sonnets on the transient reconciliation, the one on lily-livered moralists, the one on the inadequacy of the poet's principles to cope with his passions, and that sonnet on the rose:

[1] *Sandra Belloni*.

              shines she gloriously,
And with that softest dream of blood, she glows:
Mild as an evening heaven round Hesper bright!
I pluck the flower, and smell it, and revive
The time when in her eyes I stood alive.
I seem to look upon it out of Night.

The letter was so discerning, and so eloquent, that it did as much for Swinburne's fame as for Meredith's own.

A few years later Britain's lion of prudery was roaring at the defender himself. It was Meredith's turn for loyalty in defence: "the compensation for injustice," he had written, "is that in that dark ordeal we gather the worthiest around us."[1] Meredith did not indeed think that Swinburne's trouncing was altogether undeserved. He delighted in his friend's attack on the organism of Christianity; but the natural idealism which could welcome scepticism hardly relished indecency. "No one is fonder of good sound bawdry than I," wrote Hardman; but Swinburne was too "strongly sensual" for Hardman to stand. Meredith's words were frank. "You have fairly deserved it," Meredith wrote to Swinburne: there are certain directions in which one does not point. And though Meredith felt intense amusement at Swinburne's skit on French novels—*Ce qui peut se passer dans un cab safety*, where Lord Whitestick, Bishop of Londres, made a criminal assault upon the heroine—Meredith would have liked to weed and prune Swinburne's

[1] *The Ordeal*. René Galland

poems. The pourer of lava was the original of Tracy Runningbrook in *Sandra Belloni*.[1]

Swinburne was a particular friend of Dante Gabriel Rossetti. Swinburne and Rossetti had taken Sir Thomas More's delightful house in Cheyne Walks, and here Meredith was to find a home a night a week, when he came up to London on business. But he slept at the house only once. There was a quarrel. It was rumoured that, when put out at night, Meredith's old boots were replaced by a new pair. It was said by others that when Meredith called Rossetti a fool, Rossetti threw a cup of milk in his face. It was said again that when Meredith saw the enormous breakfast Rossetti ate, it raised his gorge. It has been suggested yet again that what disgusted Meredith was a woman Rossetti, now a young widower, had in the house. In any case, it was agreed that, whatever happened, the admired original of Rossetti's merciful Redeemer was disgusted, and walked out of the house never to return. There was undoubtedly a quarrel. That a cup of milk, or ham and eggs, or old boots, or a woman was the cause of it is gossip, not authenticated fact. Meredith himself attributed the difference to his solicitude for the artist eating and painting without sufficient exercise. "Devotion to his work, in contempt of our nature, killed him."

§ 4

Other friends of this period were the Wyses. Sir Thomas Wyse, who had been Minister in Athens,

[1] *The Ordeal*. René Galland.

had married Princess Letitia, daughter of Lucien Bonaparte, and had two sons, Napoleon and Bonaparte. Bonaparte, a mixture of Corsican and Irish, was himself a poet, a follower of Mistral, for whom he awoke an admiration in Meredith. Victor Hugo praised Wyse's Provençal poetry as true and touching: he complimented Wyse's noble ease in a living and luminous idiom. Besides being a poet and something of a cynic, Wyse was a walker; he was altogether a man after Meredith's heart, which soon opens to him its central loves: "The cuckoo has been heard. And through the gates of his twin notes, we enter the heart of spring. We will have rare poetising, no laughter, no base cynical scorn, but all honest uplifting of the body and soul of us to the calm-flowing central Fire of things."[1]

At the third week-end in May of 1861 Meredith was to start with Maxse and Wyse, as he went a year later with Hardman, on a walk from Esher to Mickleham. But Wyse disappointed him. They were to do a greater walk together in the summer. Meredith went to Zurich in July, and met his friend at Innsbruck at the end of the month. Wyse was a cheerful companion and one with heart and spirit to join Meredith in that first intimate communion with the Alps, which was one of the great events of Meredith's life; he needed then as much as ever a walker who could keep up to thirty miles in the hot summer day, dangle bare feet above the mountain streams, raise a warm heart to the white glories above them which made earth's barren-

[1] This appears only in the suppressed edition of Mr. Ellis's book.

ness heavenly, and share an intense appreciation of human life of the noblest. But something went wrong on the trip; Wyse thought, his stomach. "It isn't fair for you to throw your stomach in my face," said Meredith, and Wyse began to get a little irritable, and then irritable continually. "He is half Prince, half Paddy," wrote Meredith, "with little pluck, a great deal of desultory reading, a wretched stomach, and no control over his nerves. He couldn't walk in the sun; he wouldn't walk after its setting; the rain he shunned as if he had been dog-bitten; in fact he was a double knapsack on my back." Meredith was not one to blunt pricking points, and thought Wyse more like a cross child than a grown man.[1]

In this Bonaparte, however, there was Ireland's good humour: it was a felicitous ending when Wyse presented Meredith to Princess Letitia in the Villa on Como. Wyse had prudently left Meredith in Venice with Arthur. In the last few weeks Meredith became intensely interested in Napoleon, and until he was seventy, when he produced his verses on Napoleon, he found absorbing anything that touched on the great genius. Venice and the Dolomites were not least in the noble company of Meredith's supreme loves: and he had no greater adventures than his intimacy with the morning and evening twilights amongst those rosy crags and shimmering waters.[2]

When he saw the Alps his first feeling was that he

---

[1] Extract from unpublished material. *Letters*.

[2] The references are again to Mr. Ellis's suppressed book.

was baffled. "Close interthreading nature with our kind," as he was wont to do, it seemed at first that his philosophy was paralysed when he found high and unfruitful rocks sublime. "Here at last," he wrote, "seems something more than earth, and visible if not tangible. They have the whiteness, the silence, the beauty and mystery of thoughts seldom unveiled within us, but which conquer Earth when once they are. In fact, they have made my creed tremble."[1] What happened was that their symbolic beauty had touched his thought that, as all human life grows from earth, so the spirit grows up from flesh. When he looked at the symbols of transcendence, he asked himself if perhaps, after all, there was not something above nature. Had he availed himself of ancient thought as to the place of nature in the world of spirit, and seen that though earth is indeed essential it has no untainted fixity to keep holiness inviolate, he would have been a more peaceful companion and a sublimer philosopher. But it was his part to show, with an abounding fullness, the nobleness of earth; he could get no further than what he realised uniquely well. "What," he asked, "if yonder Alp does touch the Heaven? Is it a rebuke to us below? In you and me there may be lofty virgin points, pure from what you call fleshliness." He listened joyfully to the solemn noise of the avalanche, and watched the clouds, like white and sulphurous masks, covering the face of the heights, or dripping moisture on the hanging meadows. "Nothing can be grander than the colossal mountains

[1] *Letters*.

of porphyry and dolomite shining purple and rosy, snow-capped here and there, with some tumultuous river noising below, and that eternal stillness overhead save where some great peak thunders." But a torrent, green as a glacier, was ever roaring down the valley also, and though its song had in it the thunder of the avalanche as it threw a silver fountain over a boulder, or dashed down the ravine in a chain of foam, yet it provided a simile of the noisy movement of men, which with their joy, their passion, and their trouble, pressed into the solitude of river, rock, and forest, guarded by mountain-walls.[1]

Here the significant dawn had deeper meanings; looking, as he had looked so often, on the glorious suffusions of the sky which come not seldom between the light's earliest grey and full sunrise, he saw in them a symbol of love irradiating the light of life and giving a detailed clearness to obscure potentialities. And this thought was to be with him till he was old. But the mountain height, with all its significance of purer and more contrasted colour, of wider and more awful prospects, of the extraordinary grandeur of peaks and gulfs, with its vivid alternatives of light and shade, gave twilight an intenser beauty, just as it added splendour to the day. In scenes so fine with radiance life did indeed become a mystery of spirit, for spirit transcended flesh. No longer could throbbing veins tell the secret of life, or the closed eye of the corpse tell the romance of death. The spirit in its nakedness burned, and joined light to immortal light, and he

[1] *Letters*. "By the Rosanna."

began to form impressions which were a solace to him in the grief of later years:

> Shall man into the mystery of breath
> From his quick beating pulse a pathway spy?
> Or learn the secret of the shrouded death
> By lifting up the lid of a white eye?
> Cleave thou thy way with fathering desire
>   Of fire to reach to fire.[1]

His nerves were sensitive to the exhilaration of rare air. And he would have been far other than he was if he had not taken in mountaineering that sportsman's pleasure which his poetic genius widened into ethics and mysticism. Sweating and kneeling were to him almost the same thing, and both essential. "Carry your fever to the Alps," he said in *Harry Richmond*, "you of mind diseased: not to sit down in sight of them, ruminating, for bodily ease and comfort will trick the soul, and set you measuring our lean humanity against Yonder sublime and infinite; but mount, rack the limbs, wrestle it out among the peaks, taste danger, sweat, earn rest; learn to discover ungrudgingly that haggard fatigue is the fair vision you have run to earth and that rest is your uttermost reward." The flowers on the heights were like vivid emblems of hope, as the zest which danger gave to life proved hope by making men love to live. To leap the green-eyed crevasses, and stretch a salt hand to the mountain cattle in the solitude of an emerald Alpine meadow, this was to taste the medicine of Zest renewed.[2]

[1] "Hymn to Colour."   [2] "By the Rosanna."

Venice was an adventure of another sort: it was a dream and a seduction to his soul. He followed the steps of Shelley and Byron, whose beloved poetry was his guide-book over the lagoon. He would spend the hot August days floating about in a gondola with his boy, noting with particular interest one amorous damsel who pressed against the bars of her window to see him pass. Each day he went over to the Lido, and bathed in the warm summer sea. The galleries were visited. These scenes he was to see again and to describe how the grandeur of the decayed sea-city, where Folly had danced Parisianly of old, spread brooding above the waters in the morning light; "beautiful, but with that inner light of history seen through the beauty, Venice was like a lowered banner. The great white dome and the Campanile watching above her were still brave emblems." To these scenes he was to return, not to paint them with a genius of personal elaboration like Ruskin, but to learn to give to love-scenes the background suggested by a name. Hardman wrote of his intense interest in the art and architecture of Venice, in her people and her history. His genius for description turned back from Venice to the Alps, and his finest recollection of his life at Venice was a morning at sea, near Trieste. This was one of his great adventures; it can be told only in his own way:

"He was awakened by light on his eyelids, and starting up beheld the many pinnacles of grey and red rocks and shadowy high white regions at the head of the gulf waiting for the sun; and the sun struck them. One by one they came out in crimson flame, till the vivid host appeared to have stepped forward. The shadows on the snow-fields deepened to purple below an irradiation of rose and pink and dazzling silver. There of all the world you might imagine gods to sit. A crowd of mountains endless in range, erect, or flowing, shattered and arid, or leaning in smooth lustre, hangs above the gulf. The mountains are sovereign Alps, and the sea is beneath them. The whole gigantic body keeps the sea, as with a hand, to right and left. . . . The Adriatic was dark, the Alps had heaven to themselves. Crescents and hollows, rosy mounds, white shelves, shining ledges, domes and peaks, all the towering heights were in illumination from Friuli into farthest Tyrol; beyond earth to the stricken senses of the gazers. Colour was steadfast on the massive front ranks: it wavered in the remoteness, and was quiet and dim as though it fell on beating wings; but there too divine colour seized and shaped forth solid forms, and thence away to others in uttermost distances where the incredible flickering gleam of new heights arose, that soared, or stretched their white uncertain curves in sky, like wings traversing infinity."[1]

§ 5

As the romance of love streamed up within him before such a vision of colour which made solid earth aerially brilliant, his mind travelled back to one friend

[1] *Beauchamp's Career. Letters.*

who he felt would understand and whom he delighted to image as a lover in those tremulous streets of Venice which filled and fell with the gentle Adriatic tide. That friend was Maxse. Maxse had been introduced to him three years before by Frederick Chapman, the publisher, as one who would take sides with him for France when France fell under the Briton's suspicion in 1859, for making war on Austria.

Maxse was a naval officer, and, soon after joining the service, had been the hero of a great exploit in the Crimean War, carrying Lord Raglan's dispatches through the enemy's lines. But the scandals had turned his patriotism into a fury against Conservative government, the weakness of well-born officers had aroused his contempt, and he had become a passionate admirer of the French. The Maxses were a merchant family of Dutch origin and had been successful in the City: the head of the family had married Lady Caroline Berkeley, whom Meredith came to know well. He was a very hard rider to hounds and appears in many contemporary pictures of celebrated runs with the Quorn. The Berkeleys had been notorious for their want of restraint. Big gamblers and wild livers, their translation of nobility was impetuousness. Whatever occupied them turned them to violence, and violence in opinions often looks very like hysteria. The patriotism of Frederick Maxse was reform of politics and opinions so radical that he was a vegetarian and an atheist; that a naval officer should want to reform at all was bad enough; his politics, however, not only horrified the Tories, they frightened the Radicals: and so keen was Maxse on denouncing abuses in Parliament that the conservative Liberals thought it better not even so much as to mention him. His name was a byword in the clubs. But his friends were touched by the frenzy of his enthusiasms, and Meredith was his friend. There have been few friendships in this world deeper, warmer, more vigorous, more consoling, or more fruitful than the friendship of Maxse and Meredith: until they were old men, their haunts echoed with the exchange of their chaff. It was Meredith's part, and not uncongenial, to counsel prudence. Maxse's fanaticism shocked him almost as much as Swinburne's indecency: he pierced its protuberances with the broadsword of his laughter.[1]

Ideas in themselves were not enough for Maxse: he became absorbed in them when he saw them as the living fountains of action, of progress or of personality. Not only Meredith, but Clemenceau, Morley and Joseph Chamberlain he singled out before the world knew them. An idealist so keen for deeds does not submit enthusiasms to the bright light of reason: he is content with their bracing effect on the imagination and the feelings. Carlyle praising heroes gave him just enough of philosophy, and where hero-worship was his religion, deeds were the fulfilment of both his law and his prophets. That a man's first thought must be his country was to him the first and great commandment. *Ich dien* was his motto. In him, as in the Elizabethans, action and imagination went hand in hand. He loved Carlyle for giving him something

[1] *Dictionary of National Biography.*

to puzzle over, and a vague feeling of great mysteries beyond. It was enough to make him devoted to realise that there was more in a book than there was in himself.

"If a thing is right, I must do it." That is the logic of sound goodness, which is however very disturbing if the moment is not right. With Maxse the moment was never right. When at last Gladstonian Liberalism had evolved and he might have been found a seat in Parliament, he swung over to the other side, and became as violent a Tory as he had ever been a Radical. Famous for his daring when almost a boy, he got nothing from it in the Navy; he was made a Rear-Admiral in 1878, on account of his seniority. Those whom he irritated saw another Zimri with all his talents ruined by unrestraint and instability.

> Blest Madman, who could every hour employ
> With something new to wish, or to enjoy!
> Railing and praising were his usual Theams,
> And both (to shew his Judgment) in Extreams.
> So over-violent, or over-civil,
> That every man to him was God or Devil.

While those who read Dryden thought of Zimri, plainer men simply said, "A crank!" Such a character could only irritate the services, and his naval career was as disappointing as his political one was vain. All his life he remained the victim of an inefficient liver!

With a short beard and wavy hair, good looks, a good figure and an air of charm, "dressed in the individual style of a naval officer of breeding, in which you can see neatness plucking at disorder," Maxse seemed certainly distinguished, as with a desire to serve, he looked out on mankind from his deep eyes with a melancholy intensity. He consulted Meredith not only on marriage but on diet: having made up his mind to follow Carlyle to the end, and to sacrifice his digestion, he gives us a picture of the hero as dyspeptic. Meredith gently reasoned with him that the principle of health is to have plenty of good blood circulating: to eat wisely, to allow a little distraction afterwards, and to take prudent exercise will keep the system from clogging.[1] Beware of vegetarianism! It can generate flatulence in a weak stomach, and do more harm than good. Better a tender chop with a glass of old Bordeaux.

These profound counsels fell on a deaf ear. Maxse once drank a bottle of bad French Burgundy at a meal, but now meat and wine were both eschewed. The vegetarian evangel had captured Maxse, and he had become an itinerant preacher of his newest religion. What was he totally to abstain from next? Clothes? "I have in fact said that we wear too much clothing—still, Fred, it is surely an excess to forswear a single garment, and rely upon hair to cover your body, as you look to impudence to protect your shivering arguments." Not clothes went next, but fish. Maxse saw that the menace to society was mackerel.

Meredith complains that one excess begets another. Maxse's disease, he said, was now mental elephantiasis. "You fancy all things as immensities: you cannot understand the value of an intermediate measure."

[1] *Dictionary of National Biography. Beauchamp's Career.* René Galland.

Wasn't it time, now, for a change in knight-errantries in the matter of religion? Pius IX was in difficulties: the preaching of vegetarianism and nakedness might be varied at this point with a little Popery. Meredith could not help asking himself if his friend Fred were a real person, or a meteorite flying from its orbit in search of ruinous collision.[1]

But if Maxse, who was now proposing marriage, was teased by his friend, he was given also the finest confidences of the lover and poet. To Wyse, who seemed too uxorious, Meredith flung out a flout or two at women: to Maxse, he opened the heart of his idealism. Love, he argued, could be distinguished from passion by its patience, its readiness for poverty, by its tenderness. But instinct, after all, in Meredith's view was more than judgment. "I believe that this plan of taking a woman, on the strength of a mighty wish for her, is the best and the safest way to find the jewel we are all in search of." Maxse's Cecilia Steel had a face that left him with the unique impression of music. "There is that softness in the curves and purity of look which move like music in my mind." Her face was a book with plates of virgin silver. To see her wedded to his friend, Meredith guaranteed to overcome his repugnance to wedding breakfasts. Marriage made the young captain full of ardour: "beauty plucked the heart out of him." But romance was not quite enough for the vehement officer about to wed. Meredith prescribed the medicine of a treatise by a man whose thought's emphasis was on the hold of the

[1] *Letters.*

material over man's psychology. He set Maxse to read a treatise on love by an acute but cynical analyst: he sent *De l'Amour*, by Stendhal.

But neither romance nor warning could make Maxse other than an extremist whose frenzies debilitated both his joy and his health. It was hardly a year after the marriage that Meredith's warning, in which chaffing was mingled first with concern and then with vexation, was dealing with the vegetarian, the atheist, the apostle of nakedness, and the victim of mental elephantiasis. For it is out of these that he created Nevil Beauchamp.[1]

§ 6

Life in the company of Maurice Fitzgerald, of Burnand, of Hardman, of Wyse, of Maxse, of Rossetti and of Swinburne gave Meredith his most congenial air. For having nothing, he possessed all things. His cottage at Esher, Copsham Cottage, one of the simplest possible, was far from resort of men, on the border of the common from which neither a hedge nor a rail divided it. It seemed, as Meredith himself said to Morley, to have grown out of the common on which it stood. Gorse and heather were its garden, and the wild stretched out into larch and pine woods: in the heart of their blue depths was a clear dark pool, guarded often by a stately heron, and a few steps from the cottage rose the mound where the heath-smells blew up among dry weeds and nettles and orchard

[1] *Letters*.

trees grown wild. This was Meredith's favourite haunt, and here he lived in unity with the changes of the season; here he wrote his *Ode to the Spirit of Earth in Autumn*, and these are the scenes which inspired the fresh vividness of the *Autumn Evensong* he wrote in his first October there.

> The long cloud edged with streaming grey
>   Soars from the West;
> The red leaf mounts with it away,
>   Showing the nest
> A blot among the branches bare:
> There is a cry of outcasts in the air.
>
> Swift little breezes, darting chill,
>   Pant down the lake;
> A crow flies from the yellow hill,
>   And in its wake
> A baffled line of labouring rooks:
> Steel-surfaced to the light the river looks.
>
> Pale on the panes of the old hall
>   Gleams the lone space
> Between the sunset and the squall;
>   And on its face
> Mournfully glimmers to the last:
> Great oaks grow mighty minstrels in the blast.
>
> Pale the rain-rutted roadways shine
>   In the green light
> Behind the cedar and the pine:
>   Come, thundering night!

Blacken broad earth with hoards of storm:
For me yon valley-cottage beckons warm.

Simple in the extreme, the cottage had the best comforts of fire and cookery and wines—all very good. He was tended by a person who, he said, was "of excellent temper, spotless principles, no sex." Gipsies haunted the common: and it was one of them who talked to him in the words of Juggling Jerry, whom he pictures dying on his favourite mound in the prime of May, when golden gorse threw out its nutty smells on the warm air. There he delighted in the open life of May, which he chanted in verses as delightful as his *Autumn Evensong:*

> Now the brown bee, wild and wise,
>   Hums abroad, and roves and roams,
> Storing in his wealthy thighs
>   Treasure for the golden combs:
>   Dewy buds and blossoms dear
>   Whisper 'tis the sweet o' the year.
>
> .   .   .   .   .   .
>
> Now all nature is alive,
>   Bird and beetle, man and mole;
> Bee-like goes the human hive,
>   Lark-like sings the soaring soul:
>   Hearty faith and honest cheer
>   Welcome in the sweet o' the year.

And here in this wholeness of spirit he welcomed Hardman, welcomed Hyndman, welcomed Maxse, welcomed Wyse. Here Maurice Fitzgerald added finesse to the kitchen's flavours, in the spirit of subtlety which made his indecent jokes so delicately so that it was indecent to perceive them so at all.[1]

Here Swinburne came, an ecstatic visionary, brandishing as it were a tract from which he poured out in wild excitement the new musical voluptuousness of the splendid paraphrase of Omar Khayyám, which he and Meredith read stanza by stanza late into the evening. And then Swinburne himself called for paper and ran to his room, with his feather pen and his red ink, and in an hour he was reading to them new verses of his own, verses in which the haunting stanza of Fitzgerald was turned to a wild beauty to rave of fleshly passion, that passion, hysterical, melodious, which is the very soul of Swinburne, for his revolutionary ardour was essentially a pæan in praise of Venus:

> . . . she came out of the naked sea
>   Making the foam as fire whereon she trod,
> And as the inner flower of fire was she.
>
> Yea, she laid hold upon me, and her mouth
> Clove unto mine as soul to body doth,
>   And, laughing, made her lips luxurious;
> Her hair had smells of all the sunburnt South,

[1] Lord Morley, *Reminiscences*. Janet Ross, *The Fourth Generation. Letters.*

> Strange spice and flower, strange savour of crushed fruit,
> And perfume the swart kings tread underfoot,
> For pleasure when their minds wax amorous,
> Charred frankincense and grated sandal-root.[1]

And the young men listened: and the zest of genius was keen on them. Meredith was indeed in a distinguished company: it was not just that one was an admiral's son, and one was to be an admiral: it was not that the old dreams of the Portsmouth shop had so soon come true in his intimacy with the grandsons of earls, or with the kinsmen of Napoleon: for even in those days Meredith was happy to be intimate with many types. But it meant he had attained freedom, a good measure of it. He moved now where he would: the world did not apply to him constraints which would have impoverished it. Striking and unconventional men, who had the freedom of the great world, met him with the sense that they were rare spirits, and he the rarest. His whole life was to be a cultivation of the novelties and rarities which came pouring in amidst surge and foam from floodgates of life. To them he gave forth in the ringing tones of physical joy his gospel of energy. Live with the world. No cloister. No languor. Play your part. Fill the day. Ponder well and loiter not. Let laughter brace you. Exist in everyday communion with Nature. Nature bids you take all, only be sure you learn how to do without.[2]

---

[1] " Laus Veneris." *Letters. George Meredith*, by G. Photiadès.

[2] Lord Morley, *Reminiscences*.

V

JANET ROSS AND "EVAN HARRINGTON"

§ 1

WHEN Thackeray was living with Mr. Macirone at Weybridge, Tom Taylor, the Editor of *Punch*, had introduced him to the Duff-Gordons, who were living at Nutfield Cottage near by. There he had met a certain M. de Haxthausen, who claimed that he had fought with the Queen of the Serpents, and who produced out of a gold box in a tiny red silk bag, which hung from a gold chain he wore round his neck, what looked like a miniature crown of amber and which was a sort of bony excrescence from a serpent's head.[1]

From this story of a Queen of Snakes Meredith made his Bhanavar the Beautiful in *The Shaving of Shagpat*. Everything about the Duff-Gordons was an inspiration to him. Sir Alexander's descent from two great Scottish families was rivalled by the remarkable gifts of the immediate forebears of his wife, Lucie Austin, the daughter of John Austin and Sarah Taylor. The Taylors of Norwich were millers with brains, and Sarah was the first woman to introduce German literature to the English public. John Austin was a jurist. As soon as Alexander Duff-Gordon met her at Lansdowne House he was attracted, and his society

[1] Janet Ross, *The Fourth Generation*.

gave her distraction from the loneliness thrust upon her by her mother's writing and her father's debility. "Miss Austin, do you know people are saying we are going to be married?" he asked one day. "Shall we make it true? " He was answered with a plain "Yes." The results were the birth of Janet and that they settled in Queen Square and gathered celebrities of the day around them. And these were the playmates of Janet. Thackeray drew pictures to amuse her. Richard Doyle gave her books. Dickens told her that *The Seven Champions of Christendom* was the most delightful book in the world. Lord Lansdowne sent her a ticket when she was nine to see Macready's last appearance as Wolsey in *Henry VIII*. She climbed on to Macaulay's knee and said "Now talk!" for the floodgates were closed till her arrival. She called Mrs. Opie her fairy godmother. She asked the Master of Trinity, Whewell, to stop her father talking "because she could not get in a word," and she came in to dessert at Roger's Sunday breakfasts. With Burke, Bentham and the Bible, her higher education had begun at the age of three. Kinglake was one of her mother's great admirers. "Can I trust myself," he wrote long afterwards to Janet, "to speak of your dear mother's beauty in the phase it had reached when I first saw her? The classical form of her features, the noble poise of her head and neck, her stately height, her uncoloured yet pure complexion, caused some of the beholders at first to call her beauty statuesque, and others to call it majestic, some pronouncing it to be even imperious." Keen, autocratic, impassioned, she laid her commanding

hold on men: but as her little girl saw her going off
to one of Dickens's parties, she looked to her like a
fairy queen. Tennyson said that he had her in mind
when he wrote *The Princess*.[1] Meredith wrote to Lucas
that he had great confidence in her judgment.

To her fifth birthday, Janet invited Mrs. Norton,
Lord Lansdowne, Thackeray, Doyle, Bayley, and Tom
Taylor, the Editor of *Punch*. Thackeray presented her
with an oyster, which she liked so well that she asked
for two more, and Watts painted her when she was a
young girl.

In the early 'fifties her people took a house at Esher,
which was frequented by the Bourbon Princes, with
whom she hunted rabbits at Claremont. And it was
here that she formed the amazing friendship with
Meredith, which he had begun with her as a child,
years before. In the meantime they had lost sight of
him. She was riding down one evening in the spring
of 1858 to meet her father at the station, when a small
boy tripped in front of her horse. He was terrified,
but fought back tears. "Papa says 'Little men ought
not to cry,' " he said. And Janet was leading him back
to the lodgings where he was staying when a handsome bearded man came out and kissed him. He looked
hard at her. "Are you not Lady Duff-Gordon's daughter?" he said, and he clasped her in his arms, she sixteen, he thirty, and cried out, "Oh, my Janet! Don't
you know me? I'm your poet."[2]

[1] *The Times*, obituary notice, 1927. Janet Ross, *The Fourth Generation*. Unpublished letters.

[2] Janet Ross, *The Fourth Generation*. René Galland

JANET ROSS AND "EVAN HARRINGTON"

For five years she was, next to Arthur, the person who meant most to him, and with whom he associated his choicest words of praise and passion. None other than she can be the "lady" of *Modern Love*. She, in fact, found him his cottage at Copsham and to be near her he planted himself in it. They took long walks together, and he would recite his poetry or discuss his novels. The Black Pool in the fir wood there was their favourite haunt. To her he wrote, to set to Schubert's exquisite *Addio*, the verses:

> I dare not basely languish,
>   Nor press your lips to mine;
> But with one cry of anguish
>   My darling I resign.
>
> Our dreams we too must smother:
>   The bitter truth is here.
> This hand is for another—
>   Which I have held so dear.
>
> I pray that at the altar
>   You may be blessed above:
> And help me if I falter,
>   And keep me true to love.

Were these his own heart's words to her? In 1860, being still only eighteen, she married Henry Ross, who was a banker and was associated with Layard as one of the earliest excavators of Nineveh, and she went to live with him in Alexandria. It was not the end of her adventures, for when he lost his money she supported him. And when she migrated to Val d' Arno some years later she farmed the property of Poggio Gherardo and frequently entertained the Duke and Duchess of Teck at a villa lent her by Count Stufa.

Meredith raved of her to his friends. Jessopp called him her "adoring worshipper," and said that Meredith used to talk of her in such words as he only could use. "Your name," wrote Jessopp to Mrs. Ross, "is to me the name of an enchantress—gifted with every grace, human and divine." Who could wonder if her godmother thought that a French maid should go as a chaperone with her and Meredith when they went on the top of a 'bus to look at the Tower?[1]

§ 2

"God bless you, my dear girl!" Meredith wrote to her when he heard of her engagement. "If you don't make a good wife, I never read a page of woman. He's a lucky fellow to get you, and the best thing that he can do is to pray that he may always know his luck." What Meredith admired about this young lady was the courage of her frankness. Her annihilating glance and startling phrases made her something of a legend in her later years, and she was known as a Union Jack flying on the slopes of Maiano or as "a chapter of archaic history." She did battle for song-birds, and when one of the assassins pointed his gun at her, she quelled him. Having written two excellent cookery books, she sold vermouth to her friends for seven lire

[1] Janet Ross, *The Fourth Generation*.

a bottle. In 1919 she routed forty communists who came to rob her of wine and oil. At the age of eighty she faced armed Fascists: in these years she recalled many intimacies with the great, and loved to explain how the old Duke and Duchess of Teck, when they were fleeing their creditors, descended on her, and ate her out of house and home in great carousals that lasted from six in the evening till midnight.[1]

This imperious lady fascinated the poet even more than her mother did, and she inspired the gayest of his books, just as Mary had inspired the most tragic: meeting Janet, in his admiration of her frankness and in the communication of gifts far superior to hers (for when all is said, Mrs. Ross will be known to history as a woman Meredith once adored), he was divided from her by thorny hedges too high to overleap and which pricked him when he pushed his way through them, leaving his mind's finery tattered. But an immense enthusiasm was there, once again foiled of hopes. Again he turned to imagination to relieve him. What was there between Janet and himself? That was the basis of his new novel, *Evan Harrington: or He would be a Gentleman*. What after all *is* a gentleman? It was a question in much debate just then. It had occasioned the eloquence of Newman in the *Idea of a University*, it had aroused Ruskin in *Modern Painters*, and it had provoked enthusiasm since 1856, when *John Halifax: Gentleman* came out. Did the word *gentleman* simply mean certain advantages of fortune, appreciated by society as ease, or did it mean some essential power of

[1] *The Times*, obituary notice, 1927.

superior character? Meredith had abundance of the one; it was not so certain that he had the other. Poverty embarrasses ease: which means a certain amplitude and a familiarity with its tastes. The social standard is applied in a thousand trifles, and sticks hard at some arbitrary prejudices. When all was said, Meredith had no claim on the world but his character and genius. Education had not done for him what it does so often for rich men's sons in England: and his forebears had their shop. Meredith faced the whole question with gaiety and candour. " All but a Gentleman," "Gentle and Genteel" and "The Tailor's Family" were among the titles he suggested for the book to Lucas. His memories of Portsmouth were rich, and it would be robustly grotesque to place their tale of life immediately against the gifts of Janet. The aunts were a fine set on the one side, Lady Duff-Gordon and her daughter were splendid on the other. Let the tailor's son woo the high-bred Amazon. His own portrait of Janet's mother was to be not inferior to Kinglake's. "In her youth she was radiantly beautiful, with dark brows on a brilliant complexion, the head of a Roman man, and features of Grecian line, save for the classic Greek wall of the nose off the forehead. Women, not enthusiasts, inclined rather to criticise, and to criticise so independent a member of their sex particularly, have said that her entry into a ball-room took the breath. . . . Whenever she appeared, she could be likened to a Selene breaking through cloud; and, further, the splendid vessel was richly freighted. Trained by a scholar, much in the society of elderly men, having an

JANET ROSS AND "EVAN HARRINGTON"

innate bent to exactitude, and with a ready tongue, docile to the curb, she stepped into the world, armed to be a match for it. She cut her way through the accustomed troops of adorers, like what you will that is buoyant and swims gallantly."[1]

§ 3

"A gentleman must have one of two things, a title or money." That was the discovery of Evan's sister, the Countess de Saldar de Sancorvo, a grand-mannered lady, with anecdotes of the great, and ghost-stories where the ghosts wore coronets; a lady who would sit at receptions between the Countess de Pel and the Duchesse Eugenia de Formosa de Fontandigua. But Evan had neither money nor a title. A rich marriage, however, would make him blaze transfigured, and there was the person for him in Rose Jocelyn, who was at that moment in Lisbon. The Countess contrives that Evan should come back and stay at Beckley Court with the Jocelyns. The book turns on his mother's sense of his obligation to pay off his father's debts by developing the business, his own frankness, the prejudice of some who guess his origin, and the determination of the Countess to secure the match by stratagem. He would be a gentleman: but as he learnt from Rose that a gentleman is a frank and open creature, Evan must prove he was a gentleman by not dissimulating the fact that he was a tailor, and the opener about his trade, the more a gentleman. The

[1] Preface to *Memoirs of Lady Duff-Gordon*.

one thing a gentleman cannot do is to have a false shame, to lie, to pass for something other than he is: for with all these go meanness, egoism, hardness of heart. Besides that, common honesty demanded he should pay the debts.

His mother drew him back from his love and ambition to the shop, a sensible business woman, who had no mind to have her husband called a rogue: she was a prim creature. She did not kiss her son: her mouth, she remarked, was for food and speech, and not for slobbering mummeries.

The Countess, however, was not yet put to rout. Under cover of a profusion of lace and veil and mantilla, she entered the house where she was born, kissed her mother, and asked for Evan. "What desolation so awful as that he has stood in a—in a—*boutique?*" That she too should have sprung from this. The thought was painful, but that it should ever be *known* she had sprung from this. Nevertheless she faces Evan. "Hark to me. I have discovered Rose's secret. *Si!* It is so. Rose loves you. You blush: you blush like a girl. She *loves* you and you have let yourself be seen in a shop! Contrast me the two things. Oh! in verity, dreadful as it is, I could almost laugh . . . and I have an invitation for you, Evan,—you unmannered boy, that you do not bow! A gentle incline forward of the shoulders, and the eyes fixed softly, your upper lids drooping triflingly, as if you thanked with gentle insincerity, but were indifferent." So the Countess worked on her brother till he was up to the neck in Purgatory but his soul saturated with visions of Bliss.

JANET ROSS AND "EVAN HARRINGTON"

She drags him back to Beckley, and does insinuating battle for him. For suspicion is a miasma in the air, and Rose has breathed it. The Countess continues her stratagems, but they would all have failed if Rose's cousin, Juliana, who was in love with Evan, had not died bequeathing him her property: for Rose was on the point of affiancing herself to the son of a peer. Once Evan had been whirled away from Beckley, society howling exclusion: "Out of our halls, degraded youth: the smiles of turbaned matrons: the sighs of delicate maids: genial wit: educated talk, refined scandal, vice in harness: dinners sentinelled by stately plush: these, the flavour of life, are not for you, though you stole a taste of them, wreathed impostor! Pay for it with years of remorse."

But with the aid of Rose's love, of fortune and of the Countess, he secures Rose in return for the estate, and a postscript to this bliss comes a year later from the Countess in Rome, announcing her reconciliation with "the infinitely maligned Jesuits." "Here you have every worldly charm, and all crowned by Religion! This is my true delight. I feel at last that whatsoever I do, I cannot go far wrong while I am within hail of my gentle priest. I never could feel so before."

Here then, as we saw, Meredith once again found emancipation in the invention of his genius. Once again he pictured things as he felt they might have been. It was not the baronet's son who was his hero now: it was just the tailor's, but the tailor's son whose sister was a Countess, who inherited an estate, and who married the daughter of a baronet. It is a subtle story: and the subtlest point in it is to introduce his aunt, to whom, as he afterwards said to Lady Milner, he owed his early training in manners, as the astute person who contrives so many stratagems for him at Beckley.

§ 4

Now to several friends who knew Meredith well in later life he was perfectly frank about his own origin and therefore about his personal material for this comedy. Was not everything avowed also to Janet, as she read the unfolding chapters and herself corrected his portrait of her, and of her family? And had Meredith ever suffered the insults thrown at Evan? Was Mr. Ross, or was some earlier suitor, another Laxley of whom the Countess wrote, "One of the noble peers among his ancestors must have been a pig"? These latter are questions which will never be answered. The fact is that he faced the facts and turned them into one of the most excellent romantic comedies that England had seen since *As You Like It*. There is no need to doubt Meredith's romantic enthusiasm for Janet. Re-reading his letters some fifty years after they were written, she was startled out of her habitual reserve to exclaim, "Good God! my poet must have been in love with me." And who can say that she was wrong?

In the meantime she had asked for permission to print the letters in her first volume of memoirs in 1890. But he spoke plainly against it. She held out, nevertheless, and they appeared after his death, when so much of his story came out in his letters. Before her own death she sold them, and they found their way to New York. In 1904 she came down to see Meredith at Box Hill, and this exchange of courtesies continued till his death. When one mentioned to her the name of Meredith, she immediately answered, "I am Rose in *Evan Harrington*." She might have added that he painted another portrait of her in Janet Ilchester.

There is more in *Evan Harrington* than a battle with false pride in himself and a response to the lessons of absolute frankness in the Duff-Gordons. For that absolute frankness had something in it not a little brutal. The Taylors of Norwich were not tailors: they were millers; but the Duff-Gordons looked on themselves as certainly not inferior to the penniless poet they entertained. Was Meredith satisfied with their standards for a gentleman? Were they not involved in that great worship of a success which enabled successful merchants to enter the aristocracy as their portion, even when they rose from the humblest positions? It must not be forgotten that Meredith was one with Evan in being without money, as well as in being a shopkeeper's son. His book is his reaction to the whole of the social atmosphere of the time, when the middle classes worshipped the nobility the more passionately as they came nearer to it. Snobbery, as Meredith had seen, was merely a form of egoism. "I see now that the natural love of a lord is less subservience than a form of self-love; putting a gold-lace hat on one's image, as it were, to bow to it." So Meredith had already written in *Richard Feverel*.[1]

[1] Chapter XXXIV.

There was one matter in which Meredith betrayed himself. It was ease with strangers. His strained manner did not escape Janet's piercing eye, and she remarked that his conversation was best only when he knew he was liked. Self-consciousness always made him fizzle like a firework, and this excessive brilliance made an unfavourable impression in later years on Sir Herbert Warren and Sir Edmund Gosse. "He is not an easy man to be yourself with," wrote Stevenson to Henry James, "there is so much of him, and the veracity and the high athletic intellectual humbug are so intermixed." Even Morley found his conversation "turbulent and strained." If he had an audience waiting to appreciate, he made every effort not to disappoint them. He took it as incumbent upon him to dazzle strangers. "Even into his best talk," said Morley, "there came now and again a sense of strain; if a newcomer joined the little circle of intimates, he was transformed, forcing himself without provocation into a wrestle for violent effects." But the effort was inevitable. "What would have seemed affectation in men of another mould was natural in him. His ready resort to high pitch in thought and startling surprise in speech came by strenuous temperament."[1]

As Hyndman noted, he was "a witty, active, powerful, good-humoured and very keen observer."[2] He talked habitually with vivacity and charm. And when with the friends he knew best, "he delivered himself,"

[1] Lord Morley's *Reminiscences*. E. V. Lucas, *The Colvins and Their Friends*.

[2] H. M. Hyndman, *Dictionary of National Biography*, "George Meredith."

as Hyndman said, "without effort or artifice, of all the really profound and poetic and humorous thoughts on men and things that welled up continually within him and in a manner that I recall with delight these long years afterwards." When he was talking so, his best friends felt that he himself was better than all his books. He struck them as an incomparably great man, and an incomparably delightful one. "Ah, George," asked Burnand, as they sat out one day at Seaford, "why don't you write as you talk?"

VI

ARTHUR'S ABDICATION

§ 1

Richard Feverel made Meredith one friend. A Cambridge undergraduate, called Jessopp, thought Meredith the greatest of rising geniuses after Tennyson, and found occasion to write to him. Meredith warmly responded. He found that Jessopp had been elected to a fellowship at Cambridge, and then made headmaster of Norwich Grammar School. He and his wife came down to Meredith at Copsham and won his entire confidence. Mrs. Jessopp he thought one of the brightest little women, in wit and blood, that one could meet, saying that she united sweetness of nature with worth and capacity. When he went over to stay with them in Norwich, Jessopp took him across to Cambridge and entertained him at St. John's, taking him twice to dine at High Table.[1] In his new friend Meredith had such confidence that, in September, 1862, he handed over to him the son he worshipped.

"This is Arthur's character," he wrote to Jessopp. "It is based upon sensitiveness, I am sorry to say. He is healthy, and *therefore* not moody. His nature is chaste: his disposition *at present* passively good. He reflects: and he has real and just ideas. He will not learn readily. He is obedient, brave, sensible. His brain

[1] *Letters.*

is fine and subtle, not capacious. His blood must move quickly to spur on, and also his heart."[1]

But Mrs. Jessopp noticed that the outfit of the widower's son was not complete. Where was his dessert-spoon, his tea-spoon and his fork? His six towels, and his pillow-cases? Were his sheets marked? Mrs. Jessopp had not thought of speaking about it to the great man while he was with her, preferring to amuse him with stories of a courtship in the kitchen, or to reassure him that in their partitioned dormitory the boys would sleep well. She reserved her courage for a letter. He in return poured out his feelings for his dear boy, whom he met in London on his way home for the Christmas holidays in 1862, and took to the Pantomime. Whatever the boy wanted he was to have, and older friends give way, and work too. But at last, fortified by oysters and pastry, he started back cheerfully to school, with a side glance at his father's forlornness. "Never mind, Papa; it's no use minding it. I shall soon be back to you." Excessive devotion is never particularly interesting to a child, who may, however, be flattered or be tactful.[2]

The boy in fact enjoyed school. Everything was to his taste except chapel. In spite of all the remonstrances of Maxse, the boy had been encouraged to say his prayers: but not, of course, the prayers of the Prayer Book. He was to say "Our Father": he was to think of the Father of all Good: and ask not for the benefits of this world, but for moral strength. All this was to

[1] Unpublished letter in Mr. Altschul's possession.
[2] *Letters.* S. M. Ellis.

be allowed at Norwich,—prayer for hours, in fact,—but not a word of dogma. One may ask, one may think, one may feel, but the traditional highway of the faithful is too dusty: their feelings and their requests, but not their thoughts. The boy must follow the counsels of the Redeemer, but not pray to Him. Meredith did not recognise that in his relations with Christianity he had but exchanged one highroad for another. His view is but the conventional one among Unitarians, and there is vital sincerity in all conventions. In his spiritual intercourse with nature, he was a devotee and a prophet: but that need not have disturbed the Christian creed. It has no immediate quarrels with Meredith's claim that beauty is our portion.

In April Arthur had the measles. Meredith compared him to a pard, a boiled cod in a napkin, a mulberry in the shade. He tended the little invalid day and night, and was only too thankful to keep him back from school till he was out of quarantine.[1] A word that all was not well with him was enough to make Meredith wild with anxiety: if Arthur dropped from too high in the gymnasium, if Jessopp said that he felt anxious for any reason, if the boy caught a complaint—like measles, the father's heart beat fast and high. *Ubi thesaurus, ibi cor.* And Meredith's passion took the form of an intense solicitude for his darling. When home for his holidays Arthur fell from a friend's horse and was dragged fifty yards. Nothing but a few

[1] Mr. Ellis is, however, quite wrong in saying he kept him away from school for a term and sent him back in *August*. He was back before the end of May. See *Letters*, vol. i, p. 106.

bruises came of it, but Meredith's concern was terrible. Arthur was going through the normal adventures of a developing boy. Jessopp's anxiety was caused apparently by his being a little loose with his Latin grammar.

§ 2

Of course the boy returned his father's love in his own way. His heart would break, he wrote once, if he thought his dearest papa was angry with him: but, like some other boys, he was not always keen on writing home. Meredith frequently complains. "I posted a letter, anyway," the boy once pleaded: but Meredith was doubtful, and advised enquiry and cross-examination. Yet in all alike Arthur was supreme. How could the father be happy with his living heart away from him? his heart was with those who watched over the boy and made him happy. "I see not only that every care is taken of him under your roof," Meredith writes to Mrs. Jessopp, "but that happiness is his vital air there." His solicitude for Arthur made Morley call him a "thoughtful, prudent, devoted father to his little son." But the prudent, devoted father could be severe. When Arthur kept begging to taste port, he was made to drink a whole tumblerful and was afterwards violently sick.[1]

Through all this, Meredith's life was lonely and rather empty. The friendship of Maxse and Hardman were much: but the friendships of married men leave

[1] Unpublished letters. S. M. Ellis, *George Meredith*.

big vacuities. There were others, of course: the young socialist from Cambridge, Hyndman, who cultivated a genius whom he felt he could patronise. He had come down to Seaford with Maurice Fitzgerald and took Meredith up to Cambridge for Newmarket Week, in 1864. There Meredith met undergraduates: there too he wrestled with Hyndman. And he was again with him in after-days in Venice. Then there was Frank Burnand, a figure of fun, a man who was to be knighted when Editor of *Punch*, one with a twinkle in his eyes and who was never weary of play, or plays upon words. And again there was Hardman's friend, "Poco" as they called him, Lionel Robinson, puckish, affectionate, droll: Lionel Robinson, who later found out Arthur in Lille, stricken with consumption after Meredith had been separated from him for years. How did this come about? It was because Arthur, and Hardman, and Hyndman, and Poco, and Frank Burnand, with Maxse, with Swinburne, with Maurice Fitzgerald, with even Mrs. Ross writing to *The Times* from Alexandria, were not enough. They had their gamesome times, their wrestling bouts, their roars of laughter: there was all the absorbing business of bringing out masterpieces of poetry and planning masterpieces of prose; there were the busy hours reading for Chapman and Hall, or writing articles for the *Ipswich Journal*; there was a trip in the finest scenery of the French Alps with Lionel Robinson in 1863, as there had been that in the Tyrol with Wyse in 1862; this time Grenoble, the Grande Chartreuse, the Col de Lautaret, Mont Genèvre, and over the Alps to Turin, the Lago

Maggiore, Geneva and Dijon; and a yachting expedition with Cotter Morison a few months later.[1]

§ 3

It was a crowded creative time, a time boisterous with life. "I desire to strike the poetic spark out of absolute human clay, and in doing so I have the fancy that I do solid human work," Meredith wrote. But he was still unsatisfied, was still yearning for something that should make all experience pulse with rapture as once it pulsed.

> I chafe at darkness in the night,
>   But when 'tis light,
> Hope shuts her eyes; the clouds are pale;
> The fields stretch cold into a distance hard:
> I wish again to draw the veil
>   Thousand-starred.
>
> Am I of those whose blooms are shed,
>   Whose fruits are spent,
> Who from dead eyes see Life half dead;—
> Because desire is feeble discontent?
> Ah no! desire and hope shall die,
>   Thus were I.
>
> But in me something clipped of wing
>   Within its ring
> Frets; for I have lost what made

[1] *Letters*.

> The dawn-breeze magic, and the twilight beam
> A hand with tidings o'er the glade
> Waving seem.[1]

Was it then merely the passing of childhood's clouds of joy? was it the evaporation of the romantic tinctures of youth? was Passion's dye fading in the common daylight of maturer age? was earth losing its hold? None of these. His philosophy of life was fixed in radiant energy:

> A star has nodded through
> The depths of the flying blue:
> Time only to plant the light
> Of a memory in the blindness,
> But time to show me the sight
> Of my life thro' the curtain of night;
> Shining a moment, and mixed
> With the onward-hurrying stream,
> Whose pressure is darkness to me;
> Behind the curtain, fixed,
> Beams with an endless beam
> That star on the changing sea.

No, he was sure of the promise of life: energy and rapture were one in him: his mind was consciously one with Nature in her constant creativeness: but he was craving for romance as he once had known it, the romance of intimate passion poured, not upon a son, but into rich exchange of soul and body in wedded

[1] *Poems*, "I chafe at darkness." And an unpublished letter to Jessopp.

love. Arthur was a most bright and intelligent boy; and certainly good-looking; he looked lovely in his shirt. "I jump with delight," wrote Meredith to Mrs. Jessopp, "at the thought of having my darling in my arms"; but not all Arthur's boyishness could make him remotely like a wedded woman.[1]

Meredith could flout to Wyse, but he wrote to his closer friend, when he wedded, of sacred raptures, such as he indeed remembered: and memory meant vividness, and vividness meant life. He was haunted by unknown fair faces:

> Though I am faithful to my loves lived through,
> And place them among Memory's great stars,
> Where burns a face like Hesper: one like Mars:
> Of visages I get a moment's view,
> Sweet eyes that in the heaven of me, too,
> Ascend, tho' virgin to my life they passed.
> Lo, these within my destiny seem glassed
> At times so bright, I wish that Hope were new.

His wishing was father to his thought: it is true that he said that he was satisfied: that he had his experience, and would not ask for more.

> Earth is too poor to hold a second chance;
> I will not ask for more than Fortune gave.

But he knew that earth was not poor: from her abundance she gives with a generosity that never fails the demands of our energies. Unconsciously, inevitably, Meredith, soon after his first wife was dead, began to love again.

[1] Unpublished letters. *Poems*.

Would Arthur like it? If Meredith asked, it was only to assure himself that Arthur would welcome a second and worthier mother. But adored only children do not worship step-mothers, even if very worthy.[1]

§ 4

A lack of vitality practically compensated by more than usual sweetness: this is the first outline in Meredith's letters of one who entered into a warmer relation than even Janet Ross. In June of 1864 the characteristic warmth which blood had given to the earlier love-poems is tinging a letter about one for whom his whole being had been waiting. Freshness and immediacy show that a warm tide has fused nature and the spirit, the outer and the inner, in a keen and rapturous mind. "He loves a woman as he never yet loved and she for the first time has let her heart escape her." So not that first sweet creature who inspired *Love in the Valley*, no Lucy Desborough, not brilliant and bewitching Mary Nicolls, certainly not Janet, in the enigma of his fervour for her, could now be thought of in comparison. Her excellence makes all things new. "I shall now first live. I shall work as I have never yet done. . . . With a wife and with such a wife by my side, I shall taste some of the holiness of this mortal world, and be new-risen in it. Already the spur is acting, and wealth comes, energy comes." A word of business. Meredith was making several hundred a year, and this fine creature was not to come to him

[1] *Poems.* Unpublished letters.

without a jointure. A passing thought for Arthur, for whom, ere this, all thought had been continuous, a thought that Arthur was to glow when his father was burning. And then romance again rushed heavenward. "I believe that I do her good. I know that she feels it. Me she fills with such deep and reverent emotion that I can hardly think it the action of a human creature merely. I seem to trace a fable thus far developed by blessed angels in the skies. She has been reserved for me, my friend. It was seen that I could love a woman, and one has been given me to love. . . ."[1]

Where was Arthur's place, for Arthur was the son of Mary? Mary too had held him, and through the sweetness of Marie came a ghostly revival of Mary's charm, a revival which tortured. Besides, her whole story had to be made known to Justin Vulliamy. "But I would pass through fire for my darling, and all that I have to endure seems little for the immense gain I hope to get. When her hand rests in mine, the world seems to hold its breath, and the sun is moveless. I take hold of eternity."[2]

So much will nature do. The worshipped boy could not generate this rapture. Can experience go further? The ardour of youth can burn so much more intensely than any hope or imagining that a being's capacity for joy is brimming, and the word *satisfied* says nothing of the wonders which are too good to guess or crave. "Have we not heaven's own sunlight within us?" He wrote the question long after, in his unpublished version of *One of Our Conquerors*. Marie Vulliamy

[1] *Letters.* [2] Unpublished letters.

was deeply touched to be the adored of such an adorer. Unable to respond with the passion of a genius, she was unable to understand; and when we cannot understand, there is something humble in accepting. The exaltation of this humility was the greatness of Marie Vulliamy. Hers was the force not of passion but of calm and common sense, of faithfulness and truth. With a beautiful complexion, blue eyes and hair of a warm brown, she was slightly taller than her husband, and her excellent carriage showed to full advantage the womanly dignity of her figure. And as Hyndman noted, she added to handsomeness, cleverness, tact and charm. "Nobody who knew her could fail to esteem, admire and like her."

And his ardour gilded her, as dawn can gild the petal of the rose. This rose was good and perfect to him—a Gloire de Dijon. "She is a very handsome person, fair, with a noble pose and full figure, and a naturally high-bred style and manner such as one meets but rarely." Once and once alone, her practical and cool sense knew a man who poured through her being love's melting tides, and she persuaded her lover that she was making the same rapturous surrender as he. "When I love, I love hotly and give the heart clean out of me." The confession opened doors upon the heart and mind of George Meredith. Was he not looking at his own reflection in her pupils when he wrote that she did likewise? There is a difference between the love that is passion and the love that is affection.[1]

---

[1] The quotations here are from letters in the suppressed edition of Mr. Ellis's book, and are otherwise unpublished.

She was the excellent mother, the considerate, attentive, patient wife, the cultured musician. It pleased Meredith to refer to her as a French Protestant, but she was no more French than he was Celtic. Old Mr. Vulliamy belonged to a Huguenot family which had been settled for generations in Geneva before they came to England, where he was a manufacturer, comfortably off. He had married a Miss Bull of Birkenhead. His house at Mickleham was delightful and roomy. Built in 1636, it had the peculiar charm of late Jacobean red brick. Creepers climbed around its ample windows, and it looked out upon a spacious garden. While the sons managed the mills at Nonancourt or Montigny near Tillières on the Eure in Normandy, and the eldest daughter had married to share the life of Dauphiné with a French officer of the *bourgeoisie*, a certain Poussielque, the three remaining lived at home. Betty, the eldest, was given to good works with such enterprise that on Sunday evenings she preached in a barn to men and women, speaking, as her sister said, so closely to the hearts of the poor that they would listen to no one else. This zeal and this success, therefore, were far from congenial to the parson. Kitty, the second one, who married a clergyman named Wheatcroft, was content to conduct a Sunday School, which Marie would in emergency take over. Marie knew the price of sheets and the price of towels, and this Meredith felt to be most captivating in her. It was a new exercise for her when, on her honeymoon, she day by day copied out the newly written pages of *Vittoria*.

Meredith frequently walked over to Mickleham: they were married in September.[1]

§ 5

Jessopp blessed them in church. Arthur was present at the final act of his dethronement. "My little boy," wrote the bridegroom, "behaved in a lovely way and took to the mother I gave him sweet as milk,"[2] but he and his step-mother soon found it difficult to make a place for one another. Meredith at his betrothal had said that she was fond of him. But more detached critics had realised that the boy's abdication was inevitable. To the new wife, the boy who had been once his father's living heart is simply "a good little fellow, whom she trusts to make her friend." Although she did her utmost, her excellence as a mother was to be recognised by her own children, to whom her existence was not a grievance, and to whom she was not an interloper. She was not "gushing" to Arthur, Meredith noted quite cheerfully. How could she be? She was never gushing to anyone.[3]

§ 6

A spoilt boy with a poor digestion and an inheritance of nerves, a handsome, clever, self-sufficient boy with a temperament sensitive and reserved, to whom his father had given the imperiousness of an idol, had no place for his step-mother's love. "We

[1] S. M. Ellis, *George Meredith*.   [2] Unpublished letters.
[3] *Letters*.

mourn and howl over him," wrote Meredith to Jessopp a few months after the marriage, but the boy was no longer more than a side issue in letters to his headmaster.

He stayed however at Norwich for another two years, when he was fourteen. Then Meredith sent him to a school at Hofwyl near Berne, and still hoped for a reconciliation with Mrs. Meredith, who did what she could. If Arthur did not care to come home, would he meet his people at the seaside, in Normandy or Brittany? A religious fervour still filled the father's heart when he thought of his proud and passionate boy. "How much I long to meet you. Keep pure in mind, unselfish of heart, and diligent in study. This is the right way of worshipping God, and is better than hymns or sermons or incense. We find it doubtful whether God blesses the latter, but cultivate the former and you are sure of Him. Heed me well when I say this. May God forever bless you, I pray it nightly."[1]

In 1869 the boy paid a visit to his step-mother's eldest sister at Pont-de-Beau-Voisin in Savoy. He had to be warned against rash forming of opinions. At the end of the summer holidays he was taken by Meredith to stay with a Professor Zeller at Stuttgart. But he did not take to Germany. He thought his new schoolfellows were sneaks. Meredith entertained the idea of his winning a scholarship in Modern Languages in Oxford. But the boy preferred reading English, and wrote in praise of Ossian. He would not mix with Germans, whom his father esteemed and gratefully

[1] *Letters*. Unpublished letters.

remembered, knowing them good and lasting friends. Meanwhile Arthur was to take care of his digestion and guard against chills. But Meredith and his wife were both ready, in spite of all, to join in making sacrifices to send the boy to Oxford.

June 13 was his birthday, and two pounds was sent him in 1871, with ten more for a trip to Vienna. His father hoped to see him in August. "I want very much to see you and shall do my utmost to come." Arthur kept on grumbling at the Germans, whom victory, in truth, did not make more charming. Bismarck was already beginning to affect them. Meredith warned Arthur against being too frank in saying what he thought of them: the boy was to find a support for reticence in religion and prayer: "Let nothing flout your sense of a Supreme Being."[1]

The temper of Arthur was undoubtedly difficult. He had his father's Celtic faults but was not a hero to persevere. He had inherited some money from the Peacock side, but finally found employment in business, first at Havre, then through his father's neighbours and friends, the Beneckes, at Lille, in a linseed warehouse. He and his father were estranged: the two sensitive men misunderstood one another, and the father felt that the son preferred to be away from him. When Meredith heard of Arthur again, it was to hear through Lionel Robinson, as we saw, that Arthur had consumption. He wrote at once a letter full of concern, affection, forgiveness, urging Arthur to come home. The boy had thought of literature. Meredith promised

[1] *Letters*, and unpublished letters from Arthur.

ARTHUR'S ABDICATION

to guide him. Morley, now editing the *Fortnightly*, would help him: he would have a home with his father for as long as he wanted. He would find a brother and sister, a little sister of ten, a good humane intelligent girl, and a brother six years older: "Will, though not brilliant, is a kindly fellow, with wits of a slow sort. . . . We shall all be overjoyed to see you." But the inducements were insufficient.[1]

Arthur, cherishing bitter memories, planned instead a tour in the Eastern Alps, and offered to meet his father there. Meredith was ill and short of money, and could not promise, though he would make every effort. The old warmth of feeling and sympathy came pouring back. "My thoughts will follow you still anxiously. It is a holiday to me to think of you soon having liberty. . . . We should all have had delight in welcoming you home but your project is in every way advisable. Try to come to us next year in May or June for the summer." The family meanwhile urged Meredith to go, and it was no fault of his wife that he did not start at once. Dyspepsia and shortness of money kept him back. But he was happy to throw himself into Arthur's feelings. "I rejoice that you have flown, and am as glad of your release as if I had personally risen singing on the free air."

Arthur did not get better. He wandered about, now in the South, now in England. His step-sister Edith, now Mrs. Clarke, and her husband were to him goodness itself. In 1889 he went for a trip to Australia as a last resort: but Meredith was to learn, to his furious

[1] *Letters.*

indignation, that he had been obliged to share a cabin with a raving inebriate.

His step-mother had now passed from this world, but Arthur was not appeased. Once again he had quarrelled with his father, and sensitive and proud to the last, he refused the money with which Meredith, now in fairly comfortable circumstances, offered to secure him little luxuries. He returned to England the next summer to die on September 3rd, at the house of his step-sister. Meredith was not with him. When he learned from his younger son that Arthur was no more, grief pierced him, as it had done at the death of Arthur's mother; but being himself unwell, he yielded to the urgings of his daughter and younger son, not to be present at the burial. They went instead. His tenderness became a great gratitude to his step-daughter who, with her husband, had been indeed devoted. "Until my breath goes," wrote Meredith, "I will bless you both."[1]

[1] *Letters.*

VII

THE FUNCTION OF WOMAN

§ 1

I F we look back at the England of the early 'sixties, the last years of Prince Albert, and think of Mid-Victorianism parading in its crinolines and its prudery, if we think of the solid commercialism which aspired for elegance, building Bayswater and extending the stale ugliness of slums wherever it was busy, if we think of Victoria widowed, and of one young officer's being "awfully jealous" of another for being placed nearer the young Alexandra in her guard of honour, if we think of the solid meals, and the solid houses built without a thought for servants, we see an orgy of irresponsible egoists. These egoists were always lurking among furniture of solid mahogany. They were thorough, and did not forgo the gratifications of their sentiments.

Meredith himself had written, "Sentimentalists are those that seek to enjoy without incurring the immense debtorship for a thing done." The luxuries of love are to be compensated by a virile activity: sweat: the right to feel must be earned. That was the one side; but there was another: crinolined women must remember that they too had all that is implied by the flesh and blood they shared, not alone with dogs and horses, but with tigers and rabbits. Man is an animal. The earth is a fact, a reality so fundamental, so pervading, so true, as to be vital to the spirit. Neither with earth on the one side nor with the open air on the other were the majority of Mid-Victorians intimate enough. Their mentality was dominated by suburban parlours, they shut themselves up in prisons of propriety. The moral life was confined to avoiding what is rough and vulgar, and this became such a refinement that waists grew waspish, digestion maimed. Good food, how gross! Money, how vile! Marriage, how unspeakable! *Les femmes savantes* lived again, and spoke with traditional scorn of the creation of homes which were the all-absorbing work of those that had them. For marriage was a very thorough thing in those days, and, though sex was never mentioned, affection faced it as unequivocally as passion. The origin of families was an Eleusinian mystery, but they mounted up, not the less, to ten or twelve. Meredith openly avowed that he was content when he had three children, separated as they were by eighteen years. He was always urging that a woman must recognise woman's unique and sovereign function, but he insisted that she should aim at something more. And through his whole career, he glorified women when they were creatures of heart and brain. He was fond of quoting in later life what he was to write in the *Egoist:* "Cleverness in women is not uncommon. Intellect is the pearl. A woman of intellect is as good as a Greek statue. She is divinely wrought and she is divinely fair."[1]

[1] This echoes a line from Tennyson's "A Dream of Fair Women."

Up to that time women had tended to take too exclusively either the one attitude or the other, like Armande and Henriette. The new Armande was still scorning marriage:

> Et de vous marier, vous osez faire fête?
> Ce vulgaire dessein vous peut monter en tête?

She was still arguing in the same tone:

> Laissez aux gens grossiers, aux personnes vulgaires,
> Les bas amusements de ces sortes d'affaires.
> A de plus hauts objets élevez vos désirs,
> Songez à prendre un goût des plus nobles plaisirs,
> Et, traitant de mépris les sens et la matière,
> A l'esprit, comme nous, donnez-vous tout entière.

But the sweet frankincense of male adoration was still welcome. They wanted it without the debtorship of generation, and in denying the body, they robbed their relation with men of the sublimity of its romance. And in this larceny, there was another, more obvious, more sinister. We cannot make a spirit without a body:

> Ne supprimez point, voulant qu'on vous seconde,
> Quelque petit savant qui veut venir au monde.

You cannot scorn sense or matter, Meredith argued, and the more you tend to do so, the more you deprive yourself of the riches of life. Face it with more courage and more, till what you shrink from is seen essential to poetry and to spirit. "Fortitude," he wrote to a woman he knew well, "is the one thing for which we may pray, because without it we are unable to bear the truth." He knew what Henriette called "*les facheux besoins des choses de la vie*," but he was no more content than Armande that a woman should set herself to be the *Hausmutter* and nothing more: *ne vous contentez point*, he would have insisted:

> De vous claquemurer aux choses du ménage
> Et de n'entrevoir point de plaisirs plus touchants,
> Qu'une idole d'époux, et des marmots d'enfants!

By giving to brain what we must also give to body and to heart, both men and women rise to the realm of spirit.

This is the problem which occupies Meredith in the early 'sixties. In *Rhoda Fleming* he urges the dignity and rights of woman against the man who would look upon her, with the sentimentality of the brute, as nothing but the toy of his feelings, whatever those might be. In his two other novels he creates an Italian singer as an example of noble womanhood amongst the attenuated sentimentalists of propriety, and he turns from the drawing-room to the air of Italy to make his Sandra Belloni the noble Vittoria, a follower of his hero Mazzini. Woman was not only essential to the man of nature: she was the fruitful and inspiring being who with him completed and ennobled the life of mind and heart. Meredith enthroned her in literature's high world of reason, passion and imagination, and gave her a scope in the realm of government. He was assured that "women of the independent mind are needed for any sensible degree of progress":

he felt even that injustice had been done to women, that in fact the race had been degraded by the constraint put upon their aptitudes and faculties.

§ 2

Mazzini had long been a hero to Meredith who was just growing out of adolescence in 1848. In the preceding years, when Meredith had come back from Neuwied, he could have read Mazzini's letters in *The Times*. Mazzini was furthermore admired by Carlyle, who declared him a man of genius and virtue, and said that his nobleness of spirit was incomparable. Mazzini's philosophy was moreover in concord with Hegel's; he taught that progress was the evolution of the thought of God. He believed that the dominant influence of the individual was passing and that the world was coming into the era of collective effort when men and women should co-operate, and when a federation of democracies, studying and promoting a grand Providential design, would have its parliament at Rome. Mazzini was a great figure, and at his greatest as portrayed by Meredith. His face contrasted with the sweet virile Italian beauty of the handsome adventurer. "He had the complexion of the student, and the student's aspect. The attentive droop of the shoulders and head, the straining of the buttoned coat across his chest, the air as of one who waited and listened, which distinguished his figure, detracted from the promise of other than contemplative energy until his eyes were fairly seen and felt. That is, until the observer became aware that those soft and large meditative eyes had taken hold of him. In them lay no abstracted student's languor, no reflex burning of a solitary lamp; but a quiet grappling force engaged the penetrating look. His eyes were dark as the forest's border is dark, not as night is dark. Under favourable lights their colour was seen to be a deep rich brown, like the chestnut, or more like the hazel-edged sunset brown which lies upon our western rivers in the winter floods when night begins to shadow them. . . . He saw far and he grasped ends beyond obstacles: he was nourished by sovereign principles. He despised material present interests and, as I have said, he was less supple than a soldier. . . . His smile was quite unclouded, and came softly as a curve in water. It seemed to flow with, and pass in and out of, his thoughts,—to be a part of his emotion and his meaning when it shone transiently full. For as he had an orbed mind, so had he an orbed nature."

§ 3

Meredith's enthusiasm for progress, for liberalism, for humanity, all drew him to identify his moral fervours with the Risorgimento, and his general ideas had found an object of enthusiasm in Lady Hornby, who began as Emilia Macirone. Emilia was being courted by Wilfred Pole, a rich young parvenu with sentimental sisters. Her father had died in exile, and she had a voice which wins her the enthusiasm of a Greek millionaire, who in the end takes her to Italy, rescuing her from her friend Powys and her lover, Pole.

THE FUNCTION OF WOMAN

She reappears in Italy as Vittoria, Emilia having changed to Sandra Belloni, who was Vittoria Alessandra. In *Vittoria*, Meredith crowded his narrative with incidents, for, as a war-correspondent in Italy for *The Morning Post*, he had much more chance of observing intrigue and action. Vittoria keeps in touch with Wilfred, who has now a commission in the Austrian army, and the patriots suspect her. But she is loved by Count Carlo Ammiani, a practical conspirator, who becomes her husband, though he lacks her larger vision.

The great zest in action, which with the passion for music marks the Italian novels, is subsidiary to the study of sentiment. This problem was at the moment uppermost in Meredith's mind. Though the comic spirit might dissolve them, sentimental feelings were the poison of humanity. He wanted to get back to passion, and to the spacious reality of natural life. Stendhal in his studies of love had spoken of it as a passion which was, in so far as it made men forget their love of self, the effort which a man makes to win his supreme good in one outside him. Sentimentality, on the other hand, was a luxury where experience was preferred to interest in another. Just as snobbishness is a form of self-worship, so rhapsody is self-indulgence, and moral rhapsody is humbug. How easy it is for ambitious women to scorn the means which made the money for them to live in cultured ease, or even the flesh which enabled them to live at all. Between the life of the successful merchant's daughters and the Italian patriot's, Meredith saw the contrast between the extremes of what to admire and what to despise. He found in Italy emancipation from the unreal values with which the English social standards were then choking. *Sandra Belloni* and *Vittoria*, therefore, are developments of the theme of *Evan Harrington*.

§ 4

He alternated these with other novels, with *The House on the Beach* and *Rhoda Fleming*. It is again his contempt of social ambition which inspires these novels. Both of them are in their way tragic stories: in the slighter, Tinman is a retired tradesman who wants to present an address to the Queen, and who wants to marry his daughter to an old friend who has fled to Tasmania and whom Tinman can blackmail. In *Rhoda Fleming*, two girls on a farm in Kent became fascinated by London, which was like a new universe to their spirits. But the one who went to live there was taken to the Continent by a young man who omitted to marry her; the story turns on the question of her being made respectable, but her life is shattered.

§ 5

In all these stories Meredith was revolving his ideas of snobbery, of sentiment, of woman. He was developing his thought that men must live as social equals with women, that all must seem as they are and not put an exaggerated value on the conventions, or worldly respect, or show, nor yet allow the pampering of their own selfish emotions to be set before the great realities of a noble, passionate, active life. He asserts, in fact, the value of a life like his own, a life set on noble and passionate action, and he feels an intense amusement at the feebleness of ordinary subterfuges to pass off another life for this, the life which puts artificial standards in place of a real assessment of men. These are the ideas which occupied his imagination in those boisterous but penurious years, when he enjoyed himself so much and when he settled down to his happy marriage. In his novels he continues to find his life of action, his means of imposing his own personality on the world.

His were not the current ideas, and there was nothing else in Meredith's method to make them popular. He knew his method, and soon became aware of its consequences. "'Tis the indifferent reader that loses his subject, not I," he might have said with Molière, and already in *The Ordeal* he was aware that an audience impatient for blood and glory scorned the stress he was putting on incidents so minute, a picture so little imposing. "An audience will come," he had assured himself however, "to whom it will be given to see the elementary machine at work; who, as it were, from some slight hint of the straws, will feel the winds of March when they do not blow . . . and they will perceive moreover that in real life all hangs together: the train is laid in the lifting of an eyebrow that bursts upon the fields of thousands."

It was this which he applied, in *Sandra Belloni*, to

the exposure of the sentimental egoist's nakedness: "My vulgar meaning might almost be twisted to convey that our sentimentalists are a variety owing their existence to a certain prolonged term of comfortable feeding. The pig, it will be retorted, passes likewise through this training. He does. But in him it is not combined with an indigestion of high German romances."

When Meredith went off on his honeymoon, he was busy with *Vittoria*. They stayed first in lodgings at Mr. Price's, in Pear Tree Green in Southampton. But before long they were settled near Bursledon on the Hamble, at Ploverfield, in the house which Maxse lent them. Love, hard exercise, and prose composition filled Meredith's rapturous days, and he was delighted with the scenery. "Fancy a salt river crystal-clear," he wrote, "winding under full-bosomed woods to a Clovelly-like village, house upon house, with ships and trawlers and yachts moored under the windows, and away the flat stream shining to the southern sun till it reaches Southampton Water, with the New Forest over it shadowy and beyond, to the left, the Solent and the Island. This is visible from our bedroom window. The air makes athletes."[1]

They settled for a time in lodgings at Esher and Kingston. Then they took Kingston Lodge, to be near the Hardmans. But Meredith did not care for this neighbourhood and in 1867 sold the lease to Frederick Jones.[2]

The taste for energy, which Meredith habitually

[1] Unpublished letters.   [2] S. M. Ellis, *George Meredith*.

released in violent exercise, found another release when, as we have seen, he went to Italy in 1866 as *The Morning Post's* War Correspondent. He thus found material to finish *Vittoria* in Venice, and wrote some vigorous war letters.

It will be seen that he was War Correspondent to a Tory paper. He had been attached to another Tory paper, *The Ipswich Journal*, since 1860. It is not a little surprising that Meredith with his radical sympathies should ever have allowed himself to write for Tories. He justified the ways of Disraeli to farmers in Norfolk and Suffolk, and poured contempt on Gladstone and Lord John Russell. Would he have said that as the barrister will plead for a client without being assured of the justice of his case so he argued for his Tories? He certainly was not prepared for insincerity. A closer view of the articles show that, though a convinced radical, and even republican, in principle, he did not always identify his thought with that of the Liberal party. He was not of course editor: he was merely a contributor, and he contributed his expression of himself. He sided with the Confederates in America, against the Federals. He can hardly have agreed with *The Ipswich Journal* on Home politics: but he found ample opportunities to express his own personal feelings. Again and again he discoursed of women and their gifts: and an article on Princess Alexandra leads him to express himself on the crinoline: "The introduction of the crinoline has been in its effects morally worse than a *coup d'état*. It has sacrificed more lives; it has utterly destroyed more tempers; it has put an immense division between the sexes. It has obscured us, smothered us, stabbed us."

§ 6

Meredith was not, of course, a journalist by choice. "Palmerston's policy," said Mr. Dolman, "was a poor exchange for the pilgrim scrip," and doubtless, in comparison with Sandra, even the Southern generals seemed rather paltry figures.

Meredith had contributed from his early years to *Household Words* and *Once a Week*. In 1867 he acted as Editor of *The Fortnightly* during Morley's absence. But it was a friend of Charnock, Foakes, who gave him a regular place on *The Ipswich Journal*. Thursday he called Foakes Day, for on that day his articles had to be written in London. Sometimes he would get Hardman to write one for him, sometimes even Morley, and he was only too thankful to give it up altogether. His feeling about it is put into the mouth of Alvan, in *The Tragic Comedians:* "Above all things I detest the writing for money. Journalism for money is Egyptian bondage. No slavery is comparable to the chains of hired journalism. My pen is my fountain: the key of me, and I give myself, I do not sell. I write when I have matter in me, and in the direction it presses for, otherwise not one word!" But it is quite another matter to say, as it has been said, that his writing was dishonest. He was not a convinced radical till 1868, when he fought Maxse's election. He said in Italy, when he was writing for *The Morning Post*, that he tried to be just to both sides. *Beauchamp's Career* gives many examples of his knowing, and—what is more—feeling, the arguments of the Tories as well as those of the Liberals. The fact is that he was not a radical pamphleteer. "Generally I am with the Liberals," he told Morley, "but I do not always take party views."

Out of his love of action grew a great interest in the art and science of war. He was an ardent student of military history, and in later years, as we shall see, would discuss strategy and tactics with Lord Haldane or Lord Ypres. He read many books on wars, especially Napoleon's wars, and though, with other correspondents, he was not allowed near the firing-line, his despatches are vigorous and vivid. Beginning at Ferrara in June of 1866, they continue from Cremona, Bozzolo, Marcaria. He arrived at the Italian headquarters at Torre Malimberti and wrote from there, on July 7. He then went on to Piadena, Gonzaga, and Noale. On July 20 he wrote from Dolo, near Venice. Two days later he was at Città Vecchia. His last despatch was written from Marseilles on July 24. His method was to collect anecdotes, and his information is rarely more than second-hand. But his narrative was put down clearly. The most startling story was that of two brigands in Naples. They walked through the street unarmed, in their peasant's dress, calling at certain houses, and opened a handkerchief one of them carried. It contained six ears! Each was ticketed with a name and address, and left to stimulate prompt payment of ransom. The police dared not interfere, for the immediate result would have been the summary execution of the hostages held by the brigands, every one of whom had themselves been captured from the police-force.[1]

But the real result of his tour in Italy was to finish *Vittoria* as true to Italy's throes at that time. The spirit of the war breathes through its crowded adventures.

"The elements of melodrama," wrote Lord Morley, "joined to strong Mazzinian moral sympathies, set Meredith's imagination on fire." The natural beauty of Italy kindled him as much as her patriotism. "Italy," he once wrote, "is where I would live if I had my choice." And there was some talk of his becoming *The Times* Correspondent; he was warmly recommended, but it came to nothing.[2]

---

[1] Memorial Edition of *Works*.
[2] *The Times*, May 19, 1909. Lord Morley's *Reminiscences*.

VIII

FIRST YEARS AT BOX HILL

§ 1

WHEN Meredith once found that his wife he had always with him, his thirsts were for sunny landscapes and for friends. Hardman, as we saw, first drew him: but Hardman was not enough. He found the home he really wanted near Dorking, at the foot of the folds of Box Hill. The heather and bracken commons around Oxshott, and the red-stemmed firs sighing deeply in the wind, were exchanged for another love, a country of beech woods and downs, and, what he prized more than these, a chance to feel the wind as it came on to meet him over viewed hills and valleys. These breathed exhilaration to him and were one with the life of the heart, as he attentively watched their changes in the late afternoon:

Sunrays, leaning on our southern hills and lighting
    Wild cloud-mountains that drag the hills along,
Oft ends the day of your shifting brilliant laughter
    Chill as a dull face frowning on a song.
Ay, but shows the South-West a ripple-feather'd bosom
    Blown to silver while the clouds are shaken and ascend
Scaling the mid-heavens as they stream, there comes a sunset
    Rich, deep like love in beauty without end.

There was nothing that so constantly charmed his thought, and found expression when he talked spontaneously, as admired women and loved winds; again and again he spoke of them together.[1]

Flint Cottage, as it was called, the cottage under Box Hill to which he went in 1867, was a small square stone house, natural to the ground in which it was placed, with three acres of garden turning into orchard, and a fir wood behind leading to beeches. With just room enough for him to live within the walls, the woods rising up from it on to the hill, and London within reach, it was a home to hold him happily for forty years. His new bride was, as he would have said, a right admirable housewife, and he found a constant joy in the son she had given him; Arthur was seldom at home.

He was not long settled when discerning neighbours found that a remarkable person was amongst them. An Eton boy, Jim Gordon, was the first to appreciate this. "I know a man who lives up on Box Hill," he called out in the dark hours of morning to his cousin, Alice Brandreth. "He's quite mad, but very amusing; he likes walks and sunrises. Let's go and shout him up." Hurrying over to the Cottage, they flung pebbles at his panes. A shout answered, "What do you mean by trying to break my window?" But an invitation to watch a sunrise was worth danger to windows. In a moment he was down with them, his nightshirt tucked into brown trousers, his feet in slippers. In such a garb, at such an hour, his soul

[1] *The Times*, Feb. 12, 1928.

emanated life. A hymn to nature, life, and obligation fell on the ears of boy and girl. "Observe, not feel," he told them. Man's part in nature must be active, and rapture greets the eye that lives at sunrise as keenly as the heart:

Happy, happy time, when the white star hovers
   Low over dim fields fresh with bloomy dew,
Near the face of dawn, that draws athwart the darkness,
   Threading it with colour, like yewberries the yew.
Thicker crowd the shades as the grave East deepens
   Glowing, and with crimson a long cloud swells.
Maiden still the morn is; and strange she is, and secret;
   Strange her eyes; her cheeks are cold as cold seashells.[1]

From these morning walks he returned to the house, as his friend Morley has written, like Apollo descending from Olympus. "He came to the morning meal, after a long hour's stride in the tonic air and fresh loveliness of cool woods and green slopes, with the brightness of sunrise upon his brow, responsive penetration in his glance, the turn of radiant irony in his lips and peaked beard, his fine poetic head bright with crisp brown hair." In this radiant man, Morley, like Alice Brandreth, rejoiced to find a friend and teacher, a friend who held out to him a cordial, indulgent, and ever-faithful hand. And this was not always easy: for the young man took himself very seriously. It was noticed of him, when he was at the

[1] *Poems. Memories of George Meredith*, by Lady Butcher.

India Office, that the thought of his own dignity came foremost. At a party at a country house, Curzon, back from his Vice-royalty, was diverting a billiard-room with an account of how often he was birched at Eton, and why. As the hearers harmonised more and more with the genial mood of the narrator, it was noticed that Morley's face grew grimmer and grimmer. "If I had a son at Eton," he said, "and I thought he had to put up with such indignities, I should take him away at once."[1]

§ 2

In the 'sixties the young man, though he had a brilliant wit and could talk and write excellently, was already at bottom very solemn. He had left Oxford with a reputation: he was a conscientious young agnostic, and he became almost at once Editor of *The Fortnightly Review*. Early in the 'seventies he wrote a number of essays on Compromise, which considered most carefully and most gravely how far expediency must affect one's sincerity in realising an opinion, and which faced with agnostic conscientiousness the fact that no subjects had ever been so fascinating to men of thought as the existence of God and the immortality of the soul. A young man who took himself so seriously was liable to affront at Meredith's boisterous chaff, or frank expressions of opinion, and at last he wrote that Meredith was alone among his friends in doing him harm. Meredith's manner of

[1] Lord Morley's *Reminiscences*.

speaking, he said, clashed with his opinions, ideas, and likings.[1]

Even if, upon the larger matters, they were one, said Morley, yet Meredith's society failed to give him new strength, and was actually baneful. For six months, it seemed, in March of 1871, Meredith had been roughing him. Such a letter coming to the sensitiveness of Meredith seemed to cut friendship to the ground. He could not but feel it. "We will see one another as little as we can for two or three years, and by and by may come together again naturally," he answered. "And if not, you will know I am glad of the old time, am always proud of you, always heart in heart with you on all the great issues of our life, and in all that concerns your health and fortunes. . . . I am ever yours faithfully and warmly." This was the end of the quarrel. Morley saw that he had lost his temper and came back to the old ardour of friendship to enjoy his friend's teasing more than before. They kept in close touch till Meredith died, and Morley became, in fact, one of his trustees. Morley found him eager to learn everything new in public things. He remained, however, independent, putting the judgments of his justice above party.[2]

Morley and Meredith worked together for Chapman & Hall. In editing *The Fortnightly*, Morley had a free hand, and he was glad to take some of his friend's novels. Meredith became reader to the firm in 1867. Each Thursday he called at the office, and, as years went on, his visits were recognised as an event. The

[1] *Letters.*   [2] Morley's *Reminiscentes. Letters.*

employees were awed at his arrival: it was, said one of them, as though the King had come in. His talk, like the alertness of his aspect, was galvanic. His scarlet tie contrasted with his greyish hair, and his chiselled features completed the fine impression of his head.[1]

In earlier days he would write his impressions in a book; in later ones a paper was sent to him for this with the manuscripts. His standard was extremely high: his judgment impersonal and inflexible, and his first thought was to apply a criterion not of popular appeal but of merit. In almost every case his word was final. His opinion was "emphatically against" *East Lynne*, of which he wrote to Lucas "that it was in the worst style of the present taste." "My principle," he wrote at another time, "is to show the events flowing from evident causes." Of William Black, he said that he exhibited strong sense and poetic perception: that he had a remarkably clear style and a commendable power of giving pathetic touches, but that he did not know much of life. Of Edwin Arnold he wrote, "I should say this man will do something"; against Ouida's *Villiers* he wrote "Decline." Mrs. Lynn Linton's books were rejected because of her "abhorrence of the emancipation of young females from their ancient rules."[2] But though Meredith always talked in this way, it was noticed that when the young female was his daughter the ancient rules were often rigidly enforced.

In January, 1869, after reading Hardy's first novel,

[1] *Fortnightly Review*, 1909, B. W. Matz.
[2] *Fortnightly Review*, B. W. Matz. Unpublished letters.

Meredith sent for him personally to tell of the hopes he had, though he rejected the novel, *The Poor Man and the Lady*, which indeed never has been published. Hardy found, in the back room of Chapman & Hall's in Piccadilly, an unusual sort of man to meet in such a place: a handsome man with hair and beard not yet grey, wearing a frock-coat buttoned at the waist and loose above. Hardy had no idea who it was; he found a critic, encouraging but acute, a man who would spare nothing to assist the promise of merit. "Don't nail your colours to the mast just yet," he said to Hardy. Hardy recognised his adviser as a friend in later years, and visited Meredith at Box Hill. But Meredith, though he recognised Hardy's merit, was to the end oppressed by his twilight view of life.[1]

Meredith did not dilute his expressions of opinion, and the words "poor," "bad" and "commonplace," and even "impossible" or "utter rubbish," occur against the names of novelists who became well known. But he would take great trouble with writers who interested him, and after two revisions he accepted Olive Schreiner's *African Farm*. He was disappointed in the letters of "Carlyle and Jane Welsh," but found some merit in *The Heavenly Twins*. In Fitzmaurice Kelly he saw a scholarly hand, a promising author.

He described *The Autobiography of a Donkey* as faithful only to the Donkey's dullness: he withheld another volume in charity to the author: of a Tasmanian he said, "He knows Van Diemen's land well

[1] *Nineteenth Century*, Feb., 1928. *Letters*. S. M. Ellis, *George Meredith*.

but is a stranger to composition"; of another, "This is laughable enough in MS. but in print the ridicule would fall upon the publishers": of another, called humorous by the author, "Cockneyish dialogue, gutter English, ill-contrived incidents, done in daubs, maintain the assertion." Of *Diverticula Amæna* submitted by Maurice Hewlett, he wrote that it was "drenched by emotions produced by paintings and scenery." He rejected W. H. Hudson's *Mr. Abel*, but found his *Naturalist in La Plata* "excellent."[1] The object in each case was to make judgment succinct. In reviews, he had a freer hand and wrote with the generous vigour which marked all his thought. In 1868, for example, he wrote a critique on Myers's little poem, "St. Paul." It had, he said, a dignity unwavering to the end. If there were in it some lackadaisical alliteration and mellifluousness, and here and there a certain dramatic unfitness, he felt his imagery to be unusually just, and at times noble. "As one loving poetry wherever I can find it, and of any kind, I have to thank him." He cited as an example of purity and conception the verse:

> Great were his fate who on the earth should linger,
>   Sleep for an age and stir himself again,
> Watching Thy terrible and fiery finger
>   Shrivel the falsehood from the souls of men.

He reviewed also the work of "Owen Meredith," and in doing so paid a magnificent tribute to Tennyson and Browning. With Tennyson, as with Dickens,

[1] *Fortnightly Review*, 1909, B. W. Matz. Material in Mr. Altschul's collection.

he was at times disappointed, to the verge of disgust. "Arthur," he said to Lady Danesfort, was "a crowned curate, and his answer to Guinevere should have been 'Get up!'" "Tennyson," Meredith wrote to Maxse in 1869, "has many spiritual indications but no philosophy, and philosophy is the palace of thought." But he could say more than that. In 1874 he wrote to Morley that he had great pleasure in reading *Queen Mary*: "I saw no trace of power, but the stateliness, the fine tone, the high tone, of some passages, hit me hard. Curiously too in him the prose is crisp, salient, excellent." Writing on Owen Meredith, he gave Tennyson with Browning the praise of an enthusiast: "Of their kind they are incomparably excellent. Poets like these must be studied by the light of their own manifested powers." Their faults came from "penetrative insight, from imaginative complexity of perception, or from defective or superabundant energy of expression."[1] And this, in Tennyson's case, was the more generous because once, in earlier days, when Meredith was but a beginner, he had gone to see Tennyson: the great bard was unable to give him the slightest attention because he was obsessed by an unfavourable criticism of his own poems by a writer hidden under the name of Apollodorus. "Apollodorus says I'm not a great poet," was Tennyson's greeting. They went for a walk. "Apollodorus says I'm not a great poet," was Tennyson's beginning in conversation, and the words echoed in a voice deep and musical as Meredith's own. Meredith came back with Tennyson's

[1] *Works*, Memorial Edition.

one sentence echoing in his ears: "Apollodorus says I'm not a great poet."[1]

Did he recall those other lines of Tennyson's—

There let the wind sweep, and the plover cry;
But thou, go by?

§ 3

About this time Meredith wrote the most charming of his short stories. It has been published, only in the memorial edition, and none but a few enthusiasts have read it. Seven chapters, the pages of each tied together by blue ribbon, remain in manuscript and tell a story not only of "The Gentleman of Fifty and the Damsel of Nineteen," but of a man who, after a deep disillusion, found that he was falling in love at the age of thirty-six with a very simple young woman much younger than himself. Marie Vulliamy was a woman of strong character and an accomplished musician. She did not, and she could not, respond to the ardour of his passion, or the swiftness of his wit, with the individual impulse which pricked him forward. But yet he loved her, and love itself was its own miracle. "We grow together and are one in heart . . . she is like music, folding through every minute of my existence."[2] So he wrote to Hardman on his honeymoon. And to second this miracle, as he saw it in his heart and hers, was the delightful task that he set himself, in *The Gentleman of Fifty*.

[1] R. Le Gallienne, *The Romantic Nineties*.
[2] Unpublished letter.

There are seven chapters, written alternately by the Gentleman and the Damsel. The first begins with the Gentleman, who is the Squire of Dayton, finding the Vicar walking fully dressed in a stream at the end of the vicarage garden. "A wise man will not squander his laughter if he can help it but will keep the agitation of it down as long as he may. The simmering of humour sends a living spirit into the mind, whereas the boiling over is but a prodigal expenditure, and the disturbance of a clear current: for the comic element is visible to you in all things, if you do but keep your mind charged with the perception of it." It was a hot morning: "even the gloom was hot and the little insects which are food for fish tried a flight, and fell on the water's surface as if panting." But while the Squire was restraining his amusement, one of the Vicar's daughters appeared, and laughed outright. The Vicar's wife fell in next. And when this absurd scene was settled, Squire and daughter went for a row.

The second chapter shows that the Damsel was not less interested in him than he in her. Supposed to be in love with his nephew Charles, who had been courting her, she found the uncle of fifty more attractive than the nephew. She might allow an interest, for was he not her godfather? In the meanwhile she was highly amused at the frank remarks of a Mrs. Romer, who had married a man thirty-one years older than herself.

The Squire is now beginning to realise his position. Was he any less free from the power of love after fifty virtuous years than the wild young nephew? "Be dilettante all your days, and you might as fairly hope to reap a moral harvest as if you had chased butterflies." But a glance from the Damsel turns his thoughts towards standing for Parliament: great events spring from little causes. "The slipper of a soubrette trips the heart of a king and changes the destiny of a nation —the history of mankind."

He fences, and finds himself as subtle as the Damsel. "There is natural art, and artificial art, and the last beats the first. Fortunately for us, women are strangers to the last." But he must confess that, though a man of the world, he was being worked on by an unmitigated girl. "I do not know her and I believe I do not care to know her, and I am thirsting for the hour to come when I shall study her. Is not this to have the poison of a bite in one's blood? The wrath of Venus is not a fable."

Her chapter tells of her experience paying a visit to Dayton Manor that she might be studied ostensibly as a possible wife for the nephew. Among his portraits, she is shown one of the Marquise de Mazardouin, a face to be loved. Her host tests her in the language of France, where he has lived for years. She feels an intense interest in him.

"I can command myself when I choose, but it is only when I choose," she tells him. "The sort of young people who have such wonderful command of themselves are not the pleasantest."

"No," he said, "they disappoint us. We expect folly from the young." He gives her a pony, which becomes the object of her passionate endearments.

In the fifth chapter he faces frankly the situation

in which he finds himself. Falling in love twenty years before with Louise de Riverolles, he had found that he could not change his religion to marry her. She had been handed over instead to Mazardouin, who was a rake. For twenty years of his life the Squire had maintained towards her an immaculate loyalty. He had submitted to her whims, he had worshipped at her feet, he had strengthened her principle; but it had not satisfied him. "For twenty years of my life," he wrote, "I have embraced the phantom of the fairest woman that ever drew breath." He revolves his situation. He knew that he adored his marquise, that in innocency of heart she preferred him, but he knew that the English would not understand. "Politically," he said, "we are the most self-conscious people upon earth and socially the frankest animals. The terrorism of our social laws is eminently serviceable, for without it such frank animals as we are might run into bad excesses." But he hears from her that Mazardouin may die, that she may be free. It hardly moves him. He thinks rather of Alice and what strikes him as the singular audacity of her ideas. "Those vivid young feminine perceptions and untamed imaginations are desperate things to encounter. There is nothing beyond their reach. Our safety from them lies in the fact that they are always seeking and imagining too wildly: so that with a little help from us they may be taught to distrust themselves: and when they have once distrusted themselves we need not afterwards fear them, their supernatural vitality has vanished."

Back at home, Alice felt herself a stranger. Her

only consolation was her beautiful pony: her love is lavished on it. She revolves the story of Madame de Mazardouin, and realises that the Squire by this time had burnt his heart to ashes. When a letter telling her that Charles was ordered over to Dauphiny by his uncle was put into her hands at breakfast, tears fell. The final letter shows that this has convinced the Squire that she loves the nephew. He will, he says, arrange Charles's nuptials for the autumn. And there the last chapter ends.

It is not difficult to consider what moved Meredith's interest in this story. He had found that, at an age when passion might seem to have been losing its ardour, he could in fact love more wholly than in early youth. He had kept through years a loyalty to the phantom of Mrs. Ross, with whom his relation was perfectly innocent. And he then found himself subjugated by a very simple woman, much younger than himself. "The extraordinary sweetness of her laughter, the freshness and musical ring of the notes of her voice took entire possession of me: an unanticipated, accidental but absolute dominion: and the mastery I gained over her young mind during our short intimacy rather confirmed my own subjugation than released me." Alice, whose quick eye read the hedges and the wood paths and named the unknown weeds, was one who aptly symbolises Marie Vulliamy, and in this story, where a girlish charm meets experienced insight, there is a picture of the new unity in Meredith's life. The work is slighter than usual, but it has also unusual charm, and there can be no doubt that Meredith would have had greater influence as a novelist if his heart had dictated simplicity as it still does in this. No story he wrote has so much naïveté.

§ 4

In letters,[1] not less charming, we see a direct picture of the tenderness and rapture which expressed themselves in the gaiety and insight of this story. They were written to Marie Meredith in August and September of 1869. Meredith had gone over with Lionel Robinson to see Arthur at his school at Hofwyl, near Berne, the Weyburn School of *Lord Ormont*, and took him on to the Obersimmenthal and the Rieder Alp, on his way to Stuttgart. Signed, "Your husband and lover, George Meredith," or "Your own George Meredith," they show their writer in the most intimate relation of which any record remains; the intimacy voices no personal endearments: it is a record of his joy in nature. Arthur he found a good swimmer, with plenty of fun in him, with good wind, and with an eye clear and honest; he was popular in the school. But away from the school, he found that the boy of fifteen had ceased to be responsive. He had a reserve which his father was never again to pierce. He liked walks alone and did not often speak. If one wanted speech from him, the subject to choose must be one only: a thoroughly exciting one for a boy: it must be philology. Then he moved a little in his chrysalis, but only a little. The father's heart was rapture in communion

[1] These are all unpublished.

with mountains and mountain air. To watch the sunset from Berne was quite as delightful as meeting Arthur. "Sitting on the terrace at Berne, eating an ice, I had a view of the Jungfrau all blushing from foot to summit in the Alpen glow—a sight of the upper heavens. After the Jungfrau had paled, the Eiger took the glow and held it long."

He looked back on Arthur's school at Hofwyl with a kindred content. "The school stands high on central ground, with a great part of the Jura chain on the left, the Jungfrau, Breithorn, Eiger, Mönch and others to the right, and immediately in front, hills covered with birch and fir, a good lake in the middle ground, and flax fields, clover meadows; and corn and pasture up to the gardens, water flowing everywhere." On August 14 he was delighting in "cool air, hot sun, high Alpine meadows, grey peaks, fir forest and glimpses of valleys."

On August 16 he wrote from An der Lenk in the Obersimmenthal. "The great high rock is veined with sinuous cascades. Now and then I see the old man of the glaciers, with one claw close to his cheek, at the descent. Vapour comes toiling up to him. Imagine a broadish valley, green where an overflowing glacier-stream has left it green; innumerable chalets on beautiful ascending pastures, pine woods intervening; here and there a peak lifting out of the vapour to right and left, and in face the tremendous precipice of the Räzli and the Wildstrubel glaciers, about three thousand feet of it visible, the sources of the stream pouring down volumes. . . . Under the glaciers are falls of water of vast length, and again lower falls, and still lower. As I mounted I had them in view from every aspect. I heard them thundering through the gorges one minute. The next they were foaming beside me, and presently shaking the harebells of the meadows above. The East Lynn magnified fifty-fold and multiplied twenty would resemble it, with the addition of mountains overhead and glaciers all about. A month of this every year would always keep me right: I felt the change as soon as I set foot on the springy turf."

A week later he climbed the Rieder Alp, delighted to be among "brooks descending with a carol of the meadow." "The clear, thin air revived me exquisitely," he wrote, "I thought of you all the while."

"We look fronting Italy but for the curtain of mountains. The rain-cloud I see hangs above the Lago Maggiore. It is an Italian sky. Daily noble weather. The scene is one of the grandest on earth, delightful to every sense, perfectly sublime. From my window in the evening I gaze on the Monte Leone, the Fletschhorn and the Mischabel, peaks, bastions and slopes of snow, with the glacier crawling below. The Monte Leone is just in face, a fine snow line rolling to Italy and dropping sheer to the North, as we observe it. What wonders of beauty are done between the light of heaven and mountain Alps! Now they are ghostly white: a little previously they were warm grey; just before the colour of the Alpine rose (I send a sprig, the last of the season); at midday they have a shadowy richness, velvet, faint, half-melting; they come trembling into view at dawn, the cloud round their necks, the impalpable whiteness scarce to be realised until the sun rises and throws them out in air, firm and majestic. We climb the Riederhorn hard by and have the whole panorama as far as the beautiful and loftiest Weisshorn, a clear point of view. Lying there on dwarf juniper, and harebell and smaller gentian, beside us innumerable herbs breathing sweet scents in the great heat but fanned by freshest air, we have the feast of Alps."

He found the beauty of the Alps transcendent, inexhaustible. "We dine at 5 and pace up and down till bedtime under Italian stars, unimaginably bright and large." He delighted in the inspiration of exercise and travel.

But rapture had left him when he left the Alps and his longing turned back to his love of his wife for inspiration. "These towns without you beside me are not enjoyable, nor is travelling at all so, apart from you, unless I have my pack on my back, and pass uninterruptedly through fresh scenes. As soon as I stop, I look for my wife and love."

§ 5

Meanwhile Meredith had been projecting an autobiography. As far back as 1864 he had written that he had it in hand, and that its name was "Harry Richmond." But it was even less an autobiography than *David Copperfield:* much less than his own *Richard Feverel* or *Evan Harrington*. It was rather a romance of his own life, in which contrasting influences were symbolised in characters. Imagination and romantic feeling, on one side; on the other, reasons and the will for fact were the two contrasting tendencies which struggled for mastery over Meredith, and were finally united in him. Had Meredith been dominated by the first of these, said M. Galland, he would have lived his novels instead of writing them. He would have been Richmond Roy, as his grandfather tended to be. He would have attempted to put into action the wild impulses of his imagination. But these mad fancies, growing up from unceasing founts of hope, to feed the gaiety of his nature, as Richmond Roy said, though they were yet no more than an unfinished work of architecture like Cologne Cathedral as it then was, might one day startle the world.

Of imagination all compact, the lunatic Roy, sometimes lover, sometimes poet, could take his imaginations for realities, and women were subjugated by the force with which he projected them into the world of actuality. This was the power which came into conflict with all that is symbolised by the robust commonsense and the resulting well-being of Squire Beltham. He has virtues profoundly rooted in the soil. Order, wise economy, hard sense, and solid affection promise life and prosperity to future generations.[1] But neither the Squire nor his daughter, though they love him, can win Harry from his loyal ardours of worship of the romantic figures, first of Richmond Roy, and then of the Princess Ottilia. High German romance fights in him against the virtues of England: but Janet, who

[1] René Galland, *George Meredith*.

again reproduces the firm frankness and commonsense of Janet Ross, becomes a finer personage in the end than Ottilia. Kiomi is the dear child of wild nature in its passion, its energy and its health. Such is the only sense in which *Harry Richmond* is Meredith's autobiography. For the rest, it is a novel, like his others, instinct with that enhancement of life which his art gave to all his personages.

Memories of his grandfather, memories of Germany, memories of country life in Hampshire flit across this story, and show it to be another reaction of Meredith against his circumstances. It is the story of *Evan Harrington*, thought out again more fully, and from another point of view. It is in fact the last novel in which the desperate tension of Meredith's princely genius and his narrow circumstances force him into creative action in direct reference to his own life. And just because his circumstances were becoming easier, because he was married to a woman with some means, because he took holidays with her at her home in Normandy, because he had found a suitable home at Box Hill, the keen tension which made *The Ordeal* and *Evan Harrington* into such excellent works of art has gone. A certain looseness and discursiveness mark *Harry Richmond*. The fresh and natural style, the flowing narrative, the clear memories of youth, the insensible gradations between the poetic imagination and the sense of immediate fact, the true mastery of description which is obtained through the glow of emotional eloquence have awakened the admiration of many. But when all is said, *Harry Richmond* is not one of the great books. It has neither the poetic force and energy of *Vittoria*, nor the delightful comedy of *Evan Harrington*, nor the tragic ardour and power of *The Ordeal*.

Meredith henceforward was to write novels which were deliberate works of art rather than expressions forced from life and ordered by the heart's hold over the will to one set end. A portentous restlessness begins to disfigure both poems and novels. The mind is obsessed with its own phenomenal activity: the sense of strain becomes more frequent: and a vast impatience shows itself in mercilessness among the most intimate relations of life. It is true that no woman in England had more of a lover in her husband than Marie Meredith. But the ardent lover was not an easy person to live with: cuts of sarcasm at his wife, and even at his children, and an increasing aloofness, which led her some years later to build a little chalet for him in the garden, were the signs of a spirit that was communing more with itself and less with human beings. But the immense genius of love and energy, of insight and zeal, of thought and sanity were there, and the love of nature lost nothing of its delicacy or its sublimity. He still walked the woods with the ardours of a young lover, and found in them freshness and peace.

> Sweet as Eden is the air,
>   And Eden-sweet the ray.
> No Paradise is lost for them
> Who foot by branching root and stem,
> And lightly with the woodland share
>   The change of night and day.

Still, when Justin Vulliamy died in 1870, Meredith recalled with an exquisite resignation the sense of calm in Nature through her changes of life and decay. He wrote for that his *Dirge in Woods*, which, as Lady Danesfort recalls, he would quote again and again as among his favourite poems:

> A wind sways the pines,
>   And below
> Not a breath of wild air;
> Still as the mosses that glow
> On the flooring and over the lines
> Of the roots here and there.
> The pine-tree drops its dead;
> They are quiet, as under the sea.
> Overhead, overhead
> Rushes life in a race,
> As the clouds the clouds chase;
>   And we go,
> And we drop like the fruits of the tree,
>   Even we,
>   Even so.

IX

FRANCE AND GERMANY

§ 1

MARRIED, as when he was unmarried, poet or politician, novelist or philosopher, Meredith found that his friendship with Maxse was always deepening. So subtle was the power of Maxse that in 1875 Meredith was himself a vegetarian. Meredith had never been much of a meat-eater, but he had not reckoned on the limited capacities of English cooks: the burden fell upon his wife who had to cope with its effect on his temper. It was an age when men stopped taking violent exercise at thirty and devoted their spare time to dietetics, sometimes of the most fantastic and perilous kind. But there was no end to Maxse's extravagances: in 1870 he took to peculiar attire, the robe of a sort of high priest which eclipsed, in Meredith's words, all that pulpit-stricken virgins ever dreamed of for their curates. And just after adopting this Maxse invaded a dinner given by the Mayor of Southampton to a party of Americans who had thought of uniting England with their States, and having broken up all the wine bottles at the party, turned a hose of water at the diners' stomachs. Others have done these things for jests. Others again might have thought the ardour of the Americans needed damping. But not Maxse. He did it in all earnestness because he believed that extremes were the chief teachers, and that here was the most solemn and effective advocacy of teetotalism. The comment of *The Times* was that the notorious captain had an inexhaustible supply of water on the brain.[1]

But just as Maxse had lent Meredith his house at Bursledon for the honeymoon, so Meredith now drew Maxse towards Dorking. The superb fanatical hero established himself at Dunley. His mother, Lady Caroline, was a mile away at Effingham Hill.

A daughter of the notorious Lord Fitzhardinge who married his cook at Berkeley Castle, Lady Caroline had been a beauty and had become a character. The aroma of many affairs hung about her. She was much already, in 1880, of what Janet Ross was to become in 1920, and spoke out unexpected opinions without equivocation. Her worst enemies, in fact, could not call her squeamish. The vulgar strain in her added robustness to her assertion of an individuality which took full advantage of her rank. Meredith and she got on excellently. She liked his wife, and from time to time invited them to stay. When she died he said of the letters "C. M."

> To them that knew her, there is vital flame
> In these the simple letters of her name.[2]

Her strong spirit he has portrayed in Charlotte Eglett, a picture which lives. Tender was not a word for her, but she could be thoughtful for "the poor foolish victims of men." When it came to the duel between

[1] *Letters.* [2] *Poems.*

man and woman, her sense of justice put her in the party of those who at other times seemed a poor match for her powers of character. She never went counter to the principles of her husband: "the fixed principles of a very wealthy man, who abhorred debt, and was punctilious in veracity, scrupulous in cleanliness of mind and body, devoted to the honour of his country, the interests of his class." With such a husband, she was enabled to lead without the need to rule. "She could be humane, even sisterly, with women whose conduct or practice did not outrage plain sense, just as the stickler for the privileges of her class was large-heartedly charitable to the classes flowing in oily orderliness round about below it—if they did so flow." And though she could read warning only in the broadest lines, she knew just what men were and how to manage them, and this gave her a strength above that of men themselves. She used to say "that the women unaware of the advantage Society gave them [as to mastering men] were fools."[1]

It is not certain whether or not she mastered her sons. She must have admired the dash and quixotry of her son Fred: she could not have been unaware of the senselessness of his excesses. She and Meredith were largely at one about him.

At the end of 1868, as we saw, Maxse stood for Parliament, in Southampton. Meredith went down and fought the election with him. "My two months down with Captain Maxse was a dead loss of time to me," he wrote to Arthur: and indeed it forced him to

[1] *Lord Ormont and His Aminta.*

write more for newspapers, less of *Harry Richmond*. But he turned the temporary loss to good advantage in accumulating material for *Beauchamp's Career*. Maxse, with his succeeding monomanias, went straight into the book as its hero. Beauchamp was irritated by opposition, and irritated instead of conciliating others because he had "given up his brains for a lodging to a single idea. It is at once a devouring dragon, and an intractable steam force. Inspired by solitude and gigantic size, it claims divine origin." Not only was he unjust with his opponents, but it led him to consider Cecilia Halkett less as a woman than as a force to be bombarded out of the Tory fort by Radical argument. What Cecilia wanted, however, was not logic but love.

Yet there is a grandeur, even a sort of poetic grandeur, in Beauchamp, as there was a real lovableness in Maxse. "He was born with so extreme and passionate a love for his country that he thought all else of mean importance in comparison." And added to this, he knew that brain must play its part in patriotism, adjusting privileges with deserts, dues with duties, and lead to a better adjustment of wealth, for the country he passionately loved was, after all, an "ill-regulated world of wrong-doing, suffering, sin." Lastly, his passion was one with his sincerity. He shunned all kinds of posturing, and most that posturing of passion which makes sentiment statuesque. In everything his influence was the reverse of Byron's.[1]

[1] *Beauchamp's Career*.

Other friends presented other materials for Meredith's creative portraiture: Grantley Berkeley, Lady Caroline's brother, for Everard Romfrey; Russell Gurney for Seymour Austin; Dr. Hearn for Dr. Shrapnel; Hardman for Tuckham; and Alice Brandreth for Cecilia Halkett. Still less than in *Harry Richmond* was it Meredith's aim now to create, in an imaginative fabric, his own world as it might have been could his genius have fitted his outward circumstances to something congenially great. He had friends that were in their own way great figures, figures on the grand scale. To live again his life with them as it was to a nature so poetically exultant, so amused at incongruities and so keen to observe the bond between inward and outward things and where, or where not, the adjustment was made according to the standards of health and truth: this would have been occupation enough; but to Meredith it was also a jest most enjoyable to weave the fact into the fanciful with all the people he knew. The characters he created were objective to him, and he roared with laughter when the figure of Richmond Roy first faced his imagination. But the figures and the stories of people he really knew he would continue into fable, till none knew whether it was a true reminiscence or fiction to which they were listening. And when Meredith had carried through his gamesome deception with listening friends, again he would roar with laughter.[1]

---

[1] J. A. Hammerton, *George Meredith*.

§ 2

In *Beauchamp's Career* flowered also a growth from another seed. His first wife had taken him to France to begin his honeymoon: his second wife kept him in constant touch with France, and took him year after year to spend his holidays at her brother's home in Normandy. The Vulliamy property at Nonancourt and Montigny was ample. There he met that cultured life which is not uncommon in the French provinces, and met some of the old French families. In the quiet, glowing beauty of Lower Normandy, he felt, in his intimacy with nature, something new and something stimulating. And there is everywhere in France, in the style of the architecture, in the very forms of the trees, in the rich variety of the scenery, a sentiment which recalls the impression of a woman, and reminds us of the great place that woman takes in the psychology of the French. We feel it particularly in the paintings of Corot, whom Meredith especially admired.

The mill of the Vulliamy family at Nonancourt has gone, but the old house on the road to Dreux still stands, with a high mound above. The little river Avre separates it from the park and château of St. Lubin-des-Joncherets, which is described in *Beauchamp's Career* as Tourdestelle. Justin Vulliamy had a key, and with him Meredith often walked through it. The valley is "one of those Norman valleys where the river is the mother of rich pasture, and runs hidden between double ranks of willows, aspens, and poplars, that mark its winding lane in the arms of trenched meadows."

There was more sun than in England, but this province was a cousin to England's opposite coast in climate, soil, and people. Meredith's imagination was soon busy in the life of the Château de St. Lubin, picturing Maxse there with one of those womanly women who give such fullness and passion to the French connotation of beauty: one something of the type of Agnes Sorel, who had lived a few miles away.[1]

All this had been melting into the profound influence which Germany had had over him for twenty-five years. A follower and an admirer of Goethe to the end, a lover of the woods of Germany and her open spaces, he began to feel the power of French humanism. Flaubert, the one man who insisted at that time that genius must not constrain its travail to the public taste, had published his first great work in the same year as *The Ordeal*. But Meredith had been reading more deeply: for humanist philosophy, Montaigne; for the comic appreciation of social life, Molière; then La Bruyère, concise and searching in his knowledge of men and women; and then, for an irony so delicate that it was almost tenderness, Renan; and for a high note of passionate feeling, Racine. Besides Renan, he read Stendhal, Victor Hugo, Dumas, George Sand, Musset, Baudelaire, and Flaubert. He loved the vivacity of the French, the lively expression of their faces and, above all, of their eyes, their quickness to catch an idea or appreciate a feeling. He loved their daring, their energy and their passion. "They are the most mixed of any nation," he wrote, "so they are

[1] René Galland. *Beauchamp's Career*.

packed with contrasts. They are full of sentiment, they are sharply logical, free thinkers, devotees; affectionate, ferocious; frivolous, tenacious; the passion of the season operating like sun or moon on these qualities; and they can reach to ideality out of sensualism." All this he recognised in them as an intrinsic fascination, but he loved them more because his bride was born among them, and he first came to France enraptured in her company.

> . . . sweet was her voice with the tongue,
> The speechful tongue of her France,
> Soon at ripple about us, like rills
> Ever busy with little: away
> Through her Normandy, down where the mills
> Dot at lengths a rivercourse, grey
> As its bordering poplars bent
> To gusts of the plains above.
> Old stone château and farms,
> Home of her birth and her love![1]

§ 3

The influences of France and Germany fought hard when the Franco-Prussian War began. Maxse threw himself with his inevitable excess of ardour on the French side which, as we saw, had had his love from the beginning. Another friend of Meredith, Cotter Morison, was thoroughly pro-German. Morley, like Meredith himself, attempted to weigh the rival causes

[1] " A Faith on Trial." *One of Our Conquerors. Letters.*

in judgment. Meredith summed up the case for Germany in *Harry Richmond*, which naturally crystallises the memories of his youth. He wrote to Arthur that he found Germans faithful friends, and in 1869, when he took Arthur to Stuttgart, he wrote back from Baden to his wife that they were "a fat, well-to-do, kindly, decorous, moral people."[1]

As a foil for a criticism of England, he found a perfectly suitable figure in Professor Julius von Karsteg. But, though still so loyal to Goethe that he was to write three novels on the theme of *Die Wahlverwandtschaften*; that the very title of *The Gentleman of Fifty* had been taken from *Der Mann von Fünfzig Jahren*; that a poem of Goethe's could hold his mind for hours in 1877; that, finding the theme of his next novel in the story of Ferdinand Lassalle, the German Socialist, in his affair with Helène von Dönniges, he adopted one extract after another from *Wilhelm Meister*; nevertheless Meredith's passion made France the subject of his poetry. He wrote a great ode in 1870. "You will see in it," he wrote years afterwards to Mlle. de Longueuil, "all that I feel for your country."

> Look down where deep in blood and mire
> Black thunder plants his feet and ploughs
> The soil for ruin: that is France:
> Still thrilling like a lyre,
> Amazed to shivering discord from a fall
> Sudden as that the lurid hosts recall

[1] Unpublished letters. *Letters of George Meredith*.

Who met in heaven the irreparable mischance.
O that is France!
The brilliant eyes to kindle bliss,
The shrewd quick lips to laugh and kiss,
Breasts that a sighing world inspire,
And laughter-dimpled countenance
Where soul and senses caught desire!

In the dark time of tyranny and superstition, she had opened to the world a benigner day, giving note to the name of humanity. But, out of this, she had inflicted new tyrannies on Europe, and must not be surprised if a just vengeance fell upon her now. Let her prove to the world her power to lead by the creative and generous spirit in which she met tribulation.

        Soaring France!
Now is Humanity on trial in thee:
Now may'st thou gather humankind in fee:
Now prove that Reason is a quenchless scroll;
Make of calamity thine aureole,
And bleeding lead us thro' the troubles of the sea.[1]

§ 4

Such were the ideas that drenched his mind like lightnings as he worked on at *Harry Richmond*, at *Beauchamp's Career*, and later at *The Tragic Comedians*. Genius, he said later in *One of Our Conquerors*, was a sort of swiftness, and the lightning pace with which he

[1] *Poems:* " France."

flung together, in feats of amazing skill, things utterly incongruous, and crowded his pictures of life with vivid memories of winds, light, water, woods and the sky, gives proof of a speed and a power of mind that are incontestably unique as they are vital. "Life is too much heightened and explained in them to be like reality," an acute observer has noted. "He seems to know what the story means better than any man could; and to all his characters he seems to impart his own divine energy and splendour of expression."[1] Music cannot convey an illusion, and Meredith does not give us the sense that we are looking direct at life: but like an overwhelming Beethoven symphony, that at the great moment masters all the quarrelling instruments and forces wildly sundered thoughts and feelings into concord, the art of Meredith plays on us, giving us a heightened sense of life, till we apprehend its significance as poetry and glory.

A man who was passionately interested in music, his work shows the influence of the great German masters. Mendelssohn's kinsmen, the Beneckes, who were his neighbours at Box Hill, were friends that shared his love of German music. He has what Beethoven had, an exulting sense of the majesty of life both in its joy and in its gloom. But he was in the world of literature what Wagner was in the world of music. "The German Emperor has done less for their lasting fame and influence than Wagner has done," is a sentence which Meredith puts into the mouth of Victor Radnor. The two great men, so closely kindred

[1] *Times Literary Supplement*, May 20, 1909.

in the spirit of their genius, met, as Lady Danesfort records, at Dannreuther's. But Wagner was not simply a musician: he was the husband of Frau Cosima.

§ 5

Meredith's unique rôle in the history of our literature was to endue fiction with the qualities of poetry. The unexpectedness and rarity of poetry mark the style which throws the beauty of nature as a new light on the hearts and minds of men and women. The experiment has left the work of a supreme genius to be assessed in the history of our prose fiction. But no one can say the result is a sustained success. Meredith himself never claimed that. Passages of letters to Jessopp and Horne open his own mind. "Consider first my scheme as a workman," he writes to Jessopp. "It is to show you the actions of minds as well as of fortunes, and here and there men and women vitally animated by their brains, at different periods of their lives—and of men and women with something of a look-out on the world and its destinies."[1] Five weeks later he was writing to Horne that he had decided to follow the lead of his own genius. "The task of forgetting the world is not so difficult. I have ceased to think what it thinks in the matter of my contributions to light literature, and aim only at satisfying my own taste. It is the happiest of all states of mind for an author, and the best for inspiring good work in time to come." But was it so happy? Can any writer apply

[1] Unpublished letter.

to himself so absolute a standard? When he thinks of his aims, is he not generally stabbed with a sense of failure which nothing can heal but the world's approval? The world's approval came very slowly to Meredith. And so he confesses to Jessopp in 1873 that his novels are too great with ideas really to live: "I cannot go on with a story and not feel that to treat of flesh and blood is to touch the sacredest; and so it usually ends in my putting the destinies of the world about it, like an atmosphere out of which it cannot subsist. So my work fails. I see it."

Indeed, he found the writing of fiction an arduous labour. When he began a novel, he worked only in the mornings—only as it wore on did he give up his afternoon walks and his evening relaxation, for the characters took possession of him and of his story, and developed, as the characters of good novelists do, into an influence on life other than their creators had first designed for them. Then he would work for hours of the day, and even late into the night, stopping only for Cole the gardener to bring up his meals to the chalet, for a long breath of clean air on the terrace outside, or for a walk in the paths which ran through the woods beside him: he would carry on conversations with himself and sing fragments of Rabelaisian song. Sitting in his armchair, with a board of teak on his knees, and always with a quill pen, he would write, hour after hour, in blue ink. The characters of his writing as he grew older grew more and more like Greek, but they never became illegible. He could never dictate. He must put his whole being into his writing. He wrote slowly. "My ideas flow with the ink from the pen," he used to say: but as years went on, he became excessively fatigued. The end of a book meant exhaustion: even a loss of health: certainly a loss of temper. But words were always his favourite playthings. When he was tired of them, they were thrown away, and his fire blazed with the refuse of genius.

The chalet which his wife had built held him more and more. He not only worked but slept there. He wrote, in *The Tragic Comedians*, that "wife" seemed to him "the word most reverberating of the secret sought after by man, fullest at once of fruit and of mystery, or of that light in the heart of mystery which makes it magically fruitful."

But the rapture was dying away as he approached the age of fifty. Was the ardour of his passion exhausted, or was his love maimed by the self-restraint which kept him from having a family larger than he felt he could afford? In marriage he was loyal to the laws of nature which he preached. It was the most natural thing in the world that Marie Meredith should think of how his sales might be increased and not merely of the quality of his work. But any such suggestion was torture to him. "A reproach of our poverty uttered by lips we have loved," as Jean-Paul noted, "darts like red-hot iron into the breast and scorches it dry with fire."

Economy forced restraint upon his temperament, and the result did not improve his temper or his nerves. He delighted in his younger children, for a daughter had been born in the same year that he brought out *Harry Richmond*. She grew up to be his "blessed dearie," and charmed him from the first. And "my boy Willie flourishes," he wrote in 1871 to Jessopp, "and is charming to look at, quick of eye and intelligence, lazy as a sunflower."[1] Yet children, as well as wife, knew that the father who lavished love on them was capable of sudden bursts of rage: rage the more furious when it provoked nothing in reply. If his chaff were not returned, his teasing became remorseless. A curious, almost sinister apartness would make his comment on his family relentless. We see it in a letter to Jessopp, a letter of October 4, 1871, on the subject of Arthur.

"He is a short man, slightly moustached, having a touch of whisker, a good walker, a middling-clear thinker, sensible, brilliant in nothing, tending in no direction, very near to what I predicted of him as a combatant in life, but with certain reserve qualities of mental vigour which may develop, and though he seems never likely to be intellectually an athlete, one may hope he will be manful. His manner of earning his bread in his earlier stages threatens to be that of the mass of us."[2] And this was he of whom he had written only a few years earlier that apart from him he could hardly live! But to his younger son, as Mr. Le Gallienne has written, he was often the most merciless of teases. If a conventional remark or an obvious statement was made, it would be greeted as the word

[1] *The Times*, Feb. 12, 1928.
[2] Unpublished letter in the possession of Mr. Frank Altschul of New York.

of an oracle. "Behold the Sagamore!" he would say in his deep booming voice. "Mark that lofty brow! Stand in awe with me before the wisdom that sits there enthroned."[1]

When he was dining with the Lewins at Parkhurst above Abinger Hammer, he noticed that his daughter was wearing roses in her hair. He waited until a chance silence fell on the table, and then, slow, deep, resonant, were heard the words: "The blessed dearie comes down to dinner wearing a wreath of roses to fascinate the military captain." There is no coping with that particular kind of social unscrupulousness. Mischief carried him away when he found anyone who was unable to respond to his chaffing, and this provoked him not least in the case of his wife. "She is a mud fort!" he said once. "You fire broadsides into her, nothing happens."

Yet this was the husband in whom his wife recognised a lover of perfect ardour. This was the man who spared himself nothing to help or encourage youth, nothing to please or delight children whom, to the very end, he loved to have around. He brought the very voices of the fairies into their waking life. At full moon in the late summer evening, he would stand on the terrace at Flint Cottage, and say to them: "Listen, do you hear the hounds—the hounds of Tanhurst chasing the ancient Briton?" Now far off, then fainter still as they streamed up from Gomshall to the white downs, then silence—till, rushing out from Bookham, the pack in full cry hunted their quarry now but a

[1] R. Le Gallienne, *The Romantic Nineties*.

mile away; almost to be seen in the clear moonlight. Through Norbury, up over Ranmer and to rest at Picket's Hole till next full moon. The image made real to them the whole ghostly chase. "Do you hear the hounds of Tanhurst?" Of course they heard them.[1]

[1] *The Times*, Feb. 12, 1928.

X

CRITICISM AND COMEDY

§ 1

IN 1875, when Meredith published *Beauchamp's Career*, he was of course forty-seven. The years from then till 1884, which made him fifty-six, saw him rise gradually into secure fame. The friends who came to see him after 1885 were friends who were coming to visit an accredited, though not a popular, genius. The turn of the tide in his reputation was marked in the closing words of the *Athenæum* review of *Beauchamp's Career:* "We do not see any reason why he should not ultimately reach a point where, in the opinion at least of those who regard novels as works of art, and not merely collections of anecdotes, he would scarcely have a rival among the writers of fiction of our generation." In *The Spectator* Hutton voiced horror no more. The friends who had begun by admiring admired with reinforced loyalty, and a band of distinguished critics began to fill the cup of praise.

It is interesting to recall the friends who came down in those days to Box Hill, to be woven into the lengthening fabric of Meredith's life. Not least was Cotter Morison, who had been Morley's friend at Oxford, and who used to come down with Morley to Copsham. Once, in those early days, Morison had taken them for a cruise in the Channel, in his yacht, a cruise which shook their stomachs; but intercourse went on, generally, in circumstances more comfortable. "Of fellowship abounding," Morison was a sympathetic man, to whom one could speak of an inefficient digestion. He was a literary man of some distinction, writing on St. Bernard at one time, at another on Madame de Maintenon, at another on Gibbon or Macaulay. In fact, among the little circle, he was named after the saint he studied. His son Theodore, a scholarly youth, fond of fishing and football, became the great friend of Meredith's younger son, and used to be brought back from Westminster, when the two were at school there together, to stay at Flint Cottage. He was later to rise to high distinction, on the Council of India.

Very different from the bearded, genial, serious Morison was Alice Brandreth. Quiet, sane, well bred, trustful, handsome, and responsive, her excellent and delightful nature answered to the word "womanly." She was the English style of girl. She liked yachting, she liked Italy, she liked painting, liked things Old English, and was fond of horses. "One can't call her a girl," wrote Meredith in 1875, "and it won't do to say Goddess, and queen and charmer are out of the question, though she's both, and angel into the bargain." If a man stood between a good and a bad action, the thought of her would keep him straight. Like Hardman, this young lady was a thorough Tory: her ideas had nothing in common with Maxse's. Her fair beauty suggested "a radiant landscape where the tall ripe wheat flashes between shadow and shine in the stately march of summer."[1]

Not long after the completion of her portrait as Cecilia Halkett, Alice Brandreth found that she and her cousin Jim Gordon were in love with each other. The passage of years had not made him a conventionalist. He divided his passions of energy and interest between his bride, horses, hounds, and electricity. Would he or would he not make his bride happy? Time would show. As her wedding-day drew near, Meredith wrote a touching epigram:

Now dawns, all waxen to your seal of life,
This day which names you bride to make you wife.
Time shows the solid stamp: then see, dear maid,
Round those joined hands our prayers for you inlaid.[2]

Between her father's house in Elvaston Place, and the Gordons' house, Pixholme, Mrs. Jim Gordon, as she moved, drew some of the choice spirits of the time about her. Knowing this, Kegan Paul the publisher thought she would be a good person to be known by his new protégé, Robert Louis Stevenson, who also already admired Meredith above all writers living. Mrs. Gordon introduced him. At Pixholme or Flint Cottage the two met constantly through the years. With his black shirt and his long hair, Stevenson made an odd figure in the garden, and always sought the sun. Meredith at once appreciated the vivid young genius whose polished finish of style so violently con-

[1] *Beauchamp's Career.*
[2] *Memories of George Meredith,* by Lady Butcher.

trasted with his own. Stevenson, when he met Meredith in 1878, had just finished *An Inland Voyage*, and sent it down to his new friends. As soon as it arrived Mrs. Meredith fell on it, but her husband snatched it from her, and ran up with it to his chalet. "I have been fully pleased," he wrote to Stevenson. "The writing is of the rare kind which is naturally simple, yet picked and choice. It is literature. The eye on land and people embraces both and does not take them in bits. I have returned to the reading and shall again. The reflections wisely tickle, they are in the right good tone of philosophy interwrought with humour." Nevertheless, he detected one or two faults. "Keep strong work in view," he wrote a year or two later, "for you are of the few who can accomplish it."

A great array of visitors found its way to the slopes of the garden at Box Hill in those days of the 'seventies. One of them was his old friend, the painter Frederick Sandys, who had done a very fine portrait of Mrs. Meredith, and who in fact, before the marriage, had once paid Meredith a three-weeks visit. They had met through Dante Gabriel Rossetti. Rossetti called him the greatest living draughtsman, and Millais said he was worth two academicians rolled into one. He used to tell inimitable stories which Meredith appreciated: "Sandys has a romantic turn that lets one feed on him." Professor York Powell would come and read Icelandic sagas. Comyns Carr, to whom he once at the chalet read *Modern Love* late into the night, would alternate with Frederick Greenwood. Like Morley, they kept him in touch with influential journalism, and General Brackenbury made a complement to Maxse, who in 1877 became a rear-admiral.[1]

Not less important than these friends was Leslie Stephen, whom Meredith had met in Vienna in 1865. Beginning as a Fellow of Trinity Hall, he turned early to journalism. From 1871 to 1882 he was editor of the *Cornhill*. His work was divided between literature and philosophical agnosticism. Some of the best books in "English Men of Letters" were written by him, and he wrote also a *History of English Thought in the Eighteenth Century*. His first wife was a daughter of Thackeray; his second, Mrs. Duckworth, was one of the Prinseps and a sister of Mrs. H. W. Fisher. When, early in life, he had taken orders, the stiffness of his clerical collar had entered into his soul. When he gave up his profession of Christianity, he said he did not lose his faith, but found he never had any. Any approach to dogma intensified the grimness which was essential to his sensitive nature. Nothing of a joke appealed to him but the sardonic in it. Yet behind his ethical fervour for purifying Christianity of religion, there was sincerity, strength, and elevation of mind. "You know where you are with him," said Crossjay Patterne of Vernon Whitford, and Meredith had learned the sentence from his knowledge of Stephen. The bearded face was noble: it was the head of a philosopher with a heart: it was the head one expected for Socrates.

But nothing in his seriousness prevented him making friends with romantic people. Stevenson was as much

[1] *Letters. The Times*, Feb. 12, 1928. Comyns Carr, *Some Eminent Victorians*.

his friend as Meredith. And, under his seriousness, he was a sportsman. He was, in fact, President of the Alpine Club from 1865 to 1868, and wrote so well of the Alps that Morley, in his *Recollections*, said that he thought some of Stephen's prose in *The Playground of Europe* as fine as any that was written at that time. When a don at Cambridge, he walked to London in twelve hours to dine. He was the first to ascend Mont Blanc from St. Gervais. His alpine writing was vivid, direct, and unpretendingly picturesque, at the same time as it was serious and reflective. He began writing for the *Saturday Review*. For the *Cornhill*, he got Stevenson, Hardy, Sully, Henry James, and Gosse to contribute. After he gave up the *Cornhill*, he devoted himself to the *Dictionary of National Biography*. "By request no flowers" was his motto for those notices, and it was one that accorded with his own grave style. It was the perfect model of the restraint Englishmen love, and Meredith himself praised it. "The memory of his work in literature," wrote Meredith, at Stephen's death, "remains with us as being the profoundest and most sober criticism we have had in our time. The only sting in it was an inoffensive human irony that now and then stole out for a roll over, like a furry cub, or the occasional ripple on a lake in grey weather. We have nothing left that is like it."[1]

In 1878 another figure appeared at Box Hill: a figure not to be ignored, it was that of Meredith's most eloquent admirer; for the greatest of the en-

[1] Meredith's *Works*, Memorial Edition. "Sir Leslie Stephen," by F. W. Maitland, *Dictionary of National Biography*.

thusiasts for the new poet of nature, energy, and spirit was the writer of *The City of Dreadful Night*. James Thomson was not an ideal character: owing to his lack of moral fibre, he had been led into an irregularity for which he had been discharged from the Army. His morbidity intensified by hardship and loneliness, he looked for solace in drinking, and soon became a hopeless sot. After a trip to Colorado in 1872 as a mining agent, and to Spain in 1873 as a war correspondent, he resumed his life of misery and vice in London. In his own words, he found "Time crawling like a monstrous snake, wounded and slow and very venomous": he used the little of it that he had, for trouble, strife, and lust.

Of this, as it happened, Meredith knew nothing. He immensely appreciated *The City of Dreadful Night*. "There is a massive impressiveness in it that goes beyond Dürer," he wrote, "and takes it into upper regions where poetry is the sublimation of the mind of man, the voice of our highest." And when Thomson brought out his complete volume in 1880 Meredith wrote: "I have found many pages that no other English poet could have written. Nowhere is the verse, nowhere is the expression insufficient: the majesty of the line has always its full colouring, and marches under a banner." And writing, after Thomson's death, to Salt his biographer, Meredith expressed himself almost more enthusiastically: "His verse was a pure well. He has, almost past example in my experience, the thrill of the worship of valiancy as well as of sensuous beauty." But Thomson's critical appreciation of Meredith had an eloquence above any verse he wrote. When Meredith brought out *Beauchamp's Career*, Thomson saw in him "this sure mark of lofty genius, that he always rises with his theme, growing more strenuous, more self-contained, more magistral, as the demands on his thought and imagination increase," and line raced after line in noble praise.[1]

This relation with Thomson recalls the earlier episode with Horne. Horne still lived, and Meredith kept in touch with him: he wrote to Horne on November 9, 1871: "Let me anticipate that your creative gifts are still as abundant as your mind and heart are strong. No one will be gladder to hear that a new work of yours is in the press than I: few readier to do justice to its merits."[1] He wrote again on August 3, 1875: "I live in Bœotia, and have the habits of the country, and never pay complimentary visits to my friends. I love them, be assured, and rejoice if I can serve them none the less."[2]

§ 2

The numerous distinguished friends who gathered at Box Hill were certainly brilliant; to what extent were they a variety? They were often unconventional, all gifted, many of that type of sceptical intellect so fashionable in that day, which, drawing a sharp distinction between religion and reason, called itself rationalist. Philosophers have their fashions, and this has gone by. But in it, as well as in dietetics, Meredith

[1] *Letters*. Cope's *Tobacco Plant*.   [2] Unpublished letter.

was the child, perhaps the victim, of his day. Of the
great tradition of acute thought, which had related
theology to metaphysics, he knew nothing; for dogma's
relation to the intellect he cared less. On the subject
of the clergy, he had what psychologists of to-day
call a *complex*, due no doubt to the boredom with which
he had listened to droning sermons, when he might
have been breathing rapture in the open air. He thought
of parsons in general in the guise of Groseman But-
termore. Of this, his connection with the Huguenot
Vulliamys did not cure him: in fact, a few years after
his marriage it was intensified. Maxse's horror that a
baby should be christened, or a child say prayers, was
logical; but on such matters Meredith preferred to
make an accommodation with the amiable inconsistency
which surrounded him. A christening could do no
harm; prayer, as he understood it, was the soul's source
of strength: but in spite of his great esteem and affection for Jessopp, for Hawkins (Anthony Hope's father),
and for Will Rogers, who were all in orders, he could
not bring himself to take seriously the views of the
average clergyman, whether a curate or a bishop. Like
many of his contemporaries, he thought that Darwin
in his theories of the origin of species had said the last
word on the book of Genesis, and that the Church
stood or fell with the theory of verbal inspiration.
Like most of his contemporaries, he saw in the Redeemer of men an example for men, and puzzled as
little as they in leaving out of the Gospel just what
they found convenient to leave out. Renan said for
them all that they wanted to say. Meredith knew how

stupidly the Old Testament was in those days put before readers, and feared for its effect on Arthur. "I have no objection to his reading the Bible," he wrote to Jessopp. "I confess I am already baffled by his comparison between the dogma of Genesis and the mild facts of geology, nor do I think the Old Testament—the Jew creed and history—can do any good to a young creature."[1]

As he looked at his pigeon, he thought it amazingly like a parson. Like Falstaff heeling over with sherry, its eye was fixed crooked on him. It was almost too prosperous for a parson, but parsons could be prosperous: well, call it a bishop.

In June, 1874, when he was staying with his wife's sister, they were all asked over to dinner by the Rector, a High Churchman, and Meredith saw an opportunity for outrageous teasing.

"Do you think it is true that there is a portrait of Jesus Christ extant?" the Rector asked him.

"Of Nazareth?" was his amazing question.

"Certainly, of Nazareth."

"Oh no, then; but it is affirmed that there is an authentic portrait of the Virgin his Mother."

"Could we trust it?" There was supplication in the Rector's tone.

"Decidedly not." Neither courtesy nor mercy toned this answer.[2]

The man or the country fighting priestcraft or priests was in fact, to his mind, striking deeper for freedom than could be struck anywhere at that time.

[1] Unpublished letter.   [2] *Letters*.

He foresaw a perilous struggle, and was heart and soul with Bismarck against Pius IX and Leo XIII. Manning certainly he admired:

> . . . one lamp that through our fen
> Goes hourly where most noisome. . . .

None the less, he looked on his faith as a tyrant creed. One would have expected vigour of thought to have revealed weakness and hammered out a substitute: but indeed he had nothing metaphysical to offer in its place. He believed that, in this life, the spirit alone really lives, but as to the meaning of the spirit, he had the vaguest ideas. "It seems to me that spirit is . . . how, where, and by what means none can say?"[1]

But if prayer is spiritual life, he was a true adorer. Toward the selfish asking for material advantage he felt nothing but contempt. What he advocated was the heart's surrender to communion with the highest Good, with true Being, that pervading Mind who was gloriously clothed in the living garment of nature. "Prayer is power within us to communicate with the desired beyond our thirsts." It is the source of courage; the recognition of law; the exercise of the highest in our living. "Cast forth the soul in prayer; you meet the effluence of the outer truth, you join with the creative elements giving breath to you: and that crust of habit, which is the soul's tomb; and custom, the soul's tyrant; and pride, our volcano peak that sinks us in a crater; and fear, which plucks the feathers

[1] *Poems:* "To Cardinal Manning." *Letters.*

from the wings of the soul . . . you are free of them, you live in the day and for the future, by this exercise and discipline of the soul's faith." Prayer proves its efficacy in its power to ennoble us. "Who rises from his knees a better man, his prayer is answered." A deep calm, or a deep joy, can themselves become communion with the end of being.

> And have we knelt,
> Or never knelt, or eyed as kine the springs
> Of radiance, the radiance enrings:
> And this is the soul's haven to have felt.[1]

The one prayer that was always to be commended was the intense desire for strength of soul. And much as Meredith hated Anglican theology, he had enough sense to see the danger of bringing children up as free-thinkers, as Maxse was bringing his children up, and as Morley recommended. Young sceptics, he observed, will probably be young cynics. Besides that, a youth without religion had no armoury against the rank emotionalism which rises like a miasma as a concomitant to the physical impulses of youth.[2]

Insistent as Meredith was on the recognition of the flesh, and its rightful place in life's healthy fullness, he was austere in his insistence upon its being disciplined by law.

> . . . till the chasing out of its last vice,
> The flesh was fashioned but for sacrifice.[3]

And this was in fact a means of discipline as efficient

[1] *Poems:* "Winter Heavens." *Lord Ormont. Beauchamp's Career.*
[2] *Letters.*
[3] "France, 1870."

as the soul's own trials. "There is nothing the body suffers that the soul may not profit by." The only abiding joy is in the spirit: the senses are no means to happiness. And the sooner people learn endurance, the better. So Dr. Middleton argues with Sir Willoughby that unwhipped boys make ill-balanced men. "They won't take rough and smooth as they come. They make bad blood, can't forgive, sniff right and left for approbation, and are excited to anger if an east wind does not flatter them." To leave flesh unchastened was to leave the field the most fertile in moralities in the world unploughed and unsown. Was Meredith thinking of Morley? He saw, at least, that in individuals, as in nations, faults are dealt with according to inexorable law.

> Forgetful is green earth; the Gods alone
> Remember everlastingly: they strike
> Remorselessly, and ever like for like.
> By their great memories the Gods are known.[1]

And what comes most in the way of perfecting life is a false pride: the pride which makes a man refuse to admit he has been in the wrong, or disinclined to repair a mistake, or greedy for admiration, or furious at criticism, or clinging at all costs to a belief in his own superior wisdom. But the peculiar subtlety of egoism is the luxury which puts personal preference in place of fact, and prefers self-satisfaction to strenuousness.

The hater of parsons was himself an ascetic preacher. He might have been a protagonist of the Church, so

[1] "France, 1870."

kindred was his ascesis to hers. But this he never recognised. And this made him the more powerful as a teacher. Had he allied himself with the traditions that bound Church to State, his diatribes would have lulled those whom he wanted to stab broad awake. The force and elevation of his thought swept through the intellectual aristocracy of England like the rush of a mighty wind.

The secret of life was to him the creative activity of nature, which out of earth is always drawing juices for wondrous creation of leaf and flower: but the life of nature comes to its perfection in man who, like the tree, draws sustenance from earth but weds it to brain, and something more than brain, to an elevation and completion of which he spoke as "spirit," and which, in comparison with the flesh, was as coloured heights of air to soil or stream. And ever in regard to nature, Meredith loved more the spirit of Virgil than that of Wordsworth. He loved first a fruitful and humanised earth. But just as nature comprehended ether, which clothed earth in transforming and magical veils, just as earth meeting with air became the breast that gives the rose, just as the bird, which was itself compounded of "the divineness of what most deem gross material substance," could wing the bright eyes of dawn and fill them with a song, so it was for man to colour life with love and energy, and by fullness of living set his aim on nobleness. Courage, patience, passion, sanity were all ingredients of a life that must be conscious of all its ranges, and of their indivisible unity in itself.

And because nobleness was our end, life itself was a joke. There is an endless charming incongruity between the poetry of earth and the egoist's absurdities. We take leave of earth and treat ourselves as angels, only to find that we are crowned windbags. The comic spirit is always leering at our elbows, and pointing cheerfully to the absurdity of our not recognising every ingredient of our nature, as nobleness alone can do.

Here then Meredith added to the philosophy of nature. Wordsworth, whom Meredith loved, had recognised in nature a transcendent presence with whom he entered into a still communion: he had felt the sentiment of Being, spread "o'er all that moves and all that seemeth still," he had had a dim sense of unknown modes of being. Matthew Arnold, on the other hand, saw in nature something that could never be fast friends with man: a power that was stubborn, cruel, and wild. Meredith understood both: he saw the tiger's claw as well as the wind-blown clouds he courted with a lover's blood: and seeing the substance of earth as itself divine, so that the earth itself mirrored the personality of God, having a fecundity of all types of loveliness and of good, he urged that man should imitate not nature's rapine but her persistent benevolence, not her individual violences, but her creative whole. Nature to Meredith therefore was spirit, and more than spirit. It was spirit informing matter, spirit supreme in intellectual law.

> Know her a thing alive,
> Whose aspects mutably serve,
> Whose laws immutably reign.

Lacking the loftiness and precision of Wordsworth's transcendentalism, Meredith's philosophy of nature was at the same time more emotional and more reasonable. It took a more searching view both of nature's ingredients, and of her scheme; and since Meredith's swift, rapturous mind was always cognisant of more than one subject at once, he was always mingling human life with that of unreasoning nature in a deliberate and fruitful confusion, so that the flesh, which consummates love, exalts the brain, just as earth grows fruitful with flowers; and life becomes radiant with love, like the grave heavenliness of the dawn with the vapours, which are the substance of water suspended as particles in the air and penetrated by light. Nature therefore is an enchanted wood, like Westermain. Taken partially, taken crudely, she will be man's worst example, and the brute in man will conquer in lust and savagery: taken as an expression of the Mind that governs her, as creative law, it will be for all men, as for Victor and Nataly Radnor, their highest praise to be told they have kept faith with her.

> Teach me to feel myself the tree,
> And not the withered leaf,

he was fond of quoting to Mrs. Gordon, from his "Ode to the Spirit of Earth in Autumn."

Shakespeare had advocated the just commingling of blood with judgment and, though Meredith certainly knew the need of brain—

> ... if I drink oblivion of a day,
> So shorten I the stature of my soul—

he insisted that brain, which must also recognise what it owed to the flesh, must, like the flesh with which it was united, be subjected to a spiritual purpose, and this spiritual purpose was best learnt by those who watched Nature busy in the constant lesson which her complex creativeness suggested to the discerning spirit.

For him the woods were a home and gave him the key
   Of knowledge, thirst for their treasures in herbs and flowers.
The secrets held by the creatures nearer than we
   To earth he sought, and the link of their life with ours:
And where alike we are, unlike where, and the veined Division, veined parallel, of a blood that flows
In them, in us, from the source by man unattained
   Save marks he well what the mystical woods disclose.

§ 3

From this time on, therefore, the work of Meredith tends to change its form. He had always been a thinker, and was acutely conscious not only that the reactions of flesh and brain and spirit were indivisible, were inevitable, but also that man attained to his full stature in recognising that they were so. So far was he before his time that he not only foresaw and expressed in literature all that psychology now associates with the name of Freud, but that he counteracted the excesses of that, and found it its proper place in the great spiritual humanism which is Christianity. Meredith is not only the poet of evolution, who sees that man has one origin in the developing material world: he is also the poet of sacramental truth, who sees that, through reorganising his intimacy with matter, the man of spirit becomes more spiritual, because matter is no more the negation of life than spirit is. And not only must body, brain, and spirit work to complete each other in abundance of life, but one must see that they can only do so in the fullness of one individual personality meeting the fullness of others, in service, in thoughts, in love. Until this happens, the wondrous fabric of the world has no significance.

Earth was not Earth before her sons appeared,
Nor Beauty Beauty ere young Love was born.

And not only so, but, fail to recognise it, fail to see how necessary, how inevitable the lower is to the higher, the higher flops ridiculously, and is so incongruous in the scheme of things that a thoughtful man cannot keep from a smile.

Such is the idea which Meredith promulgated in 1877, in a lecture in London. Satire, he said, was ridicule without kindliness: and to sting the ridiculous man, under a semi-caress which tempts him to think that you are flattering him, is irony. If you pity him as much as you expose, and drop a tear when you have smacked him, you are a humorist: but "the test of true comedy is that it shall awaken thoughtful laughter."

"If you believe that our civilisation is founded on common sense (and it is the first condition of society to believe it), you will, when contemplating men, discern a spirit overhead: not more heavenly than the light flashed upward from glassy surfaces, but luminous and watchful; never shooting beyond them, nor lagging in the rear, so closely attached to them it may be taken for a slavish reflex, until its features are studied. It has the sage's brows, and the sunny malice of a fawn lurks at the corner of the half-closed lips drawn in an idle weariness of half-tension. . . . Men's future upon earth does not attract it, their honesty and shapeliness in the present does, and, whenever they wax out of proportion, overflown, affected, pretentious, bombastical, hypocritical, pedantic, fantastically delicate, whenever it sees them self-deceived or hoodwinked, given to run riot in idolatries, drifting into vanities, congregating in absurdities, planning short-sightedly, plotting dementedly; whenever they are at variance with their professions, and violate the unwritten laws binding them in consideration one to another, whenever they offend sound reason, fair justice, are false in humility or mined with conceit, individually or in the bulk—the spirit overhead will look humanely malign and cast an oblique light on them, followed by a volley of silvery laughter. That is the comic spirit."

To see the contrasts which that spirit perceives, one cannot but believe, he repeats, that society is founded on common sense. Not to distinguish it is to be bull-blind to the spiritual and to deny the existence of a mind of Man when minds of men are working in conjunction. Common sense is the measure even of imaginative truth. With its comic rapier it pierces us as spiritual lightnings cleave us. It finds no more truth in dull or repulsive things than in the shows of the hypocrite, or of the egoist.

And the lecture on the idea of Comedy marks a knowledge of life and an attitude towards it which mean that in his view of it, as in his view of himself, he was more searching and more stern. He gave to the world the short stories over which he had long been busy. There he turned to two brilliant studies of men. The first of these was the egoist as a country gentleman, the second was the egoist as the genius of reform. The method in both is exactly similar: it was to take a figure and read himself to it. I take my characters from life, he said, "but not till I have them by heart."

He found in the figures of Ferdinand Lassalle and Helène von Dönniges two superb creatures who attracted every side of his sympathies and whom therefore he thoroughly understood. And who was the subject of the earlier study? There was an original to Sir Willoughby Patterne, and it was an original into which Meredith read a consummate knowledge of men and of himself. Sir Willoughby would be outdone by no one, and it is the presence of rivals that leads him to the declaration of love. The theme of this book is that "the love season is the carnival of egoism." Meredith had argued out with himself *how much of his ardent worship as a lover was a demand for self-*

satisfaction, how much of it was real devotion to another human being. In *The Egoist*, love is a claim for worship by a person nurtured in idolatry. He does not care for women, but only for his own reflection in adoring eyes. His final reward, therefore, is to find himself accepted by no woman but one who has seen through him.

It has been of course suggested that, in Sir Willoughby, Meredith was painting a portrait of himself. But the time when he was the hero of his own novels was long gone by: he had reached the stage now when his aim was to read himself into the lives of other people. He still admired men and women greatly gifted, still shared enough in their weakness to understand them, and made them far more vivid than the worthy men for whom he reserved his heroines. Vernon Whitford and Redworth are very dull creatures in comparison with Sir Willoughby. Meredith was disposed to take men like Stephen and Morley very much as they took themselves. It was not the solemn men, but men of the world, who were the subjects which made really magnificent portraits. Willoughby, then, is the pattern of correctness in which all the monotonous members of a class which was nothing but well-bred found themselves mirrored. It is not only the exposure of a remarkable individual: it is a satire on English social standards: it is Meredith's denial of all that in himself craved for general appreciation amongst the entrenched class. The acid test was a man's relation to women, to the woman he thought he loved. Did he look on them as beings equal to him, though different, or did he look on them merely as a foil to himself? *The Egoist* could not have been written before Meredith's passion for Marie Vulliamy had faded in the common day of marriage, before faithfulness on her side and his had survived when romance had paled. But it could not have been written either unless he had learnt the lesson of his failures with Mary Peacock, and seen how all the raptures of romance are intoxication in comparison with that service and that sacrifice which all men owe to all women, and which each man owes especially to the woman who is, or even is to be, his wife.

§ 4

And what of women? Even women sometimes fail. Meredith indeed pictured them as creatures which women are happy in failing to be. Fearful of making them the foils of egoism, he portrayed them not independent of men, but heroic with man's independence rather than with the self-effacement by which the noblest women prove their characters great as the mothers or wives of great men. Meredith created seldom the sweet womanly type of Lucy Desbrough. Generally his heroines were Amazons: splendid ornamental women, like Janet Ross, full like her of masculine activity, and lacking, like her, in the creative genius of woman. On this point Adeline Sergeant, writing in 1889, spoke subtly. Meredith, she said, thinks of woman as of a lesser man, who is unfairly treated because she is not judged by a man's standard, nor allowed his liberty to think or act. But "the same laws and the same moralities will never fit the two. George Meredith forgets that where there are root differences of physical constitution, there are also sure to be root differences of mind and temper. . . . We shall more closely follow nature's lead if we expand rather than seek to lessen the differences between men and women." There was in Meredith something of the woman: his mother, he said: but he never quite freed his thought from his experience enough to see that in women there is, and should be, something of which there was nothing in himself.

He does, however, face the problem of the woman egoist, Clotilde von Rüdiger is as self-centred as Alvan. His indispensable requirement was that she should be absorbed in his personality. Hers was to find one who would satisfy to the full her own capacity for passionate experience. Neither of them could understand the meaning of the splendid aphorism: "barriers are for those that cannot fly."

In the last novel of this period, *Diana of the Crossways*, Meredith made another study of a well-known character; it is perhaps unnecessary to recall the story of Mrs. Norton, the brilliant Irish beauty who was accused of adultery with Melbourne and then of selling a secret to *The Times*. This, Diana is made to do, though, at the instance of Dufferin, Meredith made it clear that his story was to be read as fiction: that the lady of distinction for wit and beauty who had supplied him with an original had come under the shadow of a calumny. The question how far she had really gone and the name of a woman so striking, so well known, so ill reputed, did for Meredith what his genius never could have done. The book became a marked success: it was praised everywhere. Three editions of it were sold in a single year. The Diana of Meredith shows herself through her whole career a female egoist, but of that he takes no account. Since she is a woman, witty, lovely, criticism must give way to admiration. And Meredith found in his sympathy for this breathing woman, who, as he said, lived within him when he wrote the book, a means to state poetically some of those great ideas which had found expression a year or two before in the *Poems and Lyrics of the Joy of Earth*. The fate of Diana had occupied him for hours alone in the Chalet and, in long arguments with Lady Lugard (Flora Shaw as she was then), he debated whether he would kill her or marry her to Redworth. Flora Shaw pleaded for her life. Tall, blonde, and remarkably gifted, this friend belonged to a well-known family of County Dublin: he relished her personality as a typification of Ireland in a fine woman's brain and person. Her manner had the grace and lively sincerity of a well-bred Irish woman. He shared her interest in imperial affairs and in the Empire's big active men, Rhodes whom he missed meeting at Oxford, and Jameson who, when met, delighted him. She, for her part, appreciated to the full the poetry and wit of the great-hearted man who loved to identify himself with Ireland and call himself a Celt. An ornament at many tables, Lady Lugard said that she remembered no dinner-party more brilliant than the trio of Stevenson and herself with Meredith at Box Hill. The cook had failed him, but with such companions, relishing such wines, she had more than any other table had ever been able to afford.

The *Poems and Lyrics of the Joy of Earth* are not easy reading. A new fuller version of "Love in the Valley," "A Ballad of Past Meridian," "Melampus," and "The Lark Ascending" are among them. But the expression was becoming congested, the poet had exchanged the song of rapture for strenuous exercise in the maze of thought: yet through all

> . . . lost on his aerial rings
> In light

the skylark brought serenity in ravishment, even though the tragic note broke in upon the dark translucence of the woods. But to the cry:

O Life, how naked and how hard when known!
Life said, As thou hast carved me, such am I.
Then memory, like the night-jar on the pine,
And sightless hope, a woodlark in night sky,
Joined notes of Death and Life till night's decline:
Of Death, of Life, those inwound notes are mine.

Life was not less poignant, not less complex to the man of fifty than it had been to the widower of thirty-five who wrote *Modern Love*. But Nature was still at hand, his companion, his philosopher, his joy. His love of exercise was as passionate as ever. In those days he could get far, not only to Epsom and Reigate Hill, with its common above, but, afternoon upon afternoon, over to the woods of Leith Hill or Ranmer. As years went on, his walks had to be shorter, but Juniper Hill and Box Hill were always within reach. From Box Hill, as he looked across to Norbury or down the Whites on Burford, or over the beech woods and upon the down looking over Dorking, or over the Weald of Sussex to the South Downs in the distance, he could recall every pathway through the landscape, and recapture every glade in the Dearleap Woods near Wotton, the woods which he had in mind as "Westermain."

Often he would walk up early, through the grove of box trees, to a corner of the woods where he could see young fox cubs play: then, down on his left through the yews to the open valley below, a valley where fritillaries grow and the flowers that love chalk hills: among these he would watch the Painted-Lady butterflies or Burnet moths. Grassy tracks would lead him home, and he would watch for every change the weather made in the life of nature; point, for example, to the white Roman snail coming out after rain. As he passed over chalk-earth or sand, he pointed out what flowers grew from each soil. But in summer he picked always a head of wild scabious to put in his buttonhole.[1] And here, still watching for every hidden beauty, and searching words to reproduce it, and associating it with some resemblance to what he saw to admire in a loved woman, exquisitely sensitive to each note of each bird, to each caress or buffet of the wind, he found the inspiration for both his novels and his poems. He felt that

[1] *The Times*, Feb. 12, 1928.

he "must have occasional movements to be fecund."[1]
"A rapid walker," as he said in *The Egoist*, "poetically minded, gathers multitudes of images on his way."

The Sunday tramps added to the pleasure of walking that of the best rationalist talk. Leslie Stephen gathered them together in 1879: Croom Robertson, Walter and Frederick Pollock, Cotter Morison, John Collier, James Sully, Judge Romer, and W. P. Ker were among some twenty others who met every Sunday from October to June, and kept the world, as well as pretty country, keenly under their review. There was one of these walks which kept for him what he called a bubbling memory till long after. With cold sausages and hock, he and his son had gone up to Leith Hill and took their lunch there with the others; the full white sunlight poured down on to the wood. Then all walked down by tiny clefts of the hill, by Friday Street, into the sloping meadows on either side of the Tillingbourne, which leaps through Evelyn's Wooton, and back under Ranmer to Flint Cottage. Dinner awaited them. And Meredith's cellar, though small, was excellent.[2] He was a true "collector" of burgundy, claret, hock, and even champagne.

§ 5

It was not the fault of his cellar, nor yet of his cook, that towards 1880 Meredith's health began to weaken. In 1879 he caught whooping-cough from his son,

[1] Extract from unpublished letters.
[2] *Letters. Life of Sir Leslie Stephen*, by F. W. Maitland.

but it was not till he got to France that doctors could tell him what was the matter. In England it was called, of all things, catarrh of the stomach, and was thought to be due to writing *The Egoist* at night. "I am lank, limp and cavern-chapped," Meredith wrote to Morison. "My chalet shakes with sneezes," he said, "my nose is as the trunk of an elephant challenging his love." He was, in his own words, "frightfully overthrown by it," and had to do a long tour through the Auvergne to Nîmes and the Riviera to get over it. No sooner was he back than he found that, apart from his old digestive trouble, a malady was beginning to affect his spine, and he could no longer walk springingly. "I can't walk any of my old strides," he wrote to Robert Louis Stevenson in 1884; " . . . am no longer lord of territory." It was the beginning of his locomotor ataxia, which in another ten years' time had become acute. It was once thought by men of science that this disease could be caused only by syphilis. The theory has been proved false. In Meredith's case it was certainly incorrect. Throughout his life there had never been a hint of moral irregularities. What he had was an intense temperament, where nerves and emotions both lived at a strain in the life of strenuous passion, seeking release in excessive exercise. Some traced his spinal trouble to his throwing the beetle. But it was not alone the beetle. It was the strain of fulness of life upon a sensitive organism.[1]

The weakening of health showed itself in his pro-

[1] *Letters* and unpublished material.

cess of thinking. In his early years his work had been moulded to a set end; but in succeeding years the activity had been almost uncontrollable, and his writing had tended to become more and more highly wrought. As we look at it, trying to express the thought which is not yet defined and concrete, nervous activity once again seems to have escaped from will. The Meredith who wrote after 1880 is a man suffering from an ataxic restlessness.

His declining health added to the bitterness of disappointment at what seemed to him the failure of his career. His prodigal genius was not yet appreciated. Till about fifteen years after his marriage, he used to add to his income by talking and reading to Mrs. Wood at Eltham. He read magnificently, with a command, as Morley noticed, of fine cadence and exultant emphasis. Not only was he still poor, but he still felt with the acuteness of youth the lack of appreciation in the critics. "I take it from all alike," he wrote to Arthur, "as the cab-horse takes the whip."

§ 6

When *Diana of the Crossways* was at last bringing him the success he had so long deserved, he fell under another and deeper calamity. His wife's health gave way. In 1884 she was found to be suffering from cancer. Twice the surgeons operated, but they could do nothing. Meredith was filled with admiration at the way she bore her suffering: but when he tried to work he could not: the machine, he said, had got crazy. He had to stay and watch the end approaching to the wife who through all had been faithfulness and full affection. And like a first gift to the grave, her voice had already gone. He turned his thoughts from time to time to his friends: back at Box Hill he watched a suffering he could not lessen. The father lived with his children, between crises and respites, knowing what was to come, and not daring to wish in any direction.

The end came on September 17. Meredith did not know it was so near. He had gone to town on business for the day: when he came back at six in the evening her hand was still warm: as he pressed it, and felt for the first time no answering pressure, his hold of life was shaken. He looked at the face which had borne months of distress and saw her Mistress of the Kingdom of Rest. "I suppose there was no hope from the first," he wrote to Morley. "I did hope."

In Dorking Cemetery he bought a grave for four. And after her body had been laid there, he talked for hours to Mrs. Gordon, and then went up to stay with Lady Caroline at Effingham Hill. His daughter went to the Morleys', his son to the uncle at Nonancourt, and then to business.

Box Hill, when he returned, was a place of withered recollections, like an old life to be lived again without sunshine. "I cross and recross it," he wrote to Morley, "sharp spikes where flowers were."[1]

---

[1] *Letters. Poems:* "A Faith on Trial."

§ 7

What had he of tangible now with her dear heart? A peace which gives a glow to sorrow by opening fresh opportunities to love, as it looks into the face of death and sees human divisions done away, comes to those who believe in prayers for their dead. Meredith, though far from that, sought solace in his own way: he faced his anguish with a will to question:

>   I caught,
> With Death in me shrinking from Death,
> As cold from cold, for a sign
> Of the life beyond ashes: I cast,
> Believing the vision divine,
> Wings of that dream of my Youth
> To the spirit beloved.

But the answer only came through an effort to apprehend life as a whole: to see her one with the great spiritual principles by which life alone is lived. As he thought of her, he could not doubt she lived. He wrote for her tombstone:

> Who call her Mother and who calls her Wife
> Look on her grave and see not Death but Life.

He wrote to his son: "There is no news. I see no one. I do not doubt that you think of your dear mother. I think of her as alive in the spirit. She is with you in your worthiest thoughts." And this conviction he gradually assumed into the ardour of his poetry:

Then of those Shadows, which one made descent
Beside me I knew not: but Life ere long
Came on me in the public ways and bent
Eyes deeper than of old: Death met I too,
    And saw the dawn glow through.

Grief forced on rationalism an acceptance of immortality.[1]

---

[1] *Poems:* "A Faith on Trial," " M. M.," " Hymn to Colour."

XI

THE LONGUEUIL EPISODE

§ 1

THE hold of women over Meredith's imagination never failed to his last days. That he thought of marrying again is out of the question, but he gave to his friendship with the women he most admired an ardour which natures less prodigally rich reserve for passion, and the passion of youth.

Four women in succession were still to hold his imagination and kindle his solicitude.

The first of these he met a year after his wife's death. She was staying at "The Nook," with Grant Allen, who had a great deal in common with Meredith. For was he not both a rationalist and a novelist? Her name was Hilda de Longueuil. She belonged to a family which had lived in Canada, and had now returned to the Pyrenees.

Meredith had made Diana write of life: "When I fail to cherish it in every fibre, the fibres within are waning." He cherished life with a passion that gave to the married unity of every sensation and emotion the force, the delicacy, and the fire of poetry. He conceived himself first a poet, and, in everything he wrote, the same love of odd ways of saying things, a love which was forced on him by the fiery quality of what he had to say, gives us, in a sure succession of flashes, the Meredithian style. No one can imitate it, no one

THE LONGUEUIL EPISODE

has succeeded even in a caricature of it. And its quality is unmistakable. The mind and personality it reveals have a force and fire that others attain only in rare passions; and that at the age of fifty-eight he should address a young lady in this style with ardour and intimacy is to keep a promise rather than to offer a surprise.

Meredith speaks of her as identified with France. A French elegance and femininity were part of her distinction, and it was one to which the great writer had been especially susceptible since his second marriage, which, as we saw, had brought associations that made him more intimate with the spirit of the country. But the distinction of this lady, both in mind and personality, did not need a Meredith to discover. Without it, he said, a woman would not attract him. "But when that same Mlle. de Longueuil is out of her shyness, and conversationally animated, I would back her, for true illumination of beauty, against the field of enchantresses—and I think I am something of a judge. . . . I remember at my second interview being astonished at her fluency and expressiveness, both of speech and feature. I remember, too, at one moment, taking a dive into an eye that sparkled pure light and still detains me."

His letters to this young lady he described, perhaps erroneously, as "more, and more copious" than he had written to any one person since he was nineteen. The correspondence lasts from December, 1886, to November, 1887.[1] In it he pours himself out in re-

[1] I published it, as a sequence, in *The Nineteenth Century*, for Meredith's Centenary, in February, 1928.—R. S.

flections on politics, on literature, and on that relation of love to life and of a dear woman to them both which was the constant magnet of his genius. To give to the woman who wakened his warm and subtle sympathies the philosophy that was born of his own vital experience was one of the ambitions which he cherished for this friendship. She could feel, she could observe, she could reason, but could she join reason and feeling and perception so that each should strengthen and stimulate the other? He would teach her. "She has not yet learnt the value, or perhaps even the meaning of the impalpably spiritual from which all else flows that is really life, and love too, of the warmest. Your positive is but a matter of moments. I fancy she has been poorly schooled by her male adorers. She has regrets for waste of time, and a sense of uselessness. Let her take to answering me, and she shall love direction and inspiriting. The correspondence will not be a task, for if she merely tells me of how she is, and what she does daily, with a fledgling thought here and there, it will satisfy me: the positive concerning her is my first request."

A more touching and revealing letter, the first of this series, gives his clearer view of her temperament in the light of those ideas which his life made into a flame: the idea that reason, wedded to nature and the spirit, arranged life's jarring notes into a pattern of ordered melody. Reason weds nature and the spirit by recognising that emotion should lead not to its own luxuries, final as their inward sweetness seems, but to a sense of a busy productiveness in which all men, all forms of life, are recognised as one in a great spiritual order, endlessly developing, and in which "we find our happiness or not at all." To bring our desires and capacities together into this crowded living spiritual order is the meaning of life; and, until we see that meaning, life, which should be joy, is hardly worth living.

"Your words to Grant Allen, upon the welcome you give to Sleep and Death, haunt me, as though they were a piece of your history: and they tell of suffering or of impatience with it. But at least they show you on the road of enquiry, though willing to repose before much way has been made. Of course the indication is that you have not yet mastered the senses under a firm grasp of the meaning of life. We are all thinking of our own, when life is a theme perplexing us to the love of slumber. But it is out of our own that we must come, before we can think over so broad a matter at all. And this being done, we perceive a world of nature that we can trim if we please, that can go on independently and healthfully because joyfully; always busily; whose death is life; whose rest is nothing but variation: we perceive also a world of men, certainly bettered by the ages but not yet in harmony between their desires and their capacities: hence the wretchedness.

"They are still in the thick of the emotional stage: that is, of the senses holding fast on the thoughts they have given berth to, but should earlier let fly for their happiness. We find as we advance in life that if this thought is independent of our personal emotions, exactly to the degree in which it is free are we nearing to be at one with Nature in her joyful activity and our view of her work. And this not even the loss of the faculties of pleasure, nor the approach of the issues most commonly dreaded can shadow (for) one who has grown to the full development of the brain. Make your cast for a clear understanding. Believe at the outset that life is joy: only let joy be read spiritually: in other words, not as a thing to claim but as a thing to share in. . . ."

Here, more clearly stated than usual, is a mastering thought of Meredith's, and there was evidently something in this friend which sharply reminded him of his own youth when, after writing "Love in the Valley," he had expressed the mood of tragic disillusion, in "Modern Love." "You have not been led out and up," he wrote to his friend. "You have the sense of higher—never the help to reach it. An unwedded woman of any warmth of blood, if her mind is not set upon high ideals, becomes the prey of bad ones and—tra-la, tra-la! she spins the wrong way. *A beau sabreur dans le champ de Mars de Venus* becomes her natural captain, and if she would not have him for the legitimate, alas for her experiences."

§ 2

A poem with the title of "Hilda's Morning and Evening Dose of Rhyme" suggests again that the young lady's heart had been engaged with someone whom Meredith felt to be unworthy of her. "It is a blissful moment," he writes, "when the sensual spell (coloured romantic) is broken, and the phœnix arises a new bird: not ungrateful for her own sake, but the stronger through her regrets." She confided in him. Of one of her letters he writes: "It has gone and had to go. It is not lost, be sure. It is like the life that goes: the good work lasts. . . . Nothing ceases. Notice in this, how loss and sweat of anguish produce a piece of writing that I tear to strips, and there seems not a vestige left. Yet it has entered into me. It changes, akins, directs me in some way." The same thoughts had been made into a more intricate weaving in "Hilda's Morning and Evening Dose." It answers the questions which arise like cries from " Modern Love."

> *Can* another love be born
> In heart that love has left outworn;
> Appearing dead to sweet desire
> Its mouths of earth once mounts of fire?
>
> Question first if thou would'st know
> This wilful heart that wasted so;
> And ask one heart that wildly went
> To ashes, why the flames are spent.
>
> Was it to our heavens bared
> Reflectively, when forth it fared?
> And knew it, when it took the leap,
> Of whether shallow, whether deep?

Loved she an angel of the light?
All meaner forms would woman slight.
Or was the Prince of Darkness he,
Her wreck was out in deepest sea.

But less than either bids the mind
Right measure of the man to find;
From wider knowledge, keener thought,
To fathom how the spell was wrought.

And has he borne his manhood high
For whom she cast that gambler's die,
Her heart? And doth her spirit through
The senses read, and love renew?

Ah, that first love! It comes to prove
How creatures of the senses love,
Before the brain has gained control
To show how they may love in soul.

Give life to Life: in turn it gives.
Believe thy heart alive: it lives.
Know Love more heavenly than of old
Revealed, and Love will not be cold.

The past is dust: thy heart is blood,
It bears thy fate upon its flood.
Set it on nobleness, and soon
A nobler love will crown thy noon.

Here are verses as fine as "The Thrush in February." Their thought has the same high worth: but furthermore, this philosophy is also a personal plea. It is

Meredith's warning against that magnetism over women which a virile type, even when not virtuous, quite commonly exerts. "O Women!" the sage had written long before, in *Richard Feverel*, while youth was still burning, "Women who like, and will have for hero a rake! how soon are you not to learn that you have taken bankrupts to your bosoms and that the putrescent gold which attracted you was the slime on the Lake of Sin."

At sixty he had not forgotten what that could mean to women. Let them know the impulses the physical organism gives to emotion, but know them as transformed to an identity with reason and the spirit in the wholeness of man's nature at its highest. Nobleness, he said, was the standard for emotion to use in trying men and "in rescuing the minds of men from the duperies practised by the male upon them." Finally, in one of those rapid turns of thought which made all life a comedy to him, he turns away the suspicion of preaching by telling Hilda to use nobleness as an amulet for protection, a magnifier, a scrubbing-brush, a smelting-furnace and a pilot star!

Nobleness was, of course, here as elsewhere, the full development of nature, not sliced to evenness by austerity, but the realising that life and spiritual laws are something greater than convention. "I deplore the case of your errant wife with the not-much-of-a-creature for whom she tossed her cap over the windmills!" he wrote. "Some women, as well as men, require the sowing of wild oats in early life if they are to walk steady or trot zealously in harness. A Devonshire old lady, having a son who had run away with a married woman returned to her husband, complained that the latter's family objected too violently to her son's behaviour: 'Why, he only had her for a fortnight.' Old ladies gain humaneness by loss of the notions of sex, I suppose. But philosophers are with them. I heard of a husband who neglected his wife for the saddle. She found a cavalier and fled, but came back before long, and he took her, saying with magnanimity that he had been the one to blame. Here and there a woman in the clutch of a ferocious egoist has only to lift an eyelid to be loathed eternally, if not banned. By and by, when possession ceases to be a masculine noun in man's grammar-book, we shall have larger ideas of purity and especially clearer as to its place of residence."

§ 3

Meredith proposed to write to Mlle. de Longueuil a series of "Letters to a Lady on the Art of Fiction," but the plan was not completed. He was less interested in such a project than in her: a woman in a room outshone all else in it, and in a room of women this one outshone the rest. He begins his letters: "My lady and dear friend," "My dear friend and best," "My friend and dearest." He concludes: "Your most faithful," "Your devoted," "I salute you, press and kiss your hand, am at your feet, and commend you to the heavens. George M."

"Feel in me your soul's home," he writes, " and

believe that you have done more for me, in so strangely making mine a habitation for you, than I could ever repay by services." And again: "Perceive that I embrace your whole existence, all that may or could in the chances have befallen you, and am, with this feeling of mind, barely of our world when I ally myself to your destinies and speculate on them, past or future. You will not think me inquisitive, probing for revelation. I ask for nothing that does not help you on to a healthier viewing and footing of the world." And to this he adds: "Your orders created the images—they are your doing." The young lady was subjected to her friend's scrutiny and he made so bold as to tell her that he used such a phrase (it was her own coining) as "starved cat with black-currant eyes" as a makeshift photograph of her. "Shall I tell you of a defect in your physical construction, explaining much to the observer?" he asked. "Well, you have not lively nostrils, they are not nervous and dilating to air; they show the want of fiery animation. Consider that physical cause of a tendency to revolve your meditations gloomily and shut your sensations from fellowship with the outer world—that of nature and human kind." The work he planned would be to some degree inspired by her. "Your enthusiasm is kindling in me." And again, "You speak of me as a magician, you little know the marvels you in comparison have done;— mine are nothing to them." For this, his return was a fervour of spiritual guardianship. "My thoughts hang over you solicitously, and tend you, body and spirit."

§ 4

Precious words on literature run through the letters: for here indeed are pictures of the poet's intimate life. "So you like Ballads," he writes. "Well, the Iliad, greatest of poems, is a great Ballad. So you choose well. And Auld Robin Gray is exquisite in simplicity. But I beg of you to learn to love the instrument, not merely certain tunes. The treasure of verse is where thought embraces feeling, as the man the woman. Then you have the highest in mind with the deepest in nature. That is why Poetry is above philosophy: it is the voice of essential Man before the Gods. You ought to have me read to you. There are pretty lines in Goldsmith, keen shafts in Pope: but in Wordsworth really draughts from Nature's fountain, here and there,—not mixt with the vinous which I expect was once your milk. Your heart is in the woods? We will enter them together, and I sing to you, for I am of the woods."

Intensely sensitive as Meredith was, he was always stung by the judicial attitude which is proper to reviewers. That these were slow to realise the splendour of his genius is too true: but it is also true that when they did recognise it, his work had become so recondite and complex that it had lost its beauty, that rich romantic beauty which intoxicated Stevenson in Hyères as he read "Love in the Valley," and which brings *Richard Feverel* to the power and rarity of *Romeo and Juliet*. His friend was herself puzzled with the later poems; but the same feeling in the critics was to Meredith yet another of those chastisements to which he so often referred.

"I have had my inaugural whipping for the publication of Poems. I rhyme 'people' and 'ripple,' and a long paragraph of the review abuses me for a French heresy or bluntness of ear. I am told that 'we English' are not so easily satisfied. The ear of the boor in fact demands the hard consonantal smash of an exact similarity of sound, together with the repetition *ad infinitum* of the one rhyme to 'people,' being 'steeple.' Poor Theodolinda is 'enigmatical.' And it reminds me that my heart's Lady thought so. Theodolinda is in a white heat." Her moods, he said, were "like an interchange of alternate black and bright."

Three weeks later he sends her the *Athenæum*, with Henley's leader reviewing *Ballads and Poems of Tragic Life*. That review was singularly discerning. That Meredith had "the whole gamut of creation" in him and could express only a fraction of it, he himself realised: his power of expression broke down. What then did he expect of Henley, who had praised the vigorous eloquence of "France," assessed its poetry as constant and sustained, who had said of the "Phaéthôn" that "it is doubtful if the peculiar genius of the metre could be recalled in alien material with greater daring or a finer prodigality of diction"? Henley had said of Meredith himself that "he has charm as well as power, and, once his rule is accepted, there is no means of shaking him off. The position is that of the antique tyrant in a commonwealth once republican and free. We resent the domination, but we enjoy it too, and, with or against our will, we admire the author of our slavery." But because the review added to this the just criticism that "there *is* genius, but there is *not* felicity," because, quoting Baudelaire, it accused him of that form of dandyism which aimed at being uninterruptedly sublime and of congestion and clottedness—he turned to this lady with one of those outbursts to which his intense sensitiveness not seldom drove him.

"It is because I do not pass among reviewers that they treat one who is so little a favourite with the public, and who courts no favour, with this form of politeness. I am termed a harlequin, a performer of antics. I choose, when I write, the expression seeming to my imagination just, and if it is not conventional, they denounce it. When there is a stress of emotion, my speech is necessarily simple, in harmony with the common human element. They admit it, yet cannot allow that at other seasons the writer's fancy (if he have any) should be allowed to play. So they pursue their course, treating each new book of mine to blows, and me to reluctantly lessening contempt confirmed in dislike, while gradually the submerged volume comes back to the surface, is demanded, and spoken of respectfully. I am told that my first volume of poems, written when I was a minor, will now sell for ten pounds. All of them go at double the original price. Yet after close on forty years of honest work, I present myself to receive the certain lash, I trouble you with my ill-temper, and shall have your sympathy assuredly, while at heart the dear girl is thinking that those reviewers do speak a criticism not impossible to share and—minus the impertinence—modesty to utter. Believe me, it is only the bad manners which I complain of. I know my faults. I know too that all writers have some. The unfairness consists in reviewing favourites on the lines of their good things, and the unfavoured in examples of their weak or unappreciated. Forgive this tirade. I suppose I shall not publish very much more, and to be lashed up to the end is wearisome, if but for the monotony. Why do I publish verse? I really cannot say. The burden of the expense falls on me, and the silly remarks. I have sent you a rather selected specimen." His consolation was the admiration of Americans, and to those who worshipped, he took pleasure in showing courtesy, even though they often bored him. When his temper had calmed down, he said to Sir James Barrie that Henley put a laurel crown on his head and then buffeted him in the stomach.

§ 5

The third subject on which he wrote to this lady was politics, and these passages recall the more famous ones from *Beauchamp's Career* and *One of Our Conquerors*. She had been suspicious of politics. Meredith replied that as a profession it could not be improved. "Politics means the business of the world," he repeated from *Diana of the Crossways*. "Consider, if you denounce political life, and turn from the arts—what is left save a choice between the priest and the manly sportsman: and bethink you of the kind of transformation you require of him after he has killed pigeons, or rivals, and soiled doves, and jumped hurdles innumerable. You must be expecting him to change into a professor of science. No, it is nature that makes the choice of his career, and this end comes of that beginning. Keep the blood in your veins. You are praying that a Lara may conclude philanthropist. Since the beginning of our semi-civilisation, the Lara figure has laid the spell on the senses of women. We are subject to our enchantresses: he is their wizard. The hope of Christianising him while his passions attract the floods of air and can consume them is futile." A later letter resolves Meredith's cryptogram: he was thinking of that tendency in people, and especially in women, to trust all to one man of the virile and magnetic type. But are women attracted by professors of science, or does not their nature turn rather to physical, or at least merely male, excellences which are insufficient to govern the world? The remedy is not in a hero who captures the imagination of womanly minds, but in a busy people. Politics, in fact, is the business of all who would not be abjects. "The poor politicians, whose honesty you doubt, and the poor people, whose intelligence you disdain, are, by the exercise of their gifts and the 'step by stumble' enlightenment under correction of the scourges they bring on themselves by that exercise, advancing gradually to a better state than that to which your *bon roi Henri* would conduct them.

"Looking back over history will help you to look forward, above and beyond the tumble of the waters.

What you do is to begin a flight with your mind, and quickly relapse on your sensations, with a sigh and a cry for capable crowned Man to come and settle affairs. And if he came, he would but passingly smooth them.

"For permanent work, the people must be active. Already it is perceptible that they are everywhere thoughtfuller than they were. Can you truly deny it? Rather let my dear Lady ask herself whether she does not too unresistingly weary of even the sight of the struggle. Her cry for the capable Man is one of the errors of democracy also. It means the cry for the Sword to cut the difficult knot. And that, as we observe in history, represents a fracture which has to be mended by many decades of labour. Democracy nevertheless is learning. I do not perceive that Royalists show so handsome a front to the lessons of the day.

"You may see in my 'Ode to France,' written in the dark days of December, 1870, what I feel for your country. . . .

"The uproar of the coming Jubilee already deafens me with throats of a thousand famished lions. I wish I were out of the country."

In the same letter Meredith announces that Admiral Maxse had become a Unionist "with Berkeley vehemence." "I tried a few sentences of serious exposition. He burst through every one midway. So I retired to an eminence and worried him with shafts, whereat he kicked and roared and lashed his tail. I composed him by informing him of the sympathy of a lady known to me by favour of august good fortune, and that she denounced a 'Liberal' intolerance that would not give him audience. He was visibly flattered. I said further that this fair lady justly expected all 'Liberals' at a meeting to have the manners of gentlemen, if only in emulation of the decorous Tories at their meetings, or that otherwise she could hang them up by their title on the gallows of inverted commas. This remark he pronounced irony. How can one argue with him?"

There is then, in this correspondence, a vivid picture of the life and mind of Meredith at the age of sixty. Marked with his extraordinary character, it is intimate and sincere. His friendship with the Leslie Stephens, his preoccupation with his daughter, and her Irish governess, and Cole the gardener, his relations with the Lawrences of Burford and Mrs. Rasch ("a saint in silver") fill the intervals of the more precious extracts that have been quoted. The unique writer is before us, with the impulsiveness, the fervour, the sensitiveness, the energy, the exaltation which were known so well to those who loved him. His pen was "lamed with digestive struggles"; but he poured out his personality, and wrote sentences that are additions to the wisdom of our literature: "The best physician is he who with faith in his medicine waits patiently"; "Suspicion is the lustiest born of silence"; "There is no life but of the spirit which has the life eternal under varying forms"; "Face to the East at morn, westwards at eve." His mature philosophy of life, the principle which at this time dominated him, was condensed into the two lines written to this friend:

> Know love more heavenly than of old
> Revealed, and love will not be cold.

One cannot but feel an envy for Mlle. de Longueuil, and marvel that when her nervous system was reeling from the toxin injected into it by a man whom it was perilous to love, she should have attracted the admiring sympathy of a sage who, with the life that came full from life's fountains, turned passion to counsels so trenchant and ennobling.

XII

WHEN AUTUMN DAYS STRIP BARE

§ 1

THE man whose thoughts could live with those he loved, and tend them body and spirit, could show the simplest kindness to many a friend. He never forgot, writes Mr. Frank Harris, that sympathetic kindness to juniors and inferiors was a duty of his position. Mr. Harris was struck by his generosity and sweetness of soul. When Sir James Barrie first came to London, he found at Box Hill the fostering enthusiasm which Stevenson had found. From the first, Meredith believed in his work and opened to him the glow of his friendship. There was indeed no trouble he would not take to encourage youthful writers with a hint of promise, and it was Meredith who first suggested to Barrie that he should try the writing of plays. Generosity itself and simplicity itself, Meredith opened the treasures of his memory to the brilliant young writer's fancy and sympathy; told him of his own early struggles and his own early life, to point to what it had in common with Barrie's; but the High Street at Portsmouth (though of course he mentioned what *Evan Harrington* owed it) was not the key to his mystery, and his talk flew back to the great interests of his life. He would begin with reminiscence, and dart again into romance.

He especially delighted in taking in Mr. Edward Clodd, whose enquiries were thought too cunning, and whom he accordingly nicknamed "Sir Reynard." Again and again his thoughts would go back to wine, to women and to winds.[1]

But he never lost sight of his new friend's career or promise, and when the success of *The Little Minister* followed that of *A Window in Thrums*, Meredith felt a new confidence in the British public. Stevenson came still, and brought down, as well as his wife, Sidney Colvin. Both were taken to the heart of Meredith, who made friends also with certain of his neighbours, and among them the Alfred Beneckes, John Deverell with Colonel and Mrs. Lewin of Parkhurst on Leith Hill, and Sir Trevor and Lady Lawrence, his near neighbours at Burford. To Sir Trevor he loved to refer as "our affable M.P." Sir Trevor's sisters, Mary and Louisa, who had a little salon in Whitehall Place, delighted to entertain the celebrity, and to do indeed anything for him that they could. They were snobs, they were chatterers, and lacked perfection of feature. One was compared to a pug dog; the other was almost like a terrier. Before Mrs. Meredith died, she had noticed a tone of adulation in these ladies, and it had not pleased her. She wrote with her pencil after her voice had gone: "*Elles sont repoussantes.*"[2]

Henley was now taken as a friend, and the garland was remembered rather than the buffet in the stomach. "All his nature," Meredith wrote to Lord Plymouth

[1] Frank Harris, *Contemporary Portraits*.
[2] *Letters*. Private Information.

after his death, "sprang up to hail the divinity of life. . . . He had the poet's passion for nature, and by reason of it, the poet's fervent devotion to humanity . . . he was one of the main supports of good literature in our time." Young Edmund Gosse, already successful in his cultivation of celebrities, succeeded for a time in making an impression, and was more than once at Box Hill. In 1890 a young man from the North, Richard Le Gallienne, brought out a whole book on Meredith, and it was a just, as well as a delightful, book. It was written with a finish of style that few young men have been able to command. It appreciated Meredith with admirable restraint and nicety: and he could not but be pleased. "It was generously conceived," he wrote to its author, "and stands for work honestly done. You have absorbed the matter before dealing with it, so that you give it out rather than appear seeking here and there. I judge consequently that the two rare great gifts of the literary consciousness and enthusiasm will animate you to excel in productions of your own. . . . I criticise myself sharply, believe me; and criticism which points out the author's achievement or failure measured by his aim is welcome."[1]

A year later Mr. Le Gallienne asked Meredith to allow poems of his to appear in an anthology: but the poet refused. He was still smarting under criticism, and could hit back. A blow fell on Mr. Le Gallienne himself when, having asked for something of Meredith's manuscript to keep, he explained that he wanted

[1] *Letters.* R. Le Gallienne, *The Romantic Nineties.*

nothing very much, only a poem. "Only a poem!" The poet took up the words, and it was not at once that the young man was forgiven for what had sounded like a lack of appreciation. Mr. Le Gallienne's next book, also, was praised: it was called "as widely garrulous as a very blackbird, limpid as a brook, promising masterpieces in the rarest style of essay."[1]

Weakening health kept Meredith more and more to his cottage. But he had some interesting encounters. In June, 1888, dining at the Blue Posts with Haldane and Asquith, he sat between Balfour and Morley. The Liberals were beginning to make him now, at the age of sixty, into another of their grand old men. He saw the danger.

In April, 1887, dining with the Eighty Club, he had met Gladstone, on whom his remorseless glance played with misgiving. He found it painful to see how obviously the orator timed and worked up his effects. He was not pleased to have from Gladstone a greeting in conventional terms which he would himself have disdained to offer to the most commonplace of men. He knew that the Liberal leader was valiant, and had prodigious gifts; when Gladstone died, Meredith wrote: "A splendid image built of man has flown"; but when Meredith met Gladstone, he found that he could not trust him. "He is, I fear me, very much of an actor."[2]

In 1891 he had to appear as a witness in an action for slander which was brought against Chapman & Hall by a certain James Pinnock. Meredith, as reader, had accepted for publication Colonel Ellis's *West*

[1] *The Romantic Nineties.*   [2] *Letters.*

African Stories, in one of which he told about one of his characters, James Peacock, stories that had also been told about James Pinnock. Curiously enough, this Colonel Ellis was a son by the second marriage of the same Sir Samuel Ellis who had first married Meredith's aunt, Catherine. Sir Charles Russell, counsel for Pinnock, cross-examined Meredith. Meredith objected to Ellis's description of the mother of James Peacock whom James Pinnock took to be himself, but it went down with the public, he said, so he had to pass it. If his own taste were final, he would have to object to so much. "Have you ever heard of the name of Pinnock?" Russell asked the witness. "Not since the days of my youth," was the answer, "when I learnt his catechism."[1]

§ 2

After the death of his second wife, Meredith's mind returned again and again to the thought of death. His son Arthur and Sir William Hardman died within a few weeks of each other in 1890. His old friend, Frederick Jones, who had been his neighbour at Norbiton and with whom he remained in frequent touch, had died the year before. He was at Browning's funeral in Westminster Abbey on the last day of 1889, as he was to be at Tennyson's in October, 1892. Stevenson died in 1894. All these, following on the loss of his wife, mellowed and matured his thoughts of death. Grief, as he found, could make his heart ring accordant chimes with many fellows:

[1] S. M. Ellis, *George Meredith*.

> When I had shed my glad year's leaf,
> I did believe I stood alone,
> Till that great company of Grief
> Taught me to know this craving heart
>   For not my own.

"In the soul of true love there is no parting," he wrote to Mrs. Jones. "Our dearest go from touch and sight, —not, forever, from the lastingly vital to us. I say this with full consciousness of the loss I too have sustained." Mrs. Jones wrote back gratefully, and Meredith wrote again of her husband as one of the few true men he had known. "And, my friend," he went on, "these men live on in us. And more, they are the higher work of Nature, which she will not let pass away. They have the eternal in them. I do not look on death as a victory over us. Death and life are neighbours, each the cause of the other: and the task for us, under stress of deprivation, is to take our loved ones into the mind, and commune with them, spirit to spirit—so will they be wedded to us, faster, closer about us than when we had the voice and eyes." And now, in the exhilaration of a night of stars, the fir trees, as he walked through them, told him that his spirit was invested not only in flesh but also superinvested in undying life:

They waken waves of thoughts that burst to foam:
The living throb in me, the dead revive.
Yon mantle clothes us: there, past mortal breath,
Life glistens on the river of the death.
It folds us, flesh and dust.

But in 1905 he wrote, at Mrs. Jessopp's death, to the old Canon: "The cutting in twain of a life after many years of happy union can bring no renewal of it, though the wound may heal."[1]

§ 3

As he revolved the thought of his wife, he thought not only of death and immortality but of marriage itself. He still worshipped the idea of woman, he still felt a chivalrous devotion to the women he most admired. He remembered the intensity of his ardour for each of the women he had married, and yet, in neither case, had marriage been sustained bliss. In the first case, it had been torture: in the second case, it had meant that his genius put a gulf between him and a faithful woman, who did her best for him in trying circumstances, and that its gradual loss of rapturous unity, which was painful, had been accelerated by his bursts of temper. Yet, of course, in each case, he had kept with exemplary strictness to his marriage vow: he had found it unpardonable in a wife not to do the same. And marriage was not only nurtured in bliss: it was part of the sacred scheme of nature. How could the sting of torment be extracted from the bee of honeyed thighs?

That was the question which now obsessed him for nine years. "I constantly brood, conjure, speculate," he had written to Hilda de Longueuil, "and to write

[1] *Letters. Poems:* "The Lesson of Grief," "Winter Heavens." Extract from an unpublished letter.

relieves me."[1] Once again he would find in writing an outlet for instincts swelling beyond the barrage of active life. The result is the three novels, *One of Our Conquerors*, *Lord Ormont and His Aminta*, and *The Amazing Marriage*. In the first, he argues that nature is more sacred than an unnatural union forced by convention and profit: in the second, that a wife is justified in running away from a husband who will not do her justice before the world, and in the third, also, that she is dispensed from loyalty to a man who puts his egoism in the place of conjugal rights. But in none of these must Meredith be taken too seriously. He let his speculations, just as he let his reminiscences, loose from fact: and his real attitude towards marriage is shown rather in his life than in his last three novels. The idea that he really advocated temporary marriages was one of the jokes which he played on an interviewer. Although, as he wrote to Lady Ulrica Duncombe, he thought there should be a way of escape from a false choice in early life, the speculation that a revision of the contract every ten years might meet the case was more a warning against taking bickerings, or disappointments, as a reason for parting finally than it was a rejection of the idea of a binding contract. "The dreams of courtship," he said, "have to be dispelled. The couple have to be *hardened* to the married life."[2]

But the question that he believed to be at the root of the problem of marriage was man's accepting for his own the woman's standards, his not asking of her

[1] See *Nineteenth Century*, Feb., 1928.
[2] *Letters*. J. A. Hammerton, *George Meredith*.

what he would not give. This is the subject of discourse between man and woman in "The Sage Enamoured and The Honest Lady." It was a ticklish subject, and bold as Meredith was, he covered the advances of his thought in every possible ambush of complexity. No one can say that in the "Ballad of Fair Ladies in Revolt" he had been easy: and there his theme was much less difficult to handle. There it was the claims of woman for essential rights to a knowledge, which itself was power, against the convention that left her respected, but ill-informed. She too had nature in her and had the right to know to the full the working of its impulses on human beings. In real life, Meredith carefully bowdlerised his conversation in the company of women; but the poem insists that it is no compliment to women to pretend that they cannot face a mention of sex. "The Sage Enamoured" was to lead up a much darker and more slippery track to his governing principle that

> . . . not till Nature's laws and man's are one,
> Can marriage of the man and woman be.

He takes the case of a woman who has in her voice the low full tones which mean a deep experience of love, which tell of its dreams and its wounds, "the richness of tone," like Carinthia's, "carrying a music through silence." She had in youth met a young lover equally ardent and with him had delivered herself up to the white heat of their passion, thinking its fire could melt the moral law.

In later years, she found a genius of a certain age in

love, a man of grey and laurelled brow, as, after his wife's death, Meredith's own was. To cure him of a love she thought indiscreet, she opened to him the secret of her past: but in opening, she sought to condone it. He listens in chilled silence: and as her tones reverberate in the void, she hears their hollowness. Seeing then that her place is not to condone, but to confess, she names her act as sin. Before the directness of her humility, judgment is transformed to reverence: at the same time the sage is forced to fit her case into the scheme of life as a whole, and therefore to talk of principles:

He passed her through the sermon's dull defile.

He pointed out that some account the impulses of sex as devilish, some as divine. Some advocate only restraint: some condone all surrender to instinct. But what is instinct really? If instinct is nature, nature is something more than the flesh; she is a whole: she is one with reason. The only way to live is to allow duly both for reason and passion: to bridge the chasm between them. Reason weighs the present with the future, and though it allows for sexual passion because its place is central in the generation of life, it puts the generation of life before immediate gratification.

To Meredith the problem was always that of the attitude of men towards morality, not that of women. He lived at a time when men tacitly filched a good deal of licence, and allowed women none: when adultery committed by a woman was a ground for divorce, adultery committed by a man was not. He saw therefore that the need was to recognise law as law, and apply it justly to both sexes: allowing indeed for the flesh, but allowing not less for moral philosophy; and realising that the problem can be solved only by common sense with elevation of mind:

> Only the rooted knowledge to high sense
> Of heavenly can mount, and feel the spur
> For fruitfullest advancement.

The true beauty for men to seek in women is what they ought to offer them: a chaste and honest soul: a soul free from the taste for self-indulgence, whether physical, emotional, or egoistic.

§ 4

Such is the general principle: but when it comes to working it out in particular cases, how many qualifications interlace. In the case, for example, of Victor Radnor: he had made the initial mistake of marrying an old woman for money, and though he ran away with a companion natural to his choice, neither he, nor she, nor their daughter could escape the social consequences. He is a man of culture, who also had become rich; he desires to give his wife a social position, only to find that their wealth can never build on the instability of their relation: always in the background is the first wife, with a revenge that will not let them develop. Would she allow them to live quietly together? Yes. To become prominent? No. Victor and Nataly can never be secure: they are always the prey of "alarms, throbbing suspicions, like those of old travellers through the haunted forest, where whispers have intensity of meaning, and unseeing we are seen, and unaware awaited." And this the more because having outraged convention, they wanted prominence in conventional society. Or, at least, Victor wanted it. He was not one to live except as a force radiant in the world of men: and the world of men cannot tolerate the flouting of its laws. There was in him from the beginning, therefore, a kink: in the first chapter, as an Australian specialist noted, he shows the symptoms of lesion of the brain, and Meredith arrived at this by the instinct of genius: for the book ends with Victor having lost his reason. His wife and daughter are the chief victims of his double weakness. They were all the victims of their inability to face the falsehood of their position.

This is the first case to which Meredith points: the second is founded on an old story, a story much older than Diana's. It was the story of the third Lord Peterborough, who, after fighting in the Spanish war in Queen Anne's time, was afterwards privately married to the singer, Anastasia Robinson. But the characteristics were those of Lord Cardigan, who led the Light Brigade at Balaclava and of whom Meredith very often heard from Maxse. Lord Ormont was described as "our general of cavalry, whose charge at the head of fifteen wounded horses in the last great battle shattered the enemy's right wing, and gave us the victory." Lord Cardigan had married Miss Adeline de Horsey at Gibraltar in 1858.

Lord Ormont's mistake was to sacrifice his wife to

his outraged pride and his grievance against his country. Having come back with her from travels abroad, he omits to make it clear that he has married her. If he gives in to her wish to be given his position in the English social world, he must make friends with people in England, and this he will not do. Dissatisfied at not being given the social rights of a wife, Aminta Ormont gradually falls in love with his secretary, Weyburn, and goes off with him to found an international school near Berne. Then, and then only, Lord Ormont realises what love owes her. Egoist till that moment, he then in grief loves with an unselfishness that forgives. The news comes to him indeed at the moment that he was telling his sister that he had decided to give in to the wishes of his wife. In the moment when he is seeking to make amends, he learns from a letter that it is too late.

" 'She's cool,' Lady Charlotte said: . . . 'will she be expecting you to answer, Rowsley?' "

" 'Will that forked tongue cease hissing!' he shouted, in the agony of a strong man convulsed both to render and conceal the terrible, shameful, unexampled gust of tears."

Meanwhile the lovers were happy. They had escaped not for self-indulgence, but for service, and unlike Victor Radnor, they recognised that the world must have its standards, and that if it were hostile, they were not to blame it. They must try and make amends to it: they had offended good citizenship: they must not do it publicly, not insolently: still less, luxuriously.

The end of the story is finely conceived, and takes

us back to the days of *The Ordeal*. In later years Lord Ormont, travelling by chance through Berne, came upon the school. He visited it. He held their futures in his hand. But so complete was his own sense of shortcoming, so thorough therefore his forgiveness, that far from denouncing the master and mistress, he sent his nephew to their school. Such was the ripe fruit of Meredith's reflections on his relations with his first wife, and all that it meant to his brain about the relation of man to woman.

§ 5

Meredith's third and last novel on marriage was the completion of a work begun years before and laid by. In it there is a portrait of Robert Louis Stevenson as Gower Woodseer, and of Shelley's Trelawney as the Old Buccaneer. In this case, the theme is a comparatively simple one. Fleetwood treats his wife outrageously, and rouses her to indignant coldness. His outrageousness is neither more nor less than a fanatical pride in his absolute choice and in his sense of right. Typical of him is the letter with which he arranges with his bride's uncle the date of his marriage:

"MY LORD: I drive to your church door on the fifteenth of the month at ten a.m. to keep my appointment with Miss C. J. Kirby, if I do not blunder the initials.

Your Lordship's obedient servant, FLEETWOOD."

His particular vanity was that he always kept his word, and this was an example of it. His wife, on the other hand, had a fine appreciation of love, a fine conception of constancy. With a rugged nature, firm in its grasp of the great truths, she could have no patience with her husband's final love, a love which grew out of conscience awakened subtly out of pride; a nature craving for confession and forgiveness, a nature deformed by wrong-doing and anxious for the graces of life, heeds sometimes the formalities of religion before it can attain to the higher task of facing things as they are. If he could have confessed to her and sought her forgiveness direct as he should have done, she would have accepted the toil of reforming him. "She would have held hot iron to the rabid wound, and come to a love of the rescued sufferer."

But here, as elsewhere, Meredith has no mercy for the creature most in need of it, the sinner too weak to attain his own repentance unaided. A scrutiny so sensitive as to be remorseless laid ever barer the pride and sentimentality of men. Taking his characters from life, when he knew them by heart he related them in every case to his experience of himself. Fitting his life into the scheme of things, he chastised every weakness of men in order that in himself he might be purified of them. His earnestness, his elevation, his austerity —these had now mastered his character, and he had become a master of the spiritual life. But he still kept his tenderness for woman, and devoted his genius to championship of the sex on which, in the most intimate relation of life, the intensity of his temperament, and the very brilliance of his genius, drove him to inflict suffering. His three last novels are his act of reparation for the sacrifice that his devotion to his work had demanded of his wives. The saint has inflicted his sacrifice upon his family before he begins his special career. Meredith had tried to be both a husband and a spiritual genius. He discovered, first, that in his love of women he had been something of an egoist, and that the raptures of falling in love safeguard nothing: that in fact they are perilous. With him, it is never the brilliant type of hero who brings true happiness to women: or at least not in the later novels. It is the Wentworth, the Redworth, the Whitford, the Merthyr Powys, the Seymour Austin, the Owain Wythan; it is even the secretary and schoolmaster, as against the cavalry officer; it is always a type very different from Meredith himself. In fact, the possession of heroic gifts tends to make men egoists, in any case. And if they dedicate these heroic gifts to a philosophic or a spiritual end, they are all the more unsatisfactory as companions: this thought was very clear to Meredith in his old age.

> Seen, too clear and historic within us, our sins of omission
>   Frown when the Autumn days strip us all ruthlessly bare.
> They of our mortal diseases find never healing physician;
>   Errors they of the soul, past the one hope to repair.
> Sunshine might we have been unto seed under soil, or have scattered
>   Seed to ascendant suns brighter than any that shone[1].

[1] *Poems*, "The Main Regret."

Sympathy failed with both his wives and his sons for this very reason, that the grandeur of genius has a claim over its possessions which, as we saw in the case of Meredith's first wife, he will defend at any cost either to himself or to anyone else. In any case, the very career by which a man provides for his wife and children will develop in him interests and capacities they can rarely share with him. And when Meredith realised that his own part in life inevitably caused a particular suffering to the relatives to whom he was indebted for his intensest joy and for whom he had been with a supreme ardour the husband and lover, his inner consciousness, working with his elevated ethics in the subtlest interaction and freshened by direct and ever-renewed contact with nature, evolved the poems and novels before and after the death of his second wife.

And this the more because even in his latest age he kept undimmed the mood of rapture. In *One of Our Conquerors* and *The Amazing Marriage* there are masterpieces in impassioned description of morning in the Alps. When we read that "air became wine that raised the breast high to breathe it": that "it seemed that the heights fronted East to eye the interflooding of colours": that "bounding waters took the leap in silvery radiance to gloom": that "the heights and dark-banded valleys were like night and morning taking hands down the sweep of their rivers": when we read of livid peaks and folds of pine wood and a dazzling pinnacle rising over high pastures—so one sees the Cimone della Pala from Paneveggio or the

Langkofl from St. Ulrich—as being "tranced, but all motion to the heart in the eye: a splendid image of striving up to crowned victory": we realise the poetic power that survived to be turned now to account by nature, now to search the inner workings of heart and mind, now to explain London, or the relation of Britain to Europe. It seemed that nothing in contemporary life escaped Meredith's attention. And as he scented the briar, the deliciousness of youth was amorous in him still:

> O briar-scents, on yon wet wing
> Of warm South-west wind brushing by,
> You mind me of the sweetest thing
> That ever mingled frank and shy:
> When she and I, by love enticed,
> Beneath the orchard-apples met,
> In equal halves a ripe one sliced,
> And smelt the juices ere we ate.
>
> That apple of the briar-scent,
> Among our lost in England now,
> Was green of rind, and redolent
> Of sweetness as a milking cow.
> The briar gives it back, well nigh
> The damsel with her teeth on it;
> Her twinkle between frank and shy,
> My thirst to bite where she had bit.[1]

---

[1] *Poems*, "Breath of the Briar."

§ 6

But one cannot read either poems or novels without recognising first that they become more complex, more crowded, and more disordered. "A quibble was to him the fatal Cleopatra for which he lost the world and was content to lose it." So Johnson wrote of Shakespeare, and it becomes truer and truer of Meredith. He becomes less and less occupied in weaving a pattern, more and more fascinated with tangling up the fringes of thought. At the same time, he was becoming more and more of a tease; his intensity of life, his electrical restlessness became more irresponsible, more arbitrary. He preached patience, because after all it is one great lesson of nature. But he did not practise it. And in his novels he began to admit incidents that were highly improbable, or even frankly absurd. The conversation in the water in *Lord Ormont*, the arbitrariness of Fleetwood, the amazing appearance of the baby born of The Amazing Marriage, and the fact that Fleetwood was allowed to enter a monastery when his moral obligation was to return to his wife, show that Meredith was growing loose in his grip of facts. Criticism apparently made him more aware of this, for an edition of *The Amazing Marriage* in the Widener Library at Harvard accounts for the appearance of the baby. According to this, before Fleetwood left his bride at the Royal Sovereign, "He pointed to an upper window, seemed to be issuing directions. Kit nodded; he understood it, whatever it was. You might have said, a pair of burglars." After leaving her, Fleetwood recalled that still "she had a look, a strange look, the look of a witch stripped of her spells, and the more human, the more ensnaring. She had caught him, but she was at his mercy. That was a thought to cast another out."

And again that: "The drive from Canleys to the Sovereign could be done by good pacers in an hour and a half, little more, with Ines and the stables ready, and some astonishment in a certain unseen chamber. Fleetwood chuckled at a vision of romantic devilry, perfectly legitimate too. Something, more to inflict, than enjoy, was due to him."[1] Meredith's mind had begun at this time to show more acutely a likeness to his nervous malady. He had lived too eagerly, too fully, too arduously. The gymnastic of mind alternating with violent physical exercise, the flood of imagination pouring through the life of passion, the sensitiveness which goaded him to cruelty, the very force of will which kept him in these circumstances so faithful to an austere ethic; and with these the not infrequent bursts of anger, developed through his whole nervous system the same disorder which showed itself

[1] On page 249 of this edition, after the words "at the supper table," in second paragraph, "and the next day he sat," are deleted. Instead, the following are inserted, "Though it is admitted he left the Ballroom at night. But the next day he was certainly in his place (among the Peers, and voted against the Government)."

Likewise it is made clear that he went into no regular monastery, for on page 550, at the head, after the first word "Feltre," one reads: "Or some say, and so it may truly be, it was an amateur monastery, established by him down among his Welsh mountains, in which he served as a simple brother without any authority over the priests or what not he paid to act as his superiors. Monk of some sort he would be."

in his ataxy. His digestion had always been poor. And in 1892 he began to suffer the tortures of stone in the bladder.

On June 20 of that year he walked into a house in Wimpole Street belonging to the leading surgeon of the day, Mr. Buckston Browne: and with the alarming suddenness of his ataxy threw himself into a chair. "Mr. Browne, I am a writer," he began. In answer, the great surgeon, opening a bookcase straight in front of him, showed a complete edition of his works.

The two men became great friends. In the writer in whom the scientist had found the poet of evolution, giving the beauty of literature to the conception of Darwin, and wedding romance to science, the surgeon now found a man whose courage conquered his phenomenal sensitiveness. Mr. Buckston Browne had no need to waste his time in combating whims and fancies. The great surgeon found his patient, whatever his state of health, always cheerful and sometimes rollicking. And at the end he said, "I do not remember a single frown."

Meredith returned the appreciation of the surgeon with all the warmth of his nature. The next book, *Lord Ormont*, was "gratefully inscribed" to Mr. Buckston Browne. "No victim of sharp instruments," wrote Meredith, "could be in skilfuller or kinder hands ... he is the ablest as well as one of the best of men." He found in Mr. Buckston Browne also a mind thoroughly congenial, because open and fearless, and one that never ignored the impulses of a heart unusually generous and warm. Three times Mr. Buckston Browne operated on Meredith: for from now on, the poet was an invalid. And through all this time friendship and appreciation deepened. Few guests were more welcome at Box Hill than the great surgeon, the wife he adored, or his charming daughter. To her he wrote on Feb. 20, 1899, "Wee violets are modest flowers, but not the Queenly Rose is surer of a welcome when she appears. So pray withhold acknowledgments of our transmission to you, and we shall be flattered the more by knowing you pleased, *of course*."[1]

---

[1] From an unpublished letter. *Letters*.

XIII

SOME LATER FRIENDS

§ 1

A FRIEND of Meredith's who shared not a little with Mr. Buckston Browne was Dr. Plimmer. Dr. Plimmer was a Fellow of the Royal Society. He had married a widow who already had three children. Mrs. Plimmer had been born at the mouth of the Elbe. She had not only a knowledge of the literature, the music and traditions of her native country; she had also the great heart, the understanding of men, the need of providing creature-comforts for them which mark the best German women. Meredith took to her as well as to her husband. With the one he threw all his enthusiasm into the exchange of ideas, in the other he relished the sweetness and goodness of a woman. "A kind heart and a sympathetic soul," he often said to her, "are worth more than the brightest intellect."

Mrs. Plimmer gave the generosity of her admiration to the great genius. How delightful it would be, she thought, to live in the house which he had shared with Rossetti and Swinburne in Cheyne Walk. "We have bought it," at last she announced. "Have you?" was his only comment, which like his "Did you?" or "Can't you?" was not a sign of approval. He had no pleasant memories of it, and though she often pressed him to go and visit it, she asked in vain.

SOME LATER FRIENDS

Meredith wrote often both to Dr. Plimmer and to his wife. He shared with them a favourite jest which referred to a friend who was deeply interested in Frau Cosima Wagner. Meredith had met Frau Cosima as well as her famous husband, and she was a personality worthy of his attention. The daughter of Countess Marie d'Agoult and Liszt, her magnetic personality, her clear profile, her noble gestures, her way of moving as though on clouds, her radiance, contrasted with the dissatisfied expression and the sharp strident voice of *Der Meister*. Yet it was to him that she was devoted, for him she lived and strove. After his death in 1883, she looked upon herself as the vehicle through which he was manifested to the world.

It was not until 1887 that, recovering from the blow, she assumed dominance at Wahnfried and Bayreuth. She radiated, she inspired, but she also commanded absolute devotion to the cause. At one moment she was all woman and all French, voice and smile aloof and yet alluring; at another, her fierce will would be enforcing unquestioning discipline in the style of a Prussian general, and all from the scene-shifter to the great stars would stand in awe at her displeasure. Richter, van Rooy, and lovely Rosa Sucher, all vied with one another to win a smile from her. Many came often to her house, but she was intimate with none except Countess Marie Wolkenstein who, as Countess Schleinitz, had persuaded the Emperor William I to come to Bayreuth in 1876 to inaugurate the *Festspiele*.

The memory of Frau Cosima delighted Meredith,

and since Dr. Plimmer was a musician, Meredith loved when with him to speak of her: it was with a quite special gusto he referred to the devotion to her given by their common friend, Frederick Jameson, who had suggested that Meredith should resume *The Amazing Marriage* and to whom, when it was finished, it was inscribed. Jameson was an excellent musician, a devoted Wagnerian and had translated part of the *Niebelungen Ring*. He used to take sun-baths in Tyrol: and Meredith delighted in the idea that in that condition he might attract the attention of Wagner's ghost. Frau Cosima took him at one time for a reincarnation of Wagner, and his position with her became rather involved. But Meredith had no qualms for him, knowing him to have "legal assistance and the most innocent of souls."[1]

Mrs. Plimmer's son played the violoncello and from that Meredith named him. His mother he called after a verandah that she built to her house in St. John's Wood. He addresses his letters to her: "Dearest Verandah." And he was charmed to go to their house to hear music, and summed up, in a little doggerel verse like those he used to make for Hardman:

> To Plimmer, Verandah and Cello,
> > Who shine as the green of the land,
> The thanks of a crippled old fellow,
> > Though why one so lost in the yellow
> Is noticed, he can't understand.

Meredith was not fond of taking presents. He would

[1] Unpublished letters supply the remainder of this material.

accept only if they were things he liked to have, and only if given by people who could afford to give them. But Mrs. Plimmer had the knack of giving things to him, and his letters to her are full of joking gratitude. In 1899 he had been "thrilled and alarmed by the arrival of a case of wine." "Remember," he added, "that it is ingratitude stirred in me by further gifts, but you will be honourable." When she sent him a box of apples, he wrote to her husband that their cheeks encouraged him to ruddiness. When, in 1908, she sent him a lamp for his bedside, he wrote:

"Why will our Verandah paint munificence which is of its nature golden? And why pile St. John's Wood on wooded Box Hill? I am overdone with gratitude. The light works excellently. I marvel at the opportuneness of the gift just when I had raised the wish for it. Let me hear how things go with the Frankfurt scheme. It concerns all who love you. Remind the doctor of my existence and accept from me all that the years can condense into assurances of affection."

"Dearest Verandah," he wrote on the shortest day of 1904, "You will be astonished to hear that there was not an idea in my dull brain that the splendid rug you placed on my knees was another of your presents. I thought it was meant to keep me warm while you were with me, and after you had gone I called aloud to have it sent after you."

On Dec. 19, 1906, he wrote:
"Dearest Verandah,

"Don't think of coming in this weather. Your repeated presents have such an effect on gratitude that the delirious old wretch has nought but a gurgle in his throat. I am reminded of your two pots of caviare, left before you left us for Asia and Africa,—a terrible story—who sold them to you should be prosecuted."

Three months later he was again addressing his "dear and most serviceable Verandah" as a cornucopia. "I have the feeling that I stand in a shower of fruits," he wrote. "No more or you lead me to think myself favoured by a protecting planet."

And again, just before his death, he sends thanks through his Verandah to her Cello. "Tell Robin that the gift of winter gloves was worth all the showers of cornucopia under which I have been smothered—excepting the grand music."

But when Mrs. Plimmer brought him down a translation of Montaigne, he refused it in the same uncompromising tone as he refused Lady Danesfort's offer of Norwegian egg-spoons. "I do not care for translations," was all he said, and as soon as he saw Mrs. Plimmer moving, he handed the book to his nurse to wrap up for the giver to take back.

For Dr. Plimmer he felt not only affection but admiration. "Give my love," he wrote once, "to the champion of the cause of science and humanity, to whom thousands are looking." And they thoroughly enjoyed the exchange of fiendish teasing with one another. With them all Meredith was thoroughly at home, and allowed himself to relax. He talked to them as he talked to Sir James Barrie or his daughter: the letters show no trace of the strained intellectualism in which he expressed himself to Mlle. de Longueuil, and he enjoyed the relaxation. "I like to be alone with the family," he said.

§ 2

When *The Amazing Marriage* was published in 1895, its author noticed one review that particularly pleased him. It appeared in the *Pall Mall Gazette*, in a column called "The Wares of Autolycus," which often attracted his attention.[1] "Poetry is the conspicuous secret of the book," it said. "As in this great book, so in life, poetry is not hidden. It is unrevealed. And there are mystics who aver that all the now unrevealed secrets of this human life are obvious things that we daily and ignorantly use—things that we know, yet do not recognise." The review compared Carinthia with Shakespeare's Helena: it called her the "new Helena." An undaunted spirit, Carinthia claimed the environment of wind and cloud which Meredith gave her, and though the book was crowded with images wild as the flying clouds, this wildness was made to serve the writer's purpose, so that as a final result the readers were awakened, and compelled to another rate, and another way, of thinking them their own, in a stress of quickening surprise, which made them intimate with nature. "Always secret, always accessible, always present, nature is the simplest thing in the most intimate book in the world."

Meredith could not resist the mingling of prose of

[1] Nov. 29, 1895.

such distinction with an appreciation so intimately discriminating. Here was a spirit after his own heart. And this spirit was the spirit of a woman: a woman whom, when poets met her, they recognised as exquisite. "Her presence," said Mr. Le Gallienne, "radiated a peculiarly lovely serenity, like a twilight gay with stars."[1]

Around the name of Alice Meynell is the finest aroma. There was in all she wrote such finish and such fineness, her touch was so delicate and firm, that she will live among our classic essayists, and among her poems were some praised by Ruskin and the highest. "One of the most charming things that a writer of English can achieve is the repayment of the united teaching by linking their results so exquisitely in his own practice that the words of the two schools shall be made to meet each other with a surprise and delight that shall prove them at once gayer strangers and sweeter companions than the world knew they were." So she wrote of the mingling of Saxon and Latin in our language, and this charm marked her own style. A sister of Lady Butler who painted "The Roll Call," she was married to Mr. Wilfrid Meynell. Sargent has drawn her. She was a creature of pathos and delight. There was longing in her looks and her features were lovely; a fine kindness and a fine distinction marked her personality. Painted by Amy Rymer, she showed to Meredith something sepulchral in pathos, "eyes looking out of the underworld, breathing of gravemould," but this was not herself. Herbert Trench

[1] *The Romantic Nineties.*

wrote of her in a delightful poem that she was, as it were, woven of rapture.[1]

Of her article on Duse in the *Pall Mall Gazette*, Meredith had said, before he met her, that it reached the high-water mark of the literary criticism of our time. He detected in it what he had noticed in her poems, "an exquisite play upon the finer chords, quite her own." Clear, compact and pregnant with rare thought, they attracted yet more by the modesty of their style. "The surprise coming on us from their combined grace of manner and sanity of thought is like one's dream of what the recognition of a new truth would be . . . she achieves the literary miracle of subordinating compressed choice language to grace of movement." He counted that she would one day rank as one of the great Englishwomen of letters.

Such were his views of her work before he had secured a meeting with her. She herself more than answered his hopes. Responsive as ever to the presence of women, at the age of sixty-eight, crippled by locomotor ataxia, he retained the ardour and the enthusiasm which found their rapturous expression in his poems of love. The homage of this he offered to Mrs. Meynell in the spring of 1896. "I shall teach you nothing that can be new to such a mind as yours," he wrote her, "but I shall be leaven to your deeper thoughts of earth and life." By April she had become the most absorbing of his friends, and a letter he wrote to her while staying with Lady Butler in the Constable's Tower at Dover Castle tells of his delight in silent

[1] *Letters of George Meredith to Alice Meynell.*

communion with her. "I think of you gladly as with your sister, drawing strength from sea-breezes, out of the cage of brick, a visible universe about you, and those winged eyes of yours abroad in it. You write of your not being a talker. I can find the substance I want in your silences, and can converse with them. Your plea in excuse makes me ashamed of my prattle. Let me tell you that my mind is not always with my tongue in the act. I do it for the sake of sociability, and I am well disposed either to listen or to worship the modest lips that have such golden reserves."[1]

By June he was addressing her as his "dearest friend," and had found a symbol for her in an iris in his garden, golden at the heart, which he named after her, Alicia Cærulea. He wrote her a series of sonnets, to be called "The Lady of the Time"; these, however, like so many other of the vessels of the love and beauty in him, were in an after-rage destroyed: for she had demanded the return of a handkerchief which he had placed beside his heart. The sonnet that survives compares her to the Iris:

> A stately flower in my garden grows,
> Whose colour is the dawn-sky's maiden blue;
> The loveliest to my lady's thinking, too.
> And when the Lord of June bids her disclose
> Her very heart, all bashfully she throws
> An inner petal o'er the orange hue,
> As one last plea; submitting to his view,
> Yet virginally majestic while he glows.

[1] *Letters of George Meredith to Alice Meynell.*

> For reasons known to us we give the name
> Alicia Cærulea to that flower,
> Sweet as the Sea-born borne on the sea-wave:
> That Innocent in shame where there is no shame;
> That proud Reluctant; that fair slave of power,
> Who conquers most when she is most the slave.

After 1900 the letters grow rarer, and occasionally admiration is exchanged for criticism. The lady is blamed for being hard on Gibbon. Although at the very last he wrote to Mrs. Meynell that his religion of life was always to be cheerful, gloom and loneliness often assailed him. The death of Admiral Maxse was the hardest blow, shaking his stoic philosophy. "Friends are the leaves of the tree of life," he wrote, "and I am getting bare, fit only for cutting down."[1]

But apart from this warm personal relation with Alice Meynell, the letters are rich in appreciations of the winds and sky; and they have pronouncements on literature which cannot be overlooked. He felt the truth of the Brownings' mutual passion so strongly that not even the "tropical wildness of the amorous iterations" arrested him. "One sees the flower in each breast." When he published his "Napoleon," he sent it to her "so that you may be under no complimentary compulsion to incur the tedium of the journey hither and thither for the flashing visit,—though I so love to see you. If you find it goodish, you are the author. If otherwise, I am the culprit. Remember that is an Ode of History, which presents us with gross matter

---

[1] *Letters of George Meredith to Alice Meynell.*

and I must deal it out to be true to the subject. I have been tempted by the rhetorical—History's pitfall for the Muse. I have avoided this as much as I could even in the Portrait, where antithesis invited strongly and was not always to be shunned." And lastly, he disclaims the aphorisms of Sir Austin Feverel as expressions of his own mind. "These aphorisms came in the run of the pen, as dramatizings of the mind of the System-maker. I would not have owned to half a dozen of them."[1]

Sincere in all things, even to the point of brusqueness, he once gave a shock to Mrs. Meynell. When she talked of writing a book on London, he burst at her with the words "You could not do it. It is beyond you." Such words are not easy to accept, and it would not be surprising if Mrs. Meynell winced.

§ 3

There were three other ladies to whom Meredith was much attracted in his old age. There was first Mrs. Walter Palmer, a lovely young creature who had wealth through her marriage to one of the partners in the well-known Reading firm, a lady of culture who would take a *Schloss* at Bayreuth for the season,— "the round world's jewel." He called her "Queen Jean" and there was the warmest tone in Meredith's letters both to her and to her husband.

Then again there was the Duchess of Rutland (Lady Granby as she was then) who drew exquisite portraits

[1] *Letters of George Meredith to Alice Meynell.*

of women he admired, and one of himself. She drew Lady Ulrica Baring, Lady Lytton ("the sweetest of unfolding wild-rose buds"), her own daughter Lady Marjorie Manners and Lady Cromer. "With all the portraits of beautiful women from your hand," Meredith wrote to her, "there is more than the beauty. *On y voit l'âme dans les traits.*" And he was delighted with a letter that Lady Diana Duff-Cooper wrote to him a year before his death. "It showed the heart in the hand of the writer."[1]

He had in those later years another great new friend. A daughter of a Yorkshire Peer, this young lady was an intellectual, as well as a youthful beauty. Meredith delighted in her, and wrote her brilliant letters, like those he had sent to Mlle. de Longueuil. He warned her very carefully against the egoism of the idealist. Just as he had said in *The Ordeal* that love of a lord was a form of self-love, so now he gives a warning against people looking at a flattering mirror of themselves in others. "We set up an ideal of the cherished object, we try our friends and the world by the standards we have raised within, supported by pride, obscured by the passions. But if we determine to know ourselves, we see that it has been open to us all along, that in fact we did but would not know, from having such an adoration of the ideal creature erected and painted by us."[2]

The letters cover almost the same ground as those he had sent to his French friend. The story of the errant wife returning is repeated, and we hear even

[1] *Letters.*   [2] *Letters.*

that the old lady who said, "What are the man's family making such a fuss about? My son only had her for a fortnight," was an old Lady Vivian. Did his friend understand love? She had been adored by a prominent prelate, whom she accepted and afterwards jilted. Later in life she married a member of a well-known family and bore him six daughters. She was heard to say after this that she had "warmed both hands beside the fire of life."

Meredith had intuitions as to her temperament. She had known, she must have known, something about love, but she did not confide it in him. He thought her capable of much liking, of warm liking, even wildish, but not passion. "Passion," he wrote to his daughter-in-law, "is noble strength on fire." And this he gave as the reason why his friend did not admire Diana. To do that, one should be more like a spinster of sixty whom he had once asked what she wanted from poetry. Turning her head, she shouted over her shoulder, "Passion."[1]

If this lady could have understood that, he would have admired her even more:

> My Lady has Diana's brow,
> Diana's deer-like step is hers;
> A goddess she by every sign,
> Then wherefore is she not divine?
> She has no ears for lovers' vows,
> For lovers' vows she has no ears.

It was all very well to talk of Goethe: to go to India

[1] *Letters.*

for the Delhi Durbar: to have the sanest views of politics and men: to understand the best English prose. But it was much better to have one's own happiness depending on another:

> Ask, is love divine,
> Voices all are, ay.
> Question for the sign,
> There's a common sigh.
> Would we, through our years,
> Love forgo,
> Quit of scars and tears?
> Ah but no, no, no!

And this is the thought that came also to him as he looked at nature in the serene summer morning:

> We see in mould the rose unfold,
> The soul through blood and tears.

But that, it seemed, was something more than he expected this brilliant young person to understand.[1]

§ 4

Admiral Maxse, until 1901, was alive, was seen, was loved. But his influence on Meredith had lessened. He and all his four children had allied themselves to the Die-hards, and Meredith, under the influence of Lord Morley and Lord Haldane, was certainly not becoming less of a Radical. Speaking of himself always as a Celt and not a Saxon, his sympathy went

[1] *Letters. Poems*, "Fragment."

fully to Ireland. In 1887 he had written on Home Rule in the *Fortnightly* and this article pleaded more urgently for Ireland than he had done in the manuscript lying for years beside him which, as *Celt and Saxon*, was published after his death. He had long known Mrs. O'Shea (from whose bedroom Parnell escaped down a rain-pipe), and Dillon made much of him. He was the one great writer who threw himself into Ireland's cause, and with Ireland he gulped down the Church of her people.

Something of an imperialist, he was ruthless on jingoism. In 1896 he wrote for the *Daily Chronicle* a sonnet on the Jameson raid: it was called "The Warning."

We have seen mighty men ballooning high,
And in another moment bump the ground.
He falls; and in his measurement is found
To count some inches o'er the common fry.
'Twas not enough to send him climbing sky,
Yet 'twas enough above his fellows crowned,
Had he less panted. Let his faithful hound
Bark at detractors. He may walk or lie.

Concerns it most ourselves, who with our gas—
This little Isle's insatiable greed
For Continents—filled to inflation burst.
So do ripe nations into squalor pass,
When, driven as herds by their old pirate thirst,
They scorn the brain's wild search for virtuous light.

He was with the Liberals in their criticism of the politics which led on to the Boer war. He protested up to the end against British excesses, and as Mr. Frank Harris has noted, persisted all through that there were faults on both sides. A letter to the papers pleaded for mercy to Kritzinger when the war was over; but with his keenness for soldiers, and all their business, Meredith watched the exploits of the British army with intense interest. No one who listened to his talk of how Englishmen were fighting imagined him anything but a patriot. It wrung his heart that they should fall in a war not unquestionably necessary.[1]

He had indeed taken up from Maxse one idea. It was the need of training the people for military service. He was heart and soul for conscription, as he was for a national training in boxing. Foreseeing a contest with Germany, he thought it vitally necessary that England should in no way be taken by surprise. Maxse's ideas were all passed on to Lord Haldane.

"I came to know him soon after I entered Parliament," wrote Lord Haldane, "and he was very good to me, inviting me to come and dine with him whenever I pleased and bring someone. I was accompanied on one occasion by Asquith, on another by Grey, on a third by John Dillon, on a fourth by Lloyd George, on a fifth by Lord French. On the latter occasion the distinguished general and the distinguished author got into a violent controversy about the disposition of troops at the battle of Magenta—Meredith certain that he knew, and French equally certain that he was quite ignorant. At last, French having

[1] Frank Harris, *Contemporary Portraits*.

said that no one with any military knowledge could have imagined that at that stage a whole division could have been brought up to the point which Meredith thought, Meredith retorted, 'General, I have observed that Cavalry leaders however distinguished are bad judges of the operations of mixed troops.'" At this point Lord Haldane hastily ordered the motor, and took the General back to Aldershot.

On another occasion Lord Haldane was staying at Durdans, and Lord Rosebery asked him whether there was anywhere he would like to drive. Haldane asked whether Rosebery would drive over to meet Meredith. When they got to Box Hill, they were told that he was walking in the wood. "We went there and came upon him," wrote Lord Haldane, "and I made two great men known. But I never saw two great personalities become suddenly and without reason so antipathetic to each other in so short a time. Ever after that Rosebery and Meredith were most critical of each other in their conversation with me."

Meredith stayed with Haldane both in London and at Cloan. As he waited for the train on the station at Auchterarder, amazed railwaymen listened to a thunderous descant on the scheme of the universe. Meredith and the old Presbyterian minister at Cloan delighted in one another; as Meredith gave himself up to his exuberance, the minister would smile and pat him on the arm with the words: "Ye're still but a laddie."[1]

[1] Lord Haldane's unpublished papers.

§ 5

Mr. Frank Harris was not the least of Meredith's admirers. The two were invited to dine together in Elvaston Place, and conversation went on until late in the night. In the morning his hostess pointed out that for once he had met a talker who outdid him in loquacity; his answer rolled off his tongue:

"But I was sober, my dear."

Mr. Harris was a great friend of Oscar Wilde who was himself a discriminating appraiser of Meredith's brilliance. No one who lived in England in the early 'nineties could ignore Wilde. Arriving at Oxford while Ruskin was a professor there, this unctuous, erudite and altogether elaborate young man immediately attracted question, and in some cases awoke emotion. The elderly Pater, who was generally so tranquil and so silent, had once knelt, white with passion, and kissed his hand. And Wilde had made an epigram: "One resists everything except temptation."

When he was in Paris, this young man met everybody from Victor Hugo to Verlaine and M. Bourget. In London, he showed that he had a genius for pose. Of philosophy he had none, and he wanted none. His aim was to be an æsthete: to use his intellect to give a novel and delicious outline to rare experiences, and so to express himself as to make an exquisite sensation. He created the world of *Patience*, where not only young women but young men would "cling passionately to one another and think of faint lilies." And at afternoon parties the tea grew cold while the guests admired the form and pattern of their cups. "He seldom had very much to say," M. Maurois has written, "but he said it with such grace and charm."[1]

Now and again he did have something to say. For, when all is said, Wilde was not only a poseur but a genius. He said some admirable things in literary criticism. He had written in the *Fortnightly* in 1891 that Meredith was an incomparable artist: "To him belongs philosophy in fiction. His people not merely live, but they live in thought. One can see them from myriad points of view. They are suggestive. There is soul in them and around them. They are interpretive and symbolic. And he who made them, those wonderful quickly moving figures, made them for his own pleasure, and has never asked the public what they wanted, has never cared to know what they wanted, has never allowed the public to dictate to him or to influence him, in any way, but has gone on intensifying his own personality and producing his own individual work. At first none came to him. That did not matter. Then the few came to him. That did not change him. The many have come now. He is still the same. He is an incomparable novelist." Of his style Wilde had already written: "Meredith had planted round his garden a hedge full of thorns and red with wonderful roses."[2]

Such a novelist could not but meet such a critic. They were invited together to stay with the Walter Palmers at Reading in a large house-party, and Mrs.

[1] André Maurois, *Etudes Anglaises*.
[2] *Nineteenth Century*, Jan., 1889.

Jopling-Rowe, who was there also, had a photograph in which the two men appeared. Meredith of course appreciated Wilde's brilliance: but between the figure of the one, now puffed and sensual, and the austere beauty of the other's face lined with its silver hair, there was a contrast which meant opposing attitudes towards life. The ideal of the one was experience: of the other it was high strenuousness.[1]

When Wilde's disaster came, there were, in spite of *Punch*, not a few intellectuals who looked upon his sentence as brutal. Enquiries were made, and it was found that the Government of the time was disposed to take into account the judgment of the intellectuals of England, whatever that might be. Mr. Frank Harris took up Wilde's case. He found that if Meredith (now Tennyson's successor as head of the Society of Authors) and a few others would address the Government in the prisoner's favour, his sentence might be remitted. Meredith, however, peremptorily refused. The issue seemed to him a central one in life. And Meredith was as inexorable as in the case of his first wife. "Abnormal sensuality in a leader of men," he said, "should be punished with severity: all greatness is based on morality." But if, at that period, the immorality had been a woman's, and this woman had been beautiful or witty, his judgment would perhaps have been more merciful.[2]

---

[1] Louisa Jopling-Rowe, *Memoirs*. S. M. Ellis, *George Meredith*.
[2] Frank Harris, *Contemporary Portraits*.

§ 6

After the death of his second wife, Meredith found his closest companion in his daughter. He delighted in seeing her grow up, and come out into the world. And the world was gracious to her. All the details of her movements interested him. But not long after she had grown up she married Mr. Henry Parkman Sturgis, a widower of American parentage who lived at Givons Grove near Leatherhead. This was in 1894. His son had already in 1892 married Miss Margaret Elliot, the daughter of his friend, Mrs. Lewin, of Parkhurst on Leith Hill. "The girl is accomplished and charming," he wrote to Chapman.[1]

The departure of his son and daughter from Box Hill threw Meredith back more and more into the company of his servants, to whose society he had never been insensible. The choicest of his epigrams and the most opulent of his fancies descended upon their heads like rain upon the earth.

If he wanted his housemaid to take away an empty wine-bottle, he would address this sort of speech to her:

"Mary, you behold here a body from which the soul has departed. A body without a soul! Mark it there empty and useless, of no value to gods or men. Once full of genial fire, golden warmth for heart and brain, alive with inspiring ichor, Hymettean fount of noble talk and soaring thought, the elixir of wit, making of man's dull brain a thing of magic and

[1] Unpublished letter.

dreams, lifting our dull mortality into the highest heaven of invention! But behold it now, a hollow echoing shell, a forlorn cadaver, its divine life all poured out of it, no laughter in it, no wisdom, no human kindness in it, any more forever. What shall be done with it, Mary? A body from which the soul is departed. What do we do with such? What is there to be done, but to bury it out of sight of gods and men, mournful reminder of feasts that are at end and dimming candles. Mary, remove the bottle."[1]

He was never unconscious of servants, and in addressing the cook he would begin a sentence on the spices of Arabia that went through equally many involutions of gorgeousness, eloquence and congestion. And the mystified woman could only ask "What does the master mean?" And Cole, the gardener, would reply, "He means put less pepper in the soup, you fool." Like other lovers of Meredith, he saw something perfectly practical in the sentences that to others were insoluble. Cole was Meredith's stand-by from 1878 to the arrival of his nurse, Bessy Nicholls. The great man gave him several of his books and wrote in one, "A good servant cancels the name of master." Cole, knowing his master's friends, was his defence against the importunate. No one who lived in close association with George Meredith could be immune from his bursts of anger, but Cole stayed with him till the end and was not ignored. "I have something of a great power and I must use it: I can put a glass to men's chests, and see what is working

[1] R. Le Gallienne, *The Romantic Nineties*.

inside." Such was the novelist's account of himself to his gardener.

The gardener never quite forgave another being put in his place. But Bessy Nicholls was also a devoted attendant, and did much to make his last crippled years endurable. To each, Meredith gave as a legacy manuscripts of his novels.

Cole's own comment on their relation was: "There warn't a happier master and man in the whole kingdom."

XIV

THE LAST FEW YEARS

§ 1

THE 'nineties saw Meredith set firmly in a place supreme in literary England. In 1892 he had been, as we saw, elected to succeed Tennyson as President of the Society of Authors, and St. Andrews gave him her LL.D. In 1899 he was offered an honorary doctorate at Oxford, but he was too frail to attend the Encænia. In 1902 he became Vice-President of the London Library. He was offered also a baronetcy, but, thinking it unsuitable, he declined it. In 1905 the Royal Society of Literature gave him its gold medal and Edward VII admitted him to the Order of Merit. The King offered to receive him and bestow the decoration privately, but even this was too much. His leg had been broken that year, and, from that time on, he could move only in a chair. However, the King broke a precedent to send his private secretary, Lord Stamfordham, to invest him with it at Box Hill: and later sent the painter Strang to make a portrait of him to hang at Windsor.[1]

Meredith was far from insensible to these attentions. But nothing could induce him to take his literary eminence too seriously. He had schooled himself so

[1] M. Sturge Gretton, "George Meredith," *The Times*, Feb. 12, 1928.

well in earlier years against adverse criticism that fame, when it enveloped him, was a luxury to which, also, he was comparatively indifferent. No one could fail to notice the number of distinguished visitors who came to Box Hill in the last years of his life: and George Meredith could hardly fail to appreciate the position which enabled him to choose his friends amongst people the most delightful and distinguished. But he always found his friends among all classes, and to the end he continued to speak of the attentions of the great as a jest. He never referred to his decoration without insisting that the letters O.M. meant that he was an Old Man. "Royal Authority," he wrote to Mrs. Plimmer, "was not needed for that to be known." If Dr. Plimmer had congratulated him, either it was irony, "or else the Doctor is in glee because his King has patted appreciation of me on the back, necessarily showing that he wanted Majesty's confirmation of a wavering opinion."[1]

He was especially pleased, as we have seen, when his fame gave him the society of interesting women: and the portraits of some of them were placed above his mantelpiece, beside that of his wife. If a motor flashed a young friend down, it never failed to delight him, and he always enjoyed it when Lady Danesfort (who had been Mrs. Gordon and was then Mrs. Butcher) drove down to take him out for a drive herself. He loved speed in a car, which gave him the same exhilaration as a high wind. And he loved Lady Danesfort herself. "You were my friend, my dear,"

[1] Unpublished letter.

he used to say, "before the great British public (who never cared to read my books) asked what I eat for breakfast or what coloured ties I generally wear."[1]

He had a little joke about an Irish lady who went into a book-shop in Dublin to ask for *The Ordination of Peter Peverel* by a writer whose name she could not remember. When the shopman failed to identify it, she inquired for another by the same author. To those, however, who really studied and cared for him, he gave the best of himself.[2] He carefully discussed with Mrs. Sturge Gretton (then Miss Henderson) her book upon him as a reformer: he went very carefully into Professor George Macaulay Trevelyan's excellent book on his poetry and philosophy, and helped the writer to make it still more excellent, and he opened his heart and mind, in the last year of his life, to a French student, M. Photiadès.

It was not many months before the death of Meredith when Photiadès, on a wet September afternoon, arrived at Flint Cottage. With a dark plaid on his knees, the poet faced a reproduction of Titian's "Sacred and Profane Love." His complexion was still marvellously fresh.[3] His hair, still abundant, rose silvery above his short white beard and moustache. But his large and mobile mouth was not hidden. As Photiadès saw the face, it struck him that Sargent had produced a much better likeness than Watts. Greenish lights shot at times from the deep blue eyes,

[1] Lady Butcher, *Memories*.
[2] J. A. Hammerton.
[3] This was especially noticed by M. Charles Du Bos, who went down about this time with Lady Dawkins to Box Hill.

which had not lost their eloquence. Eloquent too were his nervous and restless hands. His memory was undimmed. His voice was still distinct and resonant, and, as he spoke, he laid on each word an extraordinary force. He still kept alive the inextinguishable ardour of the energy which had made him walk miles tireless and carry on a dazzling conversation.[1]

For reporters the grand old man said he had no taste: Browning indeed had not ignored his critics. Dickens and Thackeray had coaxed them as a good rider takes a horse up to a fence. Tennyson had drawn panegyrics from them, but it was not Meredith's way to court them.

Later he turned to talk of himself: "My thought is spontaneously united to my prose and to my poetry as my body to my intelligence and my soul," he said. Critics assumed the arbitrariness of absolute monarchs. To the writers they reviewed, they behaved as sultans or czars: but they were at the best really only the slave who whispered *Memento mori* to Cæsar in his triumph. "To foreigners I am illustrious but unknown," said Meredith. "As for my countrymen, I shun them and they flee."[1]

§ 2

"Live in the open and study nature." It was still Meredith's idea when malady had overtaken him and he was chained to his chair. "I have always loved

[1] Constantin Photiadès, *George Meredith*.

the face of Nature," he said, "and consented to her spirit. She loves us no better than her other productions but she signifies clearly that intelligence can make her subservient to our needs; and one proof of that is the joy in a healthy body causing increased lucidity of the mind. Therefore exercise of the body is good, and sport of all kind to be encouraged. Sport will lead of necessity to observation of nature. Let us be in the open air as much as possible, engaged in healthy rivalry with our fellows, or with the instructive, elusive game we are after."[1]

Such were the ideas of a lifetime that poured out once more from the veteran as he thought of the prowess of his youth. It would alternate especially with reflections on politics and literature.

Wit, humour, description, analysis, invention and high poetic aspiration poured out one after the other, and, as his friend noted, the ensemble was a marvel.[2] Whether one agreed with all he said or not, there was no mistaking what he meant. It was easy to speak of artificiality in his amazing phrases: but the friends who knew him best insisted that his fecundity was not artificiality. If he was amused at his vivid imaginings, he laughed. He laughed till his friends could not help laughing too. But if he was stirred by some tragic episode, or moved by some noble conception, his deep resonant voice was thrilled by the wakened feelings and told his listeners that the man whose outward indifference was taken by strangers as cynicism was

[1] *Fry's Magazine*, Nov., 1904.
[2] Hyndman, *Sunday Times*, Jan. 6, 1919.

of a nature so deeply sensitive that it needed, to save it from the world's ruthlessness, the *chevaux-de-frise* of artificial brilliancy.

No matter how elaborately fanciful his talk might be, it never escaped from fact. It was, indeed, knotted with abundant growth from earth, and Mr. Le Gallienne has well compared it to a thicket of thorns hung with sudden starry blossoms.[1]

In the last few years of his life, deafness added to the difficulty and made his talk more of a soliloquy, but deafness was the least of afflictions to one who could scarcely keep pace with the swiftness of his own ideas. If give and take were desired, it was not possible to have it. He would never allow people to write their talk for him, nor would he use an ear-trumpet. There was in him till the last a certain devil of independence. Magnetised by the rush and verve of his resonant voice, his listeners were silently rapt into another, and more vital, sphere. The loud booming voice, now deep as thunder, now swift as the wind, addressing a silent and invisible audience, could be heard far beyond the door. Once they entered, his visitors found the pitch too high, and the pace too swift for interruption. The great mouth opened and shut as though on pivots! Passing from metaphor to metaphor, building phrase on phrase, he derided, denounced and extolled with a vigour and a gusto which made it appear that even if such brilliance were not natural, it was at least extremely enjoyable to himself. The words poured out in a spontaneous flow, full of strange fancies, but

[1] *The Romantic Nineties.*

keeping close within the deep channels of wisdom. His conversation was still equal to his books in wit, equal in grandeur of thought; perhaps superior, because simpler, in expression. It is easy for great men in their old age to be spectacular, but Meredith wished always to give of his best, especially if a stranger entered the room. His claim that he read character from the slightest hints, and constantly observed it, was shown to be true by tokens difficult to describe, but impossible to mistake. His manner might seem artificial to strangers, but to none was there anything frigid about it: in everything he was alert, and secretly, one guessed, upon the look-out. If this vitality and press of ideas, this intense intellectual activity and the sometimes fantastic shapes which it took were so singular as to arouse suspicion, it can be recorded that, after leaving Meredith's presence, the whole world seemed to have fallen under a ban of silence and stupidity. The people in the train looked only half-alive, their talk was as primitive as the talk of sheep. People after meeting him for the first time would go away, awed into silence, as after hearing great music or a tragic close. Nevertheless, Meredith did not talk incessantly. He stopped quite suddenly, as if something had struck him. His mind seemed to pass into another region. He appeared a little relieved that his visitors must catch their train. Waving an affectionate, but already slightly absent-minded farewell, he turned directly to a consideration of his thought, which he seemed to pursue with the greatest intensity, pacing slowly in front of his house alone, or, when he could no longer walk, fixing his darting eyes on such views as his room afforded him.

The poet himself, among the knick-knacks of a little Victorian room, in which the hangings were a little frowsy, suggested an Athenian of the age of Pericles. Some thought him like a bust of Euripides brought to life. Some again compared him to Hermes grown old. Age had given ruggedness to the fine features, which since ten years before had become still finer, and, as Mrs. Meynell said, more august. But the nose retained the delicacy which marks the Duchess of Rutland's portrait, and the blue eyes still glittered with their old radiant irony. Unable to move from his armchair, he gave the impression not only that his mind was alert, but that his whole being had retained its vigour. He surrendered his whole heart to the delight of talk, for it was the one exercise which remained to him. It did not matter to him whether the people who came to see him were famous or not, he talked to the commonest as elaborately as to the most intelligent, and "compliments that would have flattered a duchess were presented with equal ceremony to a child. Never did he lapse into commonplace colloquialism. But all the time this highly wrought artificial conversation moved on a current of laughter. His laugh curled round his sentences as though he himself enjoyed their humorous exaggeration. The master of language was splashing and diving in his element of words."[1] He kept to the last the splendour and the brilliance of the genius which we can never

[1] *Times Literary Supplement*, Feb. 9, 1928.

THE LAST FEW YEARS

escape even when his books are most difficult and most perverse. His "genius made itself unmistakably felt in his voice and manner of speaking," said Colvin. "If I were asked to define in one word the most notable quality of Meredith's utterance, whether in recitation or everyday talk, that one word would be 'authority.' Authority along with striking finish and fullness." No one could come near him without recognising the portentous electrical force, the intellectual keenness, the warmth of heart which made the figure of George Meredith the most striking of all the great Victorian writers, or that his spirit was conceived by the

> fathering desire
> Of fire, to reach to fire.

"He had," said Sir James Barrie, "the finest face I ever saw on a man." "I was astonished," wrote Sir Ray Lankester, "by the beauty of his face, and enchanted by his talk. George Meredith stands unsurpassed as an imaginative creator, and unequalled as an original and independent master of expression. He was also a great humorist, a teacher and a prophet."[1] "He was," said Lord Haldane, "a most brilliant figure, and everything he did was all his own."[2]

---

[1] I owe most of the matter in this section to impressions collected by Mr. Buckston Browne in his scrap-book. I am indebted also to Mr. E. V. Lucas's *The Colvins and Their Friends*.—R. S.

[2] Extract from an unpublished MS.

§ 3

It would be easy to think of such a figure as a portent rather than as a human being. It is a mistake which has been made by many: whether they attempt to fathom his philosophy, to follow his novels or to enjoy his poetry, they feel that the great tease was more than anything else an incomparable Saltimbanco. Those who get no further have not known George Meredith. It was not so that he appeared to those that knew him best, and who leave a record not only of fellowship but of tenderness. There are few relations of closer understanding than those of a daughter with her father. The account of Meredith's daughter was that he was, above all things, human. He was never self-absorbed: he was occupied always with things and lives outside him, which he united with his own. The little trivial details of life, as they are lived for ordinary people, never escaped him.

We see this first in a poem in which the memories of his wife came back to him in close association with all the familiar things that she had taken into the heart of her life, and which were taken with hers into his.

> I stood at the gate of the cot
> Where my darling, with side-glance demure,
> Would spy, on her trim garden-plot,
> The busy wild things chase and lure,
> For these with their ways were her feast;
> They had surety no enemy lurked.
> Their deftest of tricks to their least
> She gathered in watch as she worked.

> I gazed: 'twas the scene of the frame,
> With the face, the dear life for me, fled.
> No window a lute to my name,
> No watcher there plying the thread.
> But the blackbird hung pecking at will;
> The squirrel from cone hopped to cone;
> The thrush had a snail on his bill,
> And tap-tapped the shell hard on a stone.[1]

And this power of feeling made nature's suggestions full not only of poignancy, but of delight. This is what gives its lyric charm to his "Song in the Songless."

> They have no song, the sedges dry,
> And still they sing.
> It is within my breast they sing,
> As I pass by.
>
> Within my breast they touch a string,
> They wake a sigh.
> There is but sound of sedges dry;
> In me they sing.

§ 4

But we see this still more clearly in the closing relations of his life, and in his interest in his grandchildren. The joy that each of his own children had been to him in their early childhood returned to him in his love of his four grandchildren, George and Margot Meredith, Joan and Dorothy Sturgis. He

[1] *Poems*, "Change in Recurrence."

delighted to have them at Box Hill, and asked them about the things on which their hearts were set, just as with Mrs. Meynell's children he had made himself one with children's ambitions and joys. "Dumplin'" Dorothy would like to have seen her young friend Julia, who was like a big pumpkin, and rolled like a ball, with only toes showing as she rolled. Margot was to have the bunny she wanted and five shillings to feed it. He wanted to know about Thompson, her brother's famous terrier, who was to have a whole biography before Meredith himself had one. Did he, or did he not, spell his name with a "p"? Let him have a friendly bark from Sandie at Box Hill.[1]

Dear and sweet old Joan he would have liked to visit at Littlehampton, but made an excuse for not coming because of his wanting a lot of extra cooking and taking up too much room. George, who was only fourteen when his grandfather died, was a little puzzled at a man of eighty saying the frank things he expected to hear only from boys at school. These relations pleased Meredith quite as much as all the politicians and writers who came down and made a fuss about him when, as he liked to pretend, he felt he was too old to care. On his seventieth birthday, thirty people of importance told him that he had attained the first rank in literature. In 1908 the congratulations were repeated on his eightieth birthday, and Herbert Trench came down with Israel Zangwill and Anthony Hope to present an address from the Society of Authors. He could not take these things too seriously, though

[1] *Letters.*

the tribute of friends touched him. With the help of Cole he fought off interviewers: those who had a claim found his old exuberance and his old courtesy. But Wilfred Scawen Blunt took the best way of approaching him when he drove up in a coach-and-four.[1]

When the papers lauded his achievements, for his eightieth birthday, they missed, he wrote to Mrs. Plimmer, "the inner me."[2] In starry eminence his spirit dwelt apart. His eyes were intent and full of fire, or rather of dreams and fire,—his fine nature, with the open head and generous heart, pitiless only to pretence and unreality, or what he called " sentimentalism," but eager always to hail true passion and true intellect wherever he might find them, as well as those other nobler qualities of youth, hope and self-devotion which he himself retained till these last days. The constant theme of his talks with Lady Danesfort during the forty years of their friendship was "You must be good."

Behind all that was a ruthless austerity of standard, which Hyndman noticed also in his expression. "His face in repose was hard, keen, eager, determined, almost menacing; the face of an intellectual gladiator who had lived in constant combat, and had always maintained a watchful self-restraint. Only when lighted up in friendly intercourse did a softer expression prevail."[3]

"Few realised," wrote Frederic Harrison, "what passionate senses of right and wrong, what a high

[1] Most of the references to Meredith in Blunt's *Diaries* are incorrect.
[2] From an unpublished letter.　　　[3] *Justice*, May 29, 1909.

heart, he could keep in all his early struggles to be recognised for what he was, what determination burned within him never to yield one jot of his own ideas and methods to any public demand, to any pecuniary effort." Still more emphatic is Mr. Frank Harris's final judgment on his character: "Nothing he ever said or did injured his reputation or tarnished the sovereign lustre of his genius."

The days went by quietly, with Bessy Nicholls always attentive, and Cole rather restive with jealousy in the background. Sandie, who was not really his own but was lent him by John Sturgis, was always with him, Sandie who had followed on a procession of dachshunds headed by Islet from Heligoland, given by Sir Fitzhardinge Maxse, who was Governor there. On October 9, 1906, he wrote to Lord Coleridge (then Mr. Stephen Coleridge): "In my household, animals are treated as one of ourselves and I have not found friendship with a beast to be profitless." Lord Coleridge had tried to get his support against vivisection, but though Meredith's sympathy was with him, he was too sane to want to overrule scientists about their own business, knowing that human life is always more precious than those of animals, even though one does, and one should, love them. "When I read of pain caused to one of the beasts," he said, "I am struck through the frame, so you can imagine that in not immediately seconding you I went against my feelings."[1] And he had written in the same tone, about traps, to the Secretary of the Humanitarian League.

[1] Reproduced in *The Times*, May 20, 1909, and not elsewhere.

THE LAST FEW YEARS

When in 1905 he went to stay at Aldeburgh, he particularly missed the company of Sandie. But of course he had his Sir Reynard, Edward Clodd, for whom he had a great affection, and he had an old fisherman to talk to. "There is no element of charm there," he wrote to Mrs. Plimmer, "only grandeur of sea and strengthening air."[1]

Indeed, the smell of the sea breathed life into him. And as he was wheeled about in his chair, he held a piece of seaweed to his nostrils, drawing in its scent with the same gusto as if it had been a rose.[2]

He could walk with fair freedom till his first operation, but as the years went on he had been able to get only to the gate, then to the door, then he rose with difficulty from his chair, and at the last he could not rise at all. The great exuberance was at times stilled, as in his last silent communings with Lady Danesfort. "Do not speak to me," he said once to Mrs. Plimmer when she came to see him in hospital. At the last she was not allowed to see him, but stealing in through the kitchen door of Flint Cottage, she snatched a glimpse in the sick room three days before the end. His friend, John Deverell, who shared his taste for natural history and for sport, often came over to see him; with Morley and William Meredith, Deverell was appointed an executor.

Up to the end, however, he kept his faculties undimmed. His last act was to pay a tribute to Swinburne. He wrote to *The Times* that Swinburne's name would "shine star-like in English Literature, a peer

[1] From an unpublished letter. [2] S. M. Ellis.

among our noblest," and in praise of Swinburne he wrote to Theodore Watts-Dunton the last of his letters: "I feel the loss of him as part of our life torn away."[1]

And all his qualities were still freshened by the dew of morning, the scent of flowers, the intimacy of wind, the constant searching of the clouds and azure, as he went in his donkey-cart up to Box Hill. In streams and woods he found a freshness of life which made his old age as vivid as his youth: as Sir Owen Seaman has said, he wore the visionary gleams of nature like a paradisal robe:

> Among her solitudes he moved apart;
> > The mystery of her clouds and star-sown skies,
> Touched by the fiery magic of his art,
> > Shone clear for other eyes.
>
> When from his lips immortal music broke
> > It was the myriad voice of vale and hill,
> "The lark ascending" poured a song that woke
> > An echo sweeter still.
>
> Seer of the soul of things, inspired to know
> > Man's heart and woman's, over all he threw
> The spell of fancy's iridescent glow,
> > The sheen of sunlit dew.[2]

The wedding of human life to nature is, as we have seen all through, the secret of his genius: it was that which gave him the sense of beauty in all human relations, and all the courage of his crippled years, and

[1] *Letters.*   [2] *Punch*, May 26, 1909.

in the very year of his death he spoke of feeling still the raptures with which, listening to the skylark in his boyhood, he had found it the tongue of the heavens:

> Once I was part of the music I heard
>   On the boughs of sweet between earth and sky,
>   For joy of the beating of wings on high
> My heart shot into the breast of the bird.
>
> I hear it now, and I see it fly,
>   And a life in wrinkles again is stirred,
>   My heart shoots into the breast of the bird,
> And it will for sheer love till the last long sigh.[1]

He breathed the last sigh in 1909, in the early dawn of the 18th of May, looking towards the dawn. His son and daughter, with the faithful nurse, were with him to the end. A few days later, they laid his ashes in the quiet grave for four in Dorking Cemetery, which he had bought twenty-three years earlier, and where the name "Marie Meredith" was graven above his own words: *not death but life*.[2] The same morning, England made for him at Westminster Abbey, in the presence of his four grandchildren, that stately memorial of sacred word and chant to which in earlier years he had himself listened for Browning and again for Tennyson. The whole country recognised the

---

[1] "Youth in Age."

[2] On his tombstone are quoted the opening words of what we have seen to be his favourite stanza:

> "Life is but a little holding, lent
>   To do a mighty labour. It is one
> With heaven and the stars when it is spent
>   To do God's aim. Else die we with the Sun."

passing of the greatest of her writers. That he had written for some and not for all was not ignored: but, of those best qualified to judge, none questioned his supremacy. While official England did him official honour, there was a sense of personal loss in hearts that knew him only from his writings. Among the many splendid tributes sent by those whose names were well known, there was a simple wreath of laurel from a boy still at school of whom none had heard, not even the poet himself. His name was Siegfried Sassoon.

George Meredith in the little holding of life had done indeed a mighty labour. The nervous and sensitive school-boy whom fancies could frighten had grown to be heroic both in endurance and in ardour. Sir James Barrie, when, long years after, he recalled his intimacy with the finest of his friends, said: "Courage is an attribute of genius and that of Meredith was splendid." His friends could at no time think of him as confined in the grave. The poet himself had written, six years earlier, to her whom in the days of his early rapture he had carried on his shoulder, to his first wife's daughter, her who had tended Arthur, "The beloved, truly loved, are not more than removed from sight. Love keeps them." Among those that live by the heart, there were, at hand and widely scattered, a company of courage who truly loved George Meredith. These found him near in what they cared for most: they felt him one with heaven and the stars.

XV

GENIUS IN ACTION

§ 1

IF we want to know the essential life of Meredith, we must know him better as a writer than as a man. The biography which speaks of him as other than we find him in the expression of his genius is false to him. The real George Meredith is in his best prose, and even more in his best poetry. It is in our unity with the spirit of his work that we first and last see really into his life. He mistrusted biographers, as he deprecated the publication of letters and obliterated written records, because he wanted men to concentrate on the impression of his ideal life he gave to all that he created. Very often, as we have seen, that ideal life flatly contradicted his other life; we see in his work his character remodelled. There, distinct from friendship, distinct from inadequate circumstances, distinct from restricted adventure, we find the man's essential self, the hero-will, the generative spirit.

To those that do find these, life is like the mountainous, indented, luxuriant landscape of Samoa transfigured by the lightning and rain of a tropic storm. He writes for those who thirst as he had thirsted for intensity of brain and heart, showing them how, by taking themselves strenuously with a due sense of humour, to make it one with noble strength in action.

This is more, no doubt, than ordinary people can stomach. Meredith himself wrote at the opening of *Modern Love:* "This is not meat for little people, or for fools."

But over those who have learned to digest his meat, Meredith's hold is firm. From him young love learns favourite hymns, which add their freshness to the woods, and make the changing skies more heavenly. With the good realities of earth he was so intimate that in themselves they told him a secret which took him far beyond the bourns of outward things, and commune with them was a sacrament. High natures are at home in life's high tides. The Nile's flood-mark records a drenching and a cleansing from which new growths burst into shoots and blooms turned by regularity of effort to nourishment, and well-nourished natures give a long loyalty to floodings of the stream.

The more fully the body lives (but grossness is not fullness) the more deeply the soul learns from living, and only when nature has become the sacrifice which initiates the soul into mysteries and feeds it with the bread of life is nature itself a living reality. The earth's highest function is the nourishment and illumination of spirits, who, before they finally give back dust to dust, will have drawn from it richer essences of eternal truth, potent in everlasting actions. This is the aim of creation.

> Earth was not Earth until her sons appeared,
> Nor Beauty Beauty ere young Love was born.

A truth so vital is itself one with what it tells of: words

which unite earth with heaven in their record of exhilaration are so much the words of life that those who know them cannot but think of them as inspired.

§ 2

That is why from those that once have caught his meaning, George Meredith commands an eagerness and an enthusiasm which are unabashed by clever criticism: for them, his sentient creations have features that neither time nor toil can mar. Henry James said, to Mr. Desmond Macarthy, that "he does the best things best," and the sense of his worth and elevation was sufficiently general with contemporary genius. Rossetti and Charles Kingsley greeted the promise of a great success; Stevenson, Browning, Sir James Barrie, and Mr. Max Beerbohm felt that he was one of the supreme masters, naming him after Shakespeare. Wilde, in a favourite aphorism, declared that: "As a writer he has mastered everything except language; as a novelist he can do everything except tell a story; as an artist he is everything except articulate." Even with the epigrammatic qualifications, the recognition is sufficient. Hardy's lines are familiar:

> He was of those whose wit can shake
> And ridicule to the very core
> The counterfeits that time will break. . . .
>   Further and further still,
> Through the world's vaporous vitiate air,
> His words wing on, as live words will.

Herbert Trench, a poet whose genius the world at large has yet to recognise, put Meredith highest among the masters of his century. Hewlett's imitation, in his earlier novels, was close enough to be sincerest compliment. Mr. Galsworthy and Mr. Wells have recorded their indebtedness. James Thomson found his style, "at its best, so beautiful in simplest Saxon, so majestic in rhythm, so noble with noble imagery, so pregnant with meaning, so vital and intense, that it must be ranked among the supreme achievements of our literature." All these men arrive at conclusions set out in 1899 by James Oliphant: "He raises us into a new and wonderful and beautiful world where every fibre of the soul is set quivering to strange and ravishing harmonies." "There can be no doubt," wrote Sir Sidney Colvin, "that his mind and imagination were among the richest and most resourceful, and above all the most rapid in working, that have ever expressed themselves in our literature,"[1] and there were many equally warm paraphrases of this judgment. All agreed with Henry James in saying, first one way, and then another, that Meredith does the best things best.

What was remarked of his work by genius is the complement of what a succession of remarkable friends noticed of his personality. From his earliest days Meredith, as we have seen, was intimate with men and women of distinction. Many of them gave him a devoted friendship, and it is from these who knew him best that we get the most intimate and therefore

[1] E. V. Lucas, *The Colvins and Their Friends*.

the truest account of his personality. Though he always spoke of himself as a Celt, he was far more of a Viking. Love of the sea, strenuousness, combativeness, exultation, marked his spirit. All leave alike an impression of a nature, vital, generous, poetic: a friend of devoted affection pouring out counsel and comment with an amazing fecundity: a brain of the rarest energy and strength: a perennial overflow of life and power and feeling and teasing and laughter: a phenomenal sensitiveness easily stung to rage, an uncompromising sincerity which could be brusque and even merciless: a love of horses, dogs, exercise and sport, an enthusiastic study of military history and a great keenness on boxing and drill, a tenderness and a ready admiration for sweet or noble women, a high courtesy towards them, an exalted spiritual eagerness: a personality which was altogether dominant and noble. "He is one of those personalities," wrote James Thomson, "who need fear no comparison with their best writings."

An outstanding genius, with the tastes and outlook of the finest of men, he was at home in a world finer than that into which his aunts married. The Early Victorian system of society which shrank from any association with trade, which regarded the shop as almost equally deplorable with the jail, which had no standards but those of tables of precedence, which bowed before "crowned windbags," survived in England till the War, and provided an endless stimulus to Meredith's taste for comedy. He was not, he could not be, blind to the powers of his own genius; and, being at home with the great, he saw through the pretensions of such aristocracy as was merely titled. Sir Thomas Browne talked of a "rabble among the gentry": Meredith chastised its pretensions, in such creations as Lord Palmet and Sir Upton Tomber; in a sense of the splendour of the sons of the earth, he found genius princely even when rising from the middle classes. When we become familiar with the march and swiftness of Meredith's genius, his power to associate dissimilar ideas and to retain a consciousness of conflicting states of mind (for these distinguish him), we can realise how he could at once recognise the constraints of the contemporary social system, and fight himself free of them in gestures that were both playful and uproarious. We cannot separate him from his friends, his naturalness, or his work. In him, the life of genius was the most real of lives; a swordsman's zest in action and adventure he found in the mastery of words. His friends figure in his novels not as themselves, but as portraits and compositions of his creation, as much his work as those of Romney or Goya were theirs. The creator stamps his heredity upon creatures that played their own part in the generative process of his mind. The characters of Meredith come to us as his creations, because all creative art is the generation of conceptions, which are the intimate intercourse of the mind with that which is outside it.

§ 3

Before Meredith, English Literature had in her family great mystics and poets of nature, great lovers.

But in Meredith the passion for the Places where desolation is the patron saint, or for the sweet growths of wild seclusion, mingled with the passion of human love, so that forever he was writing of one in terms of the other. His swift, rapturous, sinewy mind saw in every scene something which harmonised with his ecstasies of human love; he saw in love the flower of earth and reason. Man, fed on the fruits of clay, made as Donne said of red earth, dealt with the world through the gifts nature had given him: but earth and reason were both one, in the composition of man, with his spirit which could rise to unspeakable exaltations and which was most exalted when the flesh added a thrill, and common sense gave sinewy stimulus, to high excitement. They it was who raised man from grassy earth to azure heaven: it was for them

> To wing our green to wed our blue.

So, in Meredith's finest passages, the rapture of musical words speaks of nature's scenes in the terms of boy or woman:

> Lo, where the eyelashes of night are raised
> Yet lowly over morning's pure grey eyes.

Or it speaks of human life as the supremest secret of nature's growth:

> . . . she is what my heart first awaking
> Whispered the world was.

And we get these two views mingling in the "Hymn to Colour," where light, darkness and dawn are compared with and finally become identified with life, death and love. These are his lines on the sunrise:

Look now where Colour, the soul's bridegroom, makes
The house of heaven splendid for the bride.

.　　　　.　　　　.　　　　.

O bloom of dawn, breathed up from the gold sheaf
Held springing beneath Orient! that dost hang
The space of dewdrops running over leaf;
They fleetingness is bigger in the ghost
　　Than Time with all his host!

Of thee to say behold, has said adieu:
But love remembers how the sky was green,
And how the grasses glimmered lightest blue;
How saint-like grey took fervour: how the screen
Of cloud grew violet; how thy moment came
　　Between a blush and flame.

It is this which gives that unspeakable mood of rapture to the love-scenes of Richard and Lucy: Richard had seen for the first time

　　The beauty that makes holy earth and air.

Associating the fields and waters with the presence and the experience, he identifies the scenes with glories not their own: and "to-morrow the place will have a memory—the river, and the meadow, and the white-falling weir: his heart will build a temple."

Returning from his beloved, the poet of "Love in the Valley" found her presence everywhere, and nature itself grew into a moving being all life and love and joy, and in doing so revealed the presence of the divine:

Could I find a place to be alone with heaven,
  I would speak my heart out: heaven is my need.
Every woodland tree is flushing like the dogwood,
  Flashing like the whitebeam, swaying like the reed.
Flushing like the dogwood crimson in October;
  Streaming like the flag-reed South-West blown;
Flashing as in gusts the sudden-lighted whitebeam:
  All seem to know what is for heaven alone

As he turns from the presence of his beloved, he finds the plants and trees flushing, swaying, flashing, as she had, when she had dropped with bright eyes into his arms. He gives the intimate rarities of nature the names of her movements; the impulse of her spirit. To such uses he could turn George Darley's metre. Then indeed in Milton's phrase, he was the poet "simple, sensuous and passionate." Would that he were always so!

Too full of energy, observation, reason, too diversely alive, he was more interested in living things than in art. He notes, in writing about Mrs. Meynell, that she was more preoccupied with art, and that, in her uses of the elements of the language, she attains to something of perfection in writing that he grew more and more apt to miss; for he lost the sense that literature is a social art, and lacking mercy for the mediocre, his sentences grew so packed that, at their worst, they become what Goethe called *Selbstgespräch*, as even Lord Morley felt.

"Yet whenever he fails," says Professor Trevelyan, "it is not through want but from excess of imagination. His metaphors sometimes strive, one on the back of another, like fierce animals in a pit, and deal each other dismembering wounds in the struggle for existence," when they come, as in later years, to be more thought than felt. His intellect was foiled by its own tirelessness, and, by over-stimulating, he can paralyse ours.

What Sir Walter Raleigh said of Shakespeare is true of Meredith: in his desire first to clear, then to fill the mind, he heaps metaphor on metaphor, and as the years went on, his flair for surprising connections took possession of him and his manner became more a habit than the vital contact of his spirit with brain and earth: "It is the excelling merit of smiles and metaphors," he once wrote, "to spring us to vault over gaps and thickets and slippery places," and this power, which had come from the keenness with which he associated his walks with his feelings and memories, was very often overdone.

Towards the end of his life, the lyric beauty often fails, and was even consciously intended, or at least deliberately allowed, to fail. " 'The Empty Purse,' " he wrote in a letter to Mrs. Gretton, "is not poetry. But I had to convey certain ideas that could not find place in the Novels." This admission gives the key to much of his verse: tune and beauty were to be sacrificed, while he used forms in which he could be poetical so as to express himself in more incoherent and nakedly suggestive phrases than could be allowed in prose.

But to do all that is not to make poems what, as

poems, they should be. *Dulcia sunto.* The poet, Sir Philip Sidney wrote, "doth not only show the way but giveth so sweet a prospect with the way as will entice any man to enter into it." If he could have kept intact the vigour of his talk, Meredith did at times make that prospect so sweet that the young Stevenson became "drunk as with wine" in repeating his verses: in prose, as in verse, he has written passages made of rapture, and expressed in so simple yet so rare an English that they carry one by force into a world which breathes in one great presence of the spring, and where enchantment was—to use one of his own metaphors—as wholesome and fruitful as a rich meadow on the borders of the heaths. At such times one might apply to him what he himself said, when he compared Shakespeare to a fruitful island:

Passions and pageants; sweet love singing bird-like above it;
Life in all shapes, aims, and fates is there warm'd by one great human heart.

But because of his complex intensity, because, as he wrote to Mrs. Meynell, his poetry was "wild, hither and thither, following nature, opposed to your classic scheme," he lost that sense of art which stamps the order and eminence of reason on the presentment of nature. To be a perfect writer, he would have had to sacrifice his abounding fulness: he tried instead the impossible experiment of reproducing the processes of mind and feeling, before the will has ordered them to a set end.

M. Ramon Fernandez, who, like his countrymen, M. Galland and M. Photiadès, sees deep into the heart of Meredith, has in his latest essay gone much further than others in explaining the peculiarities of his style and genius. He sees that, in him, thought and intuition are one process, which M. Fernandez calls "dramatic analysis." It is a suggestive criticism, for Meredith portrays people thinking and acting both at once, and both in relation to his philosophy of life. "His men and women," says M. Fernandez, "flash like waves in the sunlight. But the centre of their action—therefore the determining factor of the balance which decides their place in life, and their power to hold it—is in themselves, and not in the zone of their outward acts."[1] Meredith attained to this power by the fulness of his life and intuition, so that when the delightfulness of beauty masters him, his images are wonderful fusions of life, giving flashes on hidden treasures: "They have all the qualities of poetry: the spontaneity, the lightness, the penetrating sharpness, the power of creating mysterious alliances through space and time."[1]

§ 4

His method was to recall through hints an impression and a vision that would have lost their magic if the details were to be recounted in an inventory, as Scott and Manzoni describe their scenes without evoking them. Meredith's way was to give the mind

[1] Ramon Fernandez, *Messages*.

that same exercise of flashing changes which the exercised body gives the attentive mind. "The art of the pen," he said, in *Diana of the Crossways*, "is to rouse the inward vision instead of labouring with a drop-scene brush as if it were to the eye, because the eye cannot contain a protracted description." So it was that this style became as Wilde said, "Chaos illumined by flashes of lightning." But as for Meredith's idea, it is indeed a secret of all art: the artist sees and recaptures, but he sees something more than the sensuous; he looks through to a world of ideas, to an informing reality which find its recognition in his own spirit, heart speaking to heart; and so there emerges a picture which the human mind drew of events or scenes or sounds or living creatures when the sensuous was informed anew by reason and the soul, and each of these becomes more exuberant because it mingles with the other; experience becomes not merely reason, nor flesh, nor spirit, but a glory of life both mortal and immortal, both seen and divined, with innumerable permutations and combinations of relationship, each of which enhances and dignifies the other. "Fervidness is the core of style," he wrote, in *Celt and Saxon*. So, like his own Melampus, Meredith perceived so eagerly and so fully that, from brooding upon the outward accidental semblance of things, he communed with them in their sacred relation to the reality which informed them:

Divinely thrilled was the man, exultingly full,
   As quick well-waters that come of the heart of the earth,

Ere yet they dart in a brook, are one bubble-pool
> To light and sound, wedding both at the leap of birth.

The soul of light vivid shone, a stream within stream;
> The soul of sound from a musical shell outflew;

Where others hear but a hum and see but a beam,
> The tongue and eye of the fountain of life he knew.

§ 5

During his lifetime and since, the question of Meredith's place in letters has occasioned the wildest guesses. Many now think that his reputation has been exaggerated.[1] He has been for the last ten years not much read either by the many, or by the few who live in the literary fashion. And yet the fact remains, that extraordinary people thought him marvellous, that many prominent Englishmen of sound culture still think him one of the supreme men of the nineteenth century, and that, as we saw, among not a few others, Stevenson and Sir James Barrie put him near Shakespeare.

It is, when all is said, the name of Shakespeare which takes us closest to deciding the question of his worth. Meredith, it is true, differed from Shakespeare in identifying himself with a deliberate philosophy of life, a sort of poetic Aristotelianism: and he had a fonder love of the ways of Olympus. But both were men of the North; neither worked in the classic Latin

[1] This is the view of Mr. T. S. Eliot, and Mr. E. M. Forster has said the same thing in his latest book.

temper, with its genius for law. Both were great romantic idealists with an impassioned appreciation of the immediate world, as one with life's majestic ranges. And both were the victims of their inundating gifts. "The Intellectual power and the creative energy wrestle as in a war embrace." So Coleridge wrote of Shakespeare: it is true of Meredith.

"I cannot say he is everywhere alike. He is many times flat and insipid. But he is always great when some great occasion is presented to him. No man can say he ever had a fit subject for his art and did not raise himself as high above his fellows, *quantum lenta solent inter viburna cupressi*." So Johnson wrote of Shakespeare. That also is true of Meredith. Both are rich in "things extreme and scattering light": in both simplicity is rare, but tells the more, when it is found, because it is like the surface of the flooding Nile which immerses, alters, and enriches the known earth which gives us rest and nourishment.

In both Shakespeare and Meredith artistic perfection could be spoiled by congestion, by the desire to press into words more of life than reason can control. Besides, Meredith was almost morbidly cautious about the use of tired phrases. And in these ways he erred far more deeply and continuously than Shakespeare. But, at his best, which is to say in the years between thirty and forty, he is full of life and sanity, and rich in an enchantingly touching beauty. It is because "he did the best things best" that even passages the most congested and obscure repay time given them. They are not only rich in salutary wisdom: they throw light on a writer who, at his best, was not less than supreme.

We find him at his best not only when he is writing his poetry of passion where the exaltation of his feeling made him both clear and musical, but in stories like *The Ordeal*, *Evan Harrington*, or even *The Tragic Comedians*, where there is nothing to repel those who find difficulty in *The Egoist*, *Beauchamp's Career* or *Diana of the Crossways*.

Whatever the faults that leaped to obviousness, a nature so rich and strong is a fine gift to the heirs of the ages, and as Oliphant reminded us, hours with Meredith, to those that give what he requires of them, are rich in time and eternity.

§ 6

He had what he himself called "a sense of the eternal in life": and this not because he had Dante's Christian philosophy or Dante's mystic vision. He had too little sense of final peace, or radiant security. Peace and order were not for him: Dante attained celestial luminance through the Church which Meredith scorned. The exultant Northerner was too busy and too thrilled by pageants and pictures of created things. He knew the English wood and meadow so well that he gives an impression of them as full of luxuriance as though they were a jungle of Nepal or Travancore. Tyrolian dawns: the fir-wood in moonlight: the plash of weirs: the swell of waves under the stars: the spring woodland's shy recesses: the country house habited by an entrenched class conscious of its power: the German forest: such were the scenes recognised with a spiritual elevation which threw over them an exhilarating glory; but though he had found earth the mother of his inspirations, his eye turned most often towards the depths of air: he drank the secret of a strengthening intoxication in courting the clouds of the Southwest with a lover's blood. Not Shelley, not Turner was more intimate with the marvels of the morning twilight. But Corot he preferred to Turner as truer in feeling to nature itself. Surveying nature with the exaltations of a poet, he braced himself to an exuberant enjoyment of the sports typical of Englishmen. Watching the air and sky with the passionate pleasure with which he watched the ringlets curling over the neck of a lovely woman, he grew intimate with air's singers and sailors. The green woodpecker, the swallows noising among the osier, the nightjar on the pine, the skylark, the nightingale, the white owl, were all, like the wild cherry and the autumn crocus, intimate friends: and he knew their ways just as he knew the ways of wild flowers. Both birds and flowers were nourished on "the divineness of what the world deems gross material substance." So among nature's scenes, an heroic company of men and women start, at his word, to life; for, in all his quarrels with Peacock's daughter, he never ceased to be a champion of the splendour of womanhood. Cheerful and natural boys, not unwhipped, keep reminding one to hold the young generation in sight, and taste "the rapture of the forward view." In the National Gallery, Furse has left us portraits of the Meredithian type: "Diana of the Uplands" and those two in "The Return from the Ride," who, wife and husband, are in fact the kinsmen of Meredith's magnificent friend, the original of Rose Jocelyn, and who now live in her villa at Poggio Gherardo above Florence. But, in his glowing gallery, figures crowd with all the complicated intensity which endears, to natures made vigorous by the mingling of brain with passion, the typical compositions of Donne and Browning, of Michelangelo and Wagner. Life was for Meredith as for them too intricate and too thrilling to be subjected to art. But the less he studied effect in composition, the more he was absorbed in the things of the spirit. His is a noble philosophy: and as we watch him moving from the woods of Westermain to the stars above the Surrey upland of his last home, we see a man who grew so intimate with men and women that, on England's common earth, he found in them the freshness and the rapture as when he was

Far away, far away, where the wandering scents
Of all flowers are sweetest, white mountains among.

§ 7

It is for Meredith the promise of life which crowns the kingly experience. He finds that hour richest which most clearly affirms the conceptions of eternity. He insists that eternity and time impregnate one another, and that what alone is salutary is the heart's hold of abundant life, given yet more abundantly. The completest is the truest. He defines the truth by images and similitudes, believing that out of knowledge of the infinite significance of outward things do our tongues and lips grow fluent in the eternal language. He was a poet for whom "the word is one with that it tells of," or, as long before Emerson, Longinus wrote, "beautiful words are indeed the very light of the mind." A latent power, Meredith's mind waited for the germinal action of sights and sounds, till it shot out in living concepts. To these he gave forth his own energy, like the ardour of the swimmer which carries him through and over waves, skimming and thrusting, with the flash of the brine he has cleft dripping from the swift swing of his arm.

www.ingramcontent.com/pod-product-compliance
Lightning Source LLC
Chambersburg PA
CBHW050856300426
44111CB00010B/1278